Texts and Monographs in Computer Science

Study Edition

Texts and Monographs in Computer Science

continued after index

Programming in the 1990s

An Introduction to the
Calculation of Programs

Edward Cohen

Springer-Verlag
New York Berlin Heidelberg
London Paris Tokyo Hong Kong

Edward Cohen
Software Logic Limited
P.O. Box 565
Brookline, Massachusetts 02146
USA

Series Editor

David Gries
Department of Computer Science
Cornell University
Ithaca, NY 14853
USA

Library of Congress Cataloging-in-Pubilcation Data
Cohen, Edward.
    Programming in the 1990s : an introduction to the calculation of
programs / Edward Cohen, — Study ed.
        p.   cm. — (Texts and monographs in computer science)
    Includes bibliographical references and index.
    1. Electronic digital computers—Programming.   I. Title.
II. Series.
QA76.6.C6235   1990
005—dc20   90-10152
                                                    CIP

Printed on acid-free paper.

Photocomposed copy prepared by the author using LaT$_E$X.

9 8 7 6 5 4 3 2 1

ISBN-13:978-0-387-97382-1   e-ISBN-13:978-1-4613-9706-9
DOI: 10.1007/978-1-4613-9706-9

To my grandmother
and to my parents.

Preface

Programming is a fascinating and challenging subject. Unfortunately, it is rarely presented as such. Most often it is taught by "induction": features of some famous programming language are given operational meaning (e.g. a loop "goes round and round"), a number of examples are shown, and by induction, we are asked to develop other programs, often radically different from the ones we've seen. Basically we are taught to guess our programs, and then to patch up our guesses. Our errors are given the cute name of "bugs". Fixing them becomes puzzle solving, as does finding tricks that exploit or avoid poorly designed features of the programming language. The entire process is time-consuming and expensive. And even so, we are never quite sure if our programs really work in all cases.

When approached in this way, programming is indeed a dull activity!

There is, however, another approach to programming, an approach in which programs can be developed reliably, with attention to the real issues. It is a practical approach based on methodically developing programs from their specifications. Besides being practical, it is exciting. Many programs can be developed with relative ease. Once difficult problems can be solved by beginners. Elegant solutions bring great satisfaction.

This is our subject. We are interested in making programming an exciting topic!

The material in this book is, of course, not pulled from thin air. It is due to a number of serious expert programmers, the best known being E.W. Dijkstra and D. Gries, and has been developed in Europe and the U.S. over many years. The examples come from a number of sources.

The text is self-contained and is designed to be comfortably explored in a single semester. It can be used in a number of ways:

> Because it is self-contained, it is well-suited for an introductory course on programming. Realizing that the recent advances in programming

are unfamiliar to many people, it is also appropriate for a second or third course, either undergraduate or graduate, or for self-study by practicing programmers interested in keeping up-to-date.

Because of its size, it can be used in a single-semester course, or can be covered slowly over two semesters. For a two-semester course, it can also be supplemented. Suggested sources of supplemental material are mentioned at the end.

Although a book about programming, and not about programming in language X (for whatever X), a notation had to be chosen for writing down programs. Dijkstra's guarded commands was the choice. (Frankly, this choice was so obvious that nothing else was considered!) They are an ideal vehicle. For one thing, they are simple (only one type of loop, only one type of if-statement), so we don't get bogged down in a myriad of (sometimes questionable) programming language features. But the main thing was that they were designed to nicely accomodate program development.

An instructor can, of course, substitute another programming language, but I wouldn't recommend it! Readers familiar with other languages can easily translate their programs. And when the text is used in an introductory course in a curriculum requiring proficiency in Pascal, say, the text can be supplemented with lectures and exercises on that language. This approach has a number of advantages. Because they will already be familiar with programming, students will be able to master the language with ease. Further, they will be in a position to evaluate its advantages and disadvantages. (We mention this because many introductory courses do not distinguish "programming" from "programming in language X". In such cases X must be taken for granted.)

The exercises are exceedingly important. This cannot be overstated. Exercises are the only way the material goes "from the head to the fingertips". I have found it beneficial to scatter certain exercises, especially those involving predicates, throughout the semester. Such reinforcement helps students become comfortable with the manipulations.

I hope that this book is enjoyable, and hope that many things are learned. My main hope, however, is that programming is revealed for what it really is — a fascinating subject worthy of further study!

ACKNOWLEDGEMENTS

My deepest gratitude goes to three people:

o Professor Wim H.J. Feijen (University of Technology, Eindhoven, The

Netherlands) whose good taste, clear writing, and ongoing quest for perfection in programming have been a great inspiration to me. It was his suggestion that I undertake this project and, while in progress, he spent many hours showing me many improvements. His influence is on every page.

o Professor David Gries (Cornell University, Ithaca NY, USA) who first taught me that programming, properly approached, is a science, and that programs can be developed in a reliable and elegant way. Without this exposure I would been bored years ago. Instead I have been continuously rewarded. In the years since, he has helped me many times.

o Professor Edsger W. Dijkstra (University of Texas, Austin TX, USA) whose lectures and writings have inspired me over many years. The central ideas in this book are his, as are most of the techniques shown. His contributions are many and are fundamental. Along the way, he has generously answered all my questions.

Very special thanks to Vit Novak, whose high standards and good sense have helped at every step, from the lectures that led to this book, to the book itself. Thanks also to Mike Sheldon, who offered excellent comments on successive drafts of each chapter, to Mark Schneider and Ted Czotter, for never being satisfied with anything that I did, always forcing me to improve my presentations and never allowing me to wave my hands. Thanks to Kaia Cornell for comments on an early draft of the manuscript, to Edgar Knapp for desperately needed LaTeX help, to Professor Fred B. Schneider (Cornell University, Ithaca NY, USA) for his comments on the (almost) final version, and to Gerhard Rossbach of Springer-Verlag.

Finally, I would like to thank the CSCI-264 students at Harvard Extension.

Edward Cohen
Boston, MA USA
April 1990

Contents

0

What can we learn from a cake?

0.0 Introduction

We are interested in programming, which in broadest terms is problem solving. There are lots of problems and we cannot solve them all. Which problems will we consider? We should delineate our topic.

- *Some problems are trivial* — it is easy to guess a solution. We will not concern ourselves with such problems, precisely for the reason that they are trivial. (Civil engineers are not interested in the problem of putting a plank over a stream).

- *Some problems are vaguely specified* — anything can be considered a solution. We dispense with these, and will only consider precisely specified problems. (A civil engineer would not look for a solution to a problem like: "get cars over water". There are millions of solutions, and presumably most are unsatisfactory. At the very least, our civil engineer will ask the questions required to formulate a precise specification).

We should also point out that some people have an uncanny ability to guess solutions. Unless good guessing can be taught, this fact is of no use to the rest of us. After all, civil engineering did not advance because some people intuitively designed successful bridges.

0.1 What can we learn from a cake?

We are given a circular cake with a number of points chosen along its circumference. A chord is drawn between every pair of points. A sharp knife cuts along each chord. Our problem is to determine the number of pieces of cake produced when the number of points equals N.

In order to simplify the problem, we require that the points are chosen so that no internal point is crossed by more than two chords. In other words, exactly two chords share each internal intersection point.[0]

Ex 0.0   Before reading on, solve the problem of the cake.   □

⋆   ⋆

We begin by examining a few cases. We start with $N = 1$, in which case there is 1 piece. For $N = 2$ there are 2 pieces:

Number of points:	1	2
Number of pieces:	1	2

Now we see a pattern. For N points there seem to be N pieces. Let's check $N = 3$, for which we find that there are 4 pieces. Our guess wasn't right. For more insight we try $N = 4$, for which we find:

Number of points:	1	2	3	4
Number of pieces:	1	2	4	8

A good guess for the number of pieces is 2^{N-1}. To be sure we try $N = 5$, for which we find:

Number of points:	1	2	3	4	5
Number of pieces:	1	2	4	8	16

For $N = 5$ we have 16 pieces. Our guess seems to work. To be absolutely certain we look at $N = 6$, for which we predict 32 pieces:

Number of points:	1	2	3	4	5	6
Number of pieces:	1	2	4	8	16	31

For $N = 6$ there are 31 pieces, not 32. Our guess was wrong! Looking for a new pattern we try $N = 7$, and find:

Number of points:	1	2	3	4	5	6	7
Number of pieces:	1	2	4	8	16	31	57

---

[0]This restriction will allow the problem to be solved without knowing anything about the (relative) positions of the points.

For $N = 7$ we have 57 pieces. We see no pattern, but are too tired of drawing pictures and counting pieces.

$\star$ $\star$

Our effort could be accurately summarized as:

> *Guess. Assume that the solution is correct until shown to be wrong.*

• *That guessing is prevalent in programming is apparent* from the fact that programmers have a special word for the activity of correcting bad guesses. This activity they call *debugging*, a word used with no embarrassment. Before bugs (i.e. errors) are found, the activity of checking a guess is called *testing*. The whole approach is one of trial-and-error. (What would happen if a civil engineer proposed building a bridge by trial-and-error?)

• *On correcting a bad guess:* We found that 2^{N-1} was incorrect for $N = 6$. How do we correct it? Perhaps we increase the exponent by 1. Perhaps we subtract 1 when N exceeds 5? This is akin to multiplying two numbers, and when the result is found to be incorrect, fiddling with its digits. No one would propose such an approach. As absurd as it may seem, many programs are "corrected" by syntactical changes like these. With guessing, there is no alternative but to guess again, all the while hoping that the new guess does the job.

• *On checking a guess:* There are often too many cases to check. With the cake problem, there are as many cases as points along the cake's circumference, namely infinity. Our second "solution" first failed at $N = 6$. Suppose it first failed at $N = 30$. Would it be likely that we would check enough? After all, we got tired of counting pieces at $N = 7$.

For another example, consider programs that respond to values from external sensors. Flight-control software responds to radar, altimeters and so on. The number of potential values, combinations of values, and sequences of combinations of values is astronomical. There is no way to check them all.

For even simple problems, there is often a huge, and usually an infinite, number of cases to check. Perhaps we can automate the case checking by using high speed computers. Consider the generation of large prime numbers, a problem of great interest in data encryption. Checking a number's primacy means factoring it. With today's technology, a 200-digit number can be factored in 1,000,000 years. Technology is no panacea: A thousand-fold improvement cuts this down to 1000 years. And we have understated our problem. The prime number generator must work for *all* cases, not just the single case we check, and our entire discussion begs the question of whether the factoring program is correct.

If we cannot check all cases, perhaps we can check selected ones. After all, an engineer can guarantee that a product is able to withstand all temperatures between 0 and 500 degrees by showing that it can withstand 0 degrees and then showing that it can withstand 500 degrees. As programmers, do we have the same luxury? In the words of C.A.R. Hoare:

> *In some ways engineers have an advantage over us. Because they are dealing in continuously varying quantities like distance, temperature, and voltage, it is possible for them to increase confidence in the reliablity of an engineering product by testing it at the extremes of its intended operating range, for example, by exposure to heat or cold, or by voltage margins. We do the same in program testing, but in our case it is futile. Firstly we have to deal with impossibly more variables and secondly these variables take on discrete values, for which interpolation and extrapolation are wholly invalid. The fact that a program works for value zero and value 65535 gives no confidence that it will work for any of the values in between . . . .*

And so we are left in a quandry: Exhaustive checking is impossible for practical reasons, and selected checking is flawed in principle.

• *Checking has nothing to do with correctness.* What is implied by the ability to check a formula? A formula can be checked if it can be evaluated. It can be evaluated if it has legal shape. Therefore the ability to check a formula depends (only) on whether the formula has legal shape. It has nothing to do with the formula's correctness.

What is implied by the ability to check a program? A program can be checked if it can be executed. It can be executed if it has legal shape. Therefore the ability to check a program depends (only) on whether the program has legal shape. It has nothing to do with the program's correctness. A computer is happy to execute any (legally shaped) program that is fed into it.

In a nutshell, the ability to check (i.e. execute) a program has no bearing on whether it is correct.

After all, Euclid wrote correct programs 2000 years ago! [1]

---

[1] The fact that programs can be executed is useful for other reasons. Professional programmers are employed because someone *wants* to execute their programs, and computer manufacturers provide machines whose value derives solely from the fact that they *can* execute these programs: *The program is an*

⋆ ⋆

So not only is *guess, test* and *guess again* impractical, the ability to test has nothing to do with correctness. The question remains, however, as to whether there is an alternative. Towards this end we examine a (correct) solution to the cake problem.

How do we start? We begin by observing that the number of pieces is increased when a chord is added. As the simplest case is when a *single* chord is added, we begin, quite naturally, by considering the increase in pieces resulting from the addition of a single chord:

increase by adding a single chord
= ⟨ A chord divides pieces in two ⟩
number of pieces divided by the chord
= ⟨ A piece is divided by a segment of the chord ⟩
number of segments on the chord
= ⟨ Segments are separated by internal intersection points ⟩
1 + number of internal intersection points on the chord

Armed with this result, we consider the increase in pieces resulting from the addition of c chords:

increase by adding c chords
= ⟨ By this last result and the requirement that each internal
intersection point is shared by exactly two chords ⟩
c + total number of internal intersection points on the new chords

Beginning with 0 points, we have 1 piece, the entire cake. Adding c chords, we increase the number of pieces by c + (total number of internal intersection points). Letting

f = number of pieces,
c = number of chords, and
p = total number of internal intersection points,

what we have derived is

$$f = 1 + c + p \tag{0}$$

---

abstract symbol manipulator, which can be turned into a concrete one by supplying a computer to it. After all, it is no longer the purpose of programs to instruct our machines; these days it is the purpose of machines to execute our programs.

– E. W. Dijkstra

Our problem, however, is to express f, the number of pieces, in terms of N, the number of points. Towards this end we observe that

$$f$$

$=$ ⟨ By (0) ⟩

  $1 + c + p$

$=$ ⟨ There is 1 chord for every pair of points, i.e.
        c = number of ways to choose N points 2 at a time ⟩

  $1 + \binom{N}{2} + p$

$=$ ⟨ There is 1 internal intersection point for every bunch
        of 4 points ⟩

  $1 + \binom{N}{2} + \binom{N}{4}$

$=$ ⟨ $\binom{n}{k} = \frac{n!}{k! * (n-k)!}$, twice ⟩

  $1 + \frac{N!}{2! * (N-2)!} + \frac{N!}{4! * (N-4)!}$

$=$ ⟨ $0! = 1$ and $z! = z * (z-1)!$; by arithmetic, lots of it ⟩

  $1 + (N^4 - 6 * N^3 + 23 * N^2 - 18 * N)/24$

This completes the development.

$$\star \qquad\qquad \star$$

If presented only with the final result, namely

$$1 + (N^4 - 6 * N^3 + 23 * N^2 - 18 * N)/24$$

we would be wholly unconvinced. We were convinced, however, when the final result was accompanied by its development. The same is true for programs. The convincingness of a program depends on the convincingness of its development, not on the program text per se. And so we focus our attention on the development.

What made the development convincing?

• *The steps were explicit.* The development was not a big essay. There was no need to parse it into its constituent steps. And each step could be understood in isolation.

- *Each step was the right size.* Each was (hopefully) small enough as to leave no doubts about its correctness.[2] To further this aim, note that each step contained an explicit hint as to why it followed from its predecessor.

- *The steps were precise.* Each step was effectively a formula manipulation. In the first part the formulae involved chords. In the end they involved arithmetic. In contrast to natural language, formulae are precise. If natural language was used, imprecision would be introduced exactly when precision was needed. Consider the phrase: "it is sunny or it is Monday". Can it be sunny on Monday? (It has been pointed out that "legalese" is an attempt to be precise in natural language.)

⋆ ⋆

We approach programming armed with these observations. We must be able to provide a convincing development as we head from problem statement (or specification) to final result (a program satisfying the specification). Each step should be explicit, and each should be the right size. Ideally, each should contain a formula manipulation.

But before we investigate the formulae we will manipulate in the course of program development, we pause to look at formula manipulation in general. In the next chapter we survey some general concepts and notations that will aid us in our future manipulations.

---

[2]We note that "guessing" is akin to a step so big that it is hardly convincing.

1

Preliminary notions, notations, and terminology

1.0 Introduction

Formula manipulation was quite effective in solving the cake problem. In fact, if we think about it, formula manipulation has been the key to success in many areas. Civil engineers manipulate formulae in bridge design, for example.

Programming has benefited from this observation. Programming, however, differs from engineering professions in a fundamental way. The civil engineer deals with continuous quantities, and therefore can err in the direction of, for example, a stronger beam. In fact, civil engineers often add "fudge factors" to compensate for the unknown properties of materials. Programmers, dealing with discrete quantities like sequences of characters, do not have this luxury. If *one* character is wrong, then most likely the entire program will be too. We must be exceedingly careful in our manipulations!

So before we investigate the manipulation of the formulae we will need to do programming, we survey some general concepts, notations, and observations that will make our future manipulations more effective.

1.1 The shapes of our calculations

A train moving at 45 feet/second is passed by a train moving in the opposite direction at 35 feet/second. A passenger in the slower train notices that the faster train takes 6 seconds to pass. We are asked to determine the length of the faster train.

Since we are after the "length of the faster train", we begin with this. What we find is that:

length of faster train
=   ⟨ The givens are in terms of rates and times, so ... ⟩
(rate faster train passed) * (time it took faster train to pass)
=   ⟨ time it took faster train to pass = 6 seconds ⟩
(rate faster train passed) * 6 seconds
=   ⟨ rate faster train passed = 45 feet/second + 35 feet/second,
        or 80 feet/second ⟩
80 feet/second * 6 seconds
=   ⟨ Arithmetic ⟩
480 feet

— which solves this (not too difficult) problem.

*   *

There are two ways to solve a problem. One is to hope for a flash of insight. It may never come. The other is to proceed slowly, step by step. Notice that the format we employed gently forced us into taking the latter approach. We started with what we were after, namely, the "length of the faster train". At each subsequent step our sole concern was where we were at and where we wanted to go. Looking carefully, we see that each "next step" was almost preordained. No cleverness was required. Notice that the format was not (simply) a way to record a solution discovered by other means, for example, by a flash of insight. It actually guided us towards the solution.

The explicit hints were useful too. They are of benefit to the reader, who no longer has to justify the validity of a step. They are also of benefit to the writer, who is less likely to make mistakes. Besides this, the hints reveal which of the "givens" have been used already, and which have yet to be employed.

Because it proved so useful even on a problem as simple as this one, we will adopt this solution format for general use. Its benefits will prove to be invaluable, especially when we encounter more challenging problems.

*   *

Remark   Our ability to solve a problem often hinges on the notations we choose. The classic example is arithmetic using roman numerals. Try multiplying LIV by VIII! With arabic numerals, however, multiplication can be taught to school children. Although inappropriate for doing arithmetic, roman numerals *are* appropriate elsewhere. They are excellent for carving into stone, for instance, an observation due to C.A.R. Hoare!   □

1.2   Laws and so on

Consider the arithmetic formulae

$$X * Y + X * Z$$

where $*$ denotes multiplication. This we can simplify to

$$X * (Y + Z)$$

by appeal to the law that "multiplication distributes over addition" — one of many arithmetic laws that should be second nature. Some other familiar laws are

Law	Name
$P = P$	$=$ is reflexive
$P * 0 = 0$	0 is the zero of $*$
$P * 1 = P$	1 is the unit (or identity element) of $*$
$P + 0 = P$	0 is the unit of $+$
$P * Q = Q * P$	$*$ is symmetric (or commutative)
$P * (Q * R) = (P * Q) * R$	$*$ is associative
$P * (Q + R) = (P * Q) + (P * R)$	$*$ distributes over $+$
$-(-P) = P$	$-$ is its own inverse
$P \leq Q$ and $Q \leq R$, then $P \leq R$	$\leq$ is transitive

This is not a complete list by any means, and we assume familiarity with other arithmetic laws and operators.

Notice that some operators take one operand, and some take two. An operator that takes one operand is called *unary*, for example $-x$. An operator that takes two is called *binary*, for example $x + y$.

We have two *types* of expressions — *arithmetic* and *boolean*. An arithmetic expression yields a number when evaluated. An example is $x + y$. An expression of type boolean, also called a boolean expression,[0] yields either the value *true* or the value *false* when evaluated. An example is $x = y$. A boolean expression equal to *true* is said to be *satisfied* or *established*. We sometimes say that it *holds*.

---

[0]Named after the 19th century mathematician George Boole. If his name was George *Boo*, we would have *boo* expressions, which would be frightening!

We will restrict ourselves to integer arithmetic. For integer division we introduce the new operator *div*. For non-negative x and positive y, x *div* y equals the largest integer at most x/y. Thus 7 *div* $3 = 2$. If x is a multiple of y we sometimes write x *div* y as the more familiar x/y.

A *law* is a boolean expression that always equals *true*. There are two kind of laws, *postulates* and *theorems*. A postulate is a law by definition. For example, we postulate that $P * 0 = 0$ always equals *true* (i.e. for any P). A theorem, being a law, also always equals *true*. The difference is that this must be proved. We can prove that formula X, say, is a theorem by a calculation having the following shape:

$$X$$
$=$ ⟨ Hint why $X = true$ ⟩
$$true$$

In other words, a theorem is a formula that can be converted to *true*.

1.3   On avoiding parentheses

To avoid writing lots of parentheses, we appeal to a few conventions:

We usually omit the parentheses around an entire expression: we write (X) as X.

We know that $X * Y + Z$ is short for $(X * Y) + Z$. We state this as "$*$ has *higher binding power, higher precedence*, or that it *binds tighter* than $+$". The unary minus, as in $-X$, binds tightest of all arithmetic operators.

We know that $X + Y \leq Z$ is short for $(X + Y) \leq Z$. In general, we state that the arithmetic operators (like $+$, $*$, and so on) bind tighter than the relational operators (like $\leq$, $=$, $>$, and so on).

As a result:

$$((W + (X * Y)) > Z)$$
$=$ ⟨ By our first convention, above ⟩
$$(W + (X * Y)) > Z$$
$=$ ⟨ By our second convention ⟩
$$(W + X * Y) > Z$$
$=$ ⟨ By our third convention ⟩
$$W + X * Y > Z$$

Starting with an expression containing 13 characters, we were able to write an equivalent expression containing only 7 characters. The result is a 50% savings and a cleaner formula. Being cleaner it is easier to read and will be easier to manipulate. Since we intend to develop our solutions in a sequence of steps, and not pull them out of thin air, such gains will serve us well.

We take this opportunity to list the relative binding powers of the operators we will use. In order of *decreasing* binding power we have:

> function application
> arithmetic operators
> relational operators
> boolean operators

We discuss function application and the boolean operators later, so don't worry about them for now. We assume familiarity with the arithmetic operators ($+$, $*$, and so on). We also assume familiarity with the relational operators. For example, we assume familiarity with the fact that $x \leq y$ is equivalent to $(x < y \ or \ x = y)$. For completeness we list them:

Relational Operator	Pronounced
$=$	equals
$<$	less than
$\leq$	at most[1]
$\geq$	at least
$>$	greater than
$\neq$	differs from

We have yet another convention, namely that

> We rarely parenthesize $W + X + Y + Z$ or $W * X * Y * Z$. In general, we omit parentheses in $W \circ X \circ Y \circ Z$ when $\circ$ is an associative operator. Being associative it can be parenthesized in any way, so why choose one way over another?

---

[1]We pronounce $\leq$ as "at most" which is much nicer than the usual "is less than or equal to". We pronounce $\neq$ as "differs from" instead of "not equal to". We tend to avoid negative terminology. In the words of A.J.M. van Gasteren: "it suggests that the positively named term is the more fundamental one and that the other one is a derived term with derived properties. Such a suggestion ... may hamper reasoning."

In summary, the conventions of binding power unclutter our formulae of parentheses. Since we intend to rely on formulae heavily, this will save us lots of writing, and will make our formulae easier to read and to manipulate.

1.4   On carrying out calculations

We introduce a new arithmetic operator, $\uparrow$, defined by the following laws:

Laws for $\uparrow$		
Law 0	$P + Q \uparrow R = P + (Q \uparrow R)$	$\uparrow$ binds tighter than $+$
Law 1	$P \uparrow (Q \uparrow R) = (P \uparrow Q) \uparrow R$	$\uparrow$ is associative
Law 2	$P \uparrow Q = Q \uparrow P$	$\uparrow$ is symmetric
Law 3	$P + Q \uparrow R = (P + Q) \uparrow (P + R)$	$+$ distributes over $\uparrow$

and would like to prove:

> Theorem A:
> $$W \uparrow X + Y \uparrow Z = (W + Y) \uparrow (W + Z) \uparrow (X + Y) \uparrow (X + Z)$$

How do we start? The straightforward approach would be to convert the entire expression to *true*. But would we prove

$$52 = (4 + 36/4) * 4 \tag{0}$$

by converting the entire expression to *true*? In other words, would we prove (0) by a calculation like

$$52 = (4 + 36/4) * 4$$
$$= \quad \langle \text{ Arithmetic } \rangle$$
$$52 = (4 + 9) * 4$$
$$= \quad \langle \text{ Arithmetic } \rangle$$
$$52 = 13 * 4$$
$$= \quad \langle \text{ Arithmetic } \rangle$$
$$52 = 52$$
$$= \quad \langle = \text{ is reflexive } \rangle$$
$$true$$

Probably not, since such an approach leads to excessive writing. Instead we would probably convert one side of the equality into the other by a calculation like

       $(4 + 36/4) * 4$
$=$ ⟨ Arithmetic ⟩
       $(4 + 9) * 4$
$=$ ⟨ Arithmetic ⟩
       $13 * 4$
$=$ ⟨ Arithmetic ⟩
       52

In general we

> | Heuristic | Prove an equality by transforming one side of the $=$ into the other.

It is unlikely, however, that we would prove (0) by converting the 52 into $(4 + 36/4) * 4$. In other words, we probably would not prove (0) by a calculation like

       52
$=$ ⟨ Arithmetic ⟩
       $13 * 4$
$=$ ⟨ Arithmetic ⟩
       $(4 + 9) * 4$
$=$ ⟨ Arithmetic ⟩
       $(4 + 36/4) * 4$

In general we

> | Heuristic | Prove an equality by transforming the more complicated side of the $=$ into the simpler side.

The reason is that there are fewer ways to simplify a complicated expression than there are to complicate a simple expression.

These observations lead us to prove our original equality by transforming the more complicated side, namely

$$(W + Y) \uparrow (W + Z) \uparrow (X + Y) \uparrow (X + Z) \tag{1}$$

into the simpler side, namely

$$W \uparrow X + Y \uparrow Z. \tag{2}$$

Proof:

$$(W + Y) \uparrow (W + Z) \uparrow (X + Y) \uparrow (X + Z)$$
=   ⟨ Our target, (2), is a shorter formula. The only law that
            shortens a formula is Law 3. We apply it twice. ⟩
$$(W + Y \uparrow Z) \uparrow (X + Y \uparrow Z)$$
=   ⟨ Our target, (2), is still shorter. Towards applying Law 3
            again, we first appeal to the fact that $+$ is symmetric. $(*)$ ⟩
$$(Y \uparrow Z + W) \uparrow (Y \uparrow Z + X)$$
=   ⟨ Law 3, with $P := Y \uparrow Z$, $Q := W$, and $R := X$ $(**)$ ⟩
$$Y \uparrow Z + W \uparrow X$$
=   ⟨ $+$ is symmetric $(*)$ ⟩
$$W \uparrow X + Y \uparrow Z$$

Thus we have proven the theorem by converting the more complicated side
of the $=$ into the simpler side using a sequence of equality-preserving steps.

⋆   ⋆

There are some observations to be made:

• When necessary, we explicitly mention how a law was used. At step $(**)$,
we indicated that Law 3, namely

$$P + Q \uparrow R = (P + Q) \uparrow (P + R)$$

was instantiated using the substitutions

$$P := Y \uparrow Z$$
$$Q := W$$
$$R := X$$

In other words we appealed to the validity of

$$Y \uparrow Z + W \uparrow X = (Y \uparrow Z + W) \uparrow (Y \uparrow Z + X).$$

We do not propose always making substitutions explicit. This would add
unnecessary clutter. We do so only when necessary.

• Had we converted the entire expression to *true* by a sequence of equality
preserving steps, we would have written:

$$W \uparrow X + Y \uparrow Z = (W + Y) \uparrow (W + Z) \uparrow (X + Y) \uparrow (X + Z)$$
$$= \quad \langle \text{ hint } \rangle$$
$$W \uparrow X + Y \uparrow Z = (W + Y \uparrow Z) \uparrow (X + Y \uparrow Z)$$
$$= \quad \langle \text{ hint } \rangle$$
$$W \uparrow X + Y \uparrow Z = (Y \uparrow Z + W) \uparrow (Y \uparrow Z + X)$$
$$= \quad \langle \text{ hint } \rangle$$
$$W \uparrow X + Y \uparrow Z = Y \uparrow Z + W \uparrow X$$
$$= \quad \langle \text{ hint } \rangle$$
$$W \uparrow X + Y \uparrow Z = W \uparrow X + Y \uparrow Z$$
$$= \quad \langle \text{ hint } \rangle$$
true

Notice how we ended up copying the left side of the equality onto every line of the proof — yielding a proof that is twice as wide as before, at no advantage to either reader or writer. Such wide proofs we would like to avoid. Our heuristics have served us well.

• The appeal to the associativity of $\uparrow$ at the first step was left implicit. This was on purpose. Its inclusion would only add clutter. Along the same lines, we normally omit steps as obvious as those marked (∗), namely rearrangements by appeals to symmetry. As a result, our proof of Theorem A can be written as

$$(W + Y) \uparrow (W + Z) \uparrow (X + Y) \uparrow (X + Z)$$
$$= \quad \langle \text{ Our target, (2), is a shorter formula. The only law that}$$
$$\text{shortens a formula is Law 3. We apply it twice. } \rangle$$
$$(W + Y \uparrow Z) \uparrow (X + Y \uparrow Z)$$
$$= \quad \langle \text{ Our target, (2), is still shorter. Law 3, with}$$
$$P := Y \uparrow Z, \; Q := W, \text{ and } R := X \rangle$$
$$Y \uparrow Z + W \uparrow X$$

Although only two steps are required, there is no disadvantage to the reader.

⋆   ⋆

Returning to our arithmetic operator $\uparrow$, we add another law:

Law 4 $P \uparrow Q \geq P$ Connection between $\uparrow$ and $\geq$

and attempt to prove

$$X \uparrow -X + Y \uparrow -Y \; \geq \; (X + Y) \uparrow -(X + Y) \qquad \text{(Theorem B)}$$

Proof: Since both sides appear equally complicated, we arbitrarily
start with the lefthand side to find:

$$X \uparrow -X + Y \uparrow -Y$$
= $\langle$ Our target has the X's and Y's "together". There are
            two ways to accomplish this: Law 3 and Theorem A. The
            last does it in one fell swoop, so we apply Theorem A. $\rangle$
$$(X + Y) \uparrow (X - Y) \uparrow (-X + Y) \uparrow (-X - Y)$$
= $\langle$ Our target has $-(X + Y)$ in it, which we lack, so
            by arithmetic $\rangle$
$$(X + Y) \uparrow (X - Y) \uparrow (-X + Y) \uparrow -(X + Y)$$
$\geq$ $\langle$ Our target is shorter. There are only three ways to shorten
            a formula: Law 3, Theorem A, and Law 4. Only Law 4 has
            a $\geq$, which we need, so we apply Law 4, with
$$P := (X + Y) \uparrow -(X + Y) \text{ and } Q := (X - Y) \uparrow (-X + Y)) \rangle$$
$$(X + Y) \uparrow -(X + Y)$$

We comment on this proof:

• When we wrote

$$A$$
= $\langle$ hint why $A = B$ $\rangle$
$$B$$
$\geq$ $\langle$ hint why $B \geq C$ $\rangle$
$$C$$

we were appealing to the validity of

$$A = B \text{ and } B \geq C, \text{ then } A \geq C.$$

Had we disallowed $\geq$ from the lefthand column of our calculation, and
allowed only $=$, we would have been forced to covert the entire expression
to *true* using a calculation like:

$$X \uparrow -X + Y \uparrow -Y \geq (X + Y) \uparrow -(X + Y)$$
= $\langle$ hint $\rangle$
$$(X + Y) \uparrow (X - Y) \uparrow (-X + Y) \uparrow (-X - Y) \geq \dots$$
= $\langle$ hint $\rangle$
$$(X + Y) \uparrow (X - Y) \uparrow (-X + Y) \uparrow -(X + Y) \geq \dots$$
= $\langle$ hint $\rangle$
true

Allowing $\geq$ in the lefthand column saved a lot of writing.

• The most important observation is that we had little choice at each step. Reading the hints reveals that each step was almost preordained. No brainstorms were required. Every step was dictated by the shape of the current expression and the shape of the target expression.

⋆   ⋆

At this point we might guess what is running through your mind: why do we bother with such small details? The reason is an empirical one: As problems become more challenging, it turns out that attention to such details is often the difference between a solution and a totally unconvincing mess.

We make a final observation. Our formulae were uninterpreted. Each step depended solely on the shape of the current expression, and the shape of the target expression. For this reason such proofs are often referred to as *syntactical* or *calculational* proofs. We will refer to them as *calculations*.

We never appealed to intuition. We never considered what $\uparrow$ meant, if it "meant" anything at all. We were given a problem and solved it by calculation. Only the person who poses a problem has to know what it means. In mathematics, vague and informal appeals to a formula's meaning is sometimes called "handwaving".

These observations lead to an exceedingly useful heuristic:

> $\boxed{\text{Heuristic}}$ Be very careful.

The reason for this heuristic is simple: We do not handwave, so must make sure that each step — each symbol manipulation — is a valid one. Write very slowly, all the while keeping one eye on the expression to be manipulated and the other on the target expression. As obvious as it sounds, this heuristic is remarkably useful.

⋆   ⋆

Ex 1.0   Prove Theorem B again, this time allowing only $=$ in the lefthand column of your calculation. Compared with our earlier proof, how many extra symbols are required? □

Ex 1.1   Using the calculation format and the laws for $\uparrow$, prove:

$$(X + Z) \uparrow (Y + Z) + (X - Z) \uparrow (Y - Z) \geq X + Y$$

□

1.5   Three new arithmetic operators

In this section we introduce three arithmetic operators that we will need
later on. Our first is the *absolute value*, where the absolute value of P,
written $|P|$, is defined by

$$|P| = P \ max \ -P \qquad\qquad \text{(Definition of absolute value)}$$

Operators *max* and *min* are defined by the following laws. To save a bit
of writing, we use m to denote that a law applies to both *max* and *min*.

Law	Name
Binding powers:	
$\quad P + Q \ m \ R = P + (Q \ m \ R)$	m has higher binding power than $+$
Basic laws:	
$\quad P \ m \ Q = Q \ m \ P$	m is symmetric
$\quad P \ m \ (Q \ m \ R) = (P \ m \ Q) \ m \ R$	m is associative
$\quad P \ m \ P = P$	m is idempotent
Distribution:	
$\quad P + Q \ m \ R = (P + Q) \ m \ (P + R)$	$+$ distributes over m
Unit and zero elements:	
$\quad P \ min \ + inf = P$	$+inf$ (or $+\infty$) is the unit for *min*
$\quad P \ max \ - inf = P$	$-inf$ (or $-\infty$) is the unit for *max*
$\quad P \ max \ + inf = +inf$	$+inf$ is the zero for *max*
$\quad P \ min \ - inf = -inf$	$-inf$ is the zero for *min*
Other laws:	Connections between:
$\quad P \ max \ Q \ \geq \ P$	*max* and $\geq$
$\quad P \ min \ Q \ \leq \ P$	*min* and $\leq$
$\quad -P \ min \ -Q = -(P \ max \ Q)$	*min* and *max*
$\quad -P \ max \ -Q = -(P \ min \ Q)$	*max* and *min*

★   ★

Ex 1.2   Using the calculation format and the appropriate laws, prove:

$$|X| + |Y| \ \geq \ |X + Y|$$

This is known as the *triangle inequality*.   □

1.6   The problem with the three dots

The sequence of N integers beginning with 3 is often written

$$3, 4, \ldots, 3 + N - 1$$

This is awfully verbose, and its meaning is hard to extract. By direct substitution for N we find:

For $N = 3$ we have : $3, 4, \ldots, 3 + 3 - 1$ or
$3, 4, \ldots, 5$.

For $N = 2$ we have : $3, 4, \ldots, 4$.

For $N = 1$ we have : $3, 4, \ldots, 3$.

For $N = 0$ we have : $3, 4, \ldots, 2$.

The notation is quite misleading! To be clear we would be forced into a case-analysis. In particular, we would have to indicate the sequence of N integers beginning with 3 using four cases:

$3, 4, \ldots, 3 + N - 1$ for $N \geq 3$
$3, 4$ for $N = 2$
3 for $N = 1$
empty   for $N = 0$

While clear, this is verbose. It is also hard to manipulate. Consider increasing each term by 7. We would have to write

$7 + 3, 7 + 4, \ldots, 7 + 3 + N - 1$ for $N \geq 3$
$7 + 3, 7 + 4$ for $N = 2$
$7 + 3$ for $N = 1$
empty   for $N = 0$

This is quite painful. Since the culprit to begin with is the three dots, "$\ldots$", we should do away with them entirely.

★   ★

For one more example, consider

1, 2, ..., 8

which might denote any of:

1, 2, 3, 4, 5, 6, 7, 8   Arithmetic progression
1, 2, 4, 8   Powers of 2 only
1, 2, 3, 5, 8   Fibonacci sequence

Yes, the three dots are quite ambiguous!

★   ★

Four alternatives present themselves for writing the sequence of $N \geq 0$ integers beginning with A, depending on whether the bounds are included:

(a) $A \leq x \leq A + N - 1$
(b) $A \leq x < A + N$
(c) $A - 1 < x \leq A + N - 1$
(d) $A - 1 < x < A + N$

Choice (b) is simplest so we adopt it. It has some nice properties. For $A \leq B$:

$A \leq x < B$ has exactly $B - A$ elements. In particular, $A \leq x < A$ is the empty sequence.

$A \leq x < B$ and $B \leq x < C$ can be combined into $A \leq x < C$.

We can add 7 to each term by writing $7 + A \leq x < 7 + A + B$ or $A \leq x - 7 < A + B$.

1.7 What are the natural numbers?

The first N natural numbers are $0 \leq x < N$. Notice that we include 0.

If we did not include 0, we would have to cast one of Newton's famous laws as

> *In the absence of an outside force, an object*
> * – stays at rest, or*
> * – moves with constant velocity.*

With 0 un-natural, an object cannot move with 0 velocity — it has to "stay at rest". Allowing 0 to be natural, we can rewrite Newton's law as

> *In the absence of an outside force, an object*
> *moves with constant velocity.*

Inclusion of 0 removes the case-analysis. Although it may seem peculiar at first, our numbering usually begins at 0. With time this too is sure to become natural!

Remark A number of famous programming languages, including some recent and well-known ones, define 1 to be the smallest array index. The designers of such languages would probably claim that "inclusion of 0 would be un-natural". Their decision has the unpleasant effect of complicating programs by forcing scattered additions and subtractions of 1 throughout program texts. What is "natural" must be learned, a fact that is well-known to athletes. Non-inclusion of 0 has other unpleasant effects as well, some of which we discuss later. □

1.8   A bit about function application

The notion of binding power allows us to unclutter formulae of parentheses, making them shorter, and easier to read and to manipulate. The traditional notation for function application, $f(x)$, can lead to lots of parentheses. To remedy this we introduce a new notation for function application, namely a lowered infix period. Thus we would write $f(x)$ as $f.x$. For more examples, we have:

Old notation	New notation
$f(x)$	$f.x$
$f(x) + f(y)$	$f.x + f.y$
$f(x) + 1$	$f.x + 1$
$f(x + 1)$	$f.(x + 1)$
$f(x, y)$	$f.x.y$ (or $f.(x, y)$)

Notice that the left column has 6 pairs of parentheses, while the right column has only 1. This is a nice improvement. (The reason why $f(x + 1)$ is written as $f.(x + 1)$, and not as $f.x + 1$, is because function application binds tighter than any other operator, hence it binds tighter than $+$.)

Function application is postulated to satisfy:

Law	Name
$f.x \circ y = (f.x) \circ y$	"." has the highest binding power
(for any operator $\circ$)	of any operator
$f.x.y = (f.x).y$	"." binds to the left
$x = y \Rightarrow f.x = f.y$	Leibniz's rule

This last postulate, Leibniz's rule, can be ignored for now. It is included for completeness only.

★   ★

A function that can be applied at any point is called *total*. A function that cannot is called *partial*. We know how to indicate function application. We need a way to indicate at which points a function can be applied.

One way is to enumerate all the points. For example, with function f, of one argument, we assert that

$$f.1, \ f.2, \ f.3, \ f.4, \ f.5, \ f.6, \ f.7, \text{ and } f.8 \tag{0}$$

are the only legal expressions. Such enumerations, however, can lead to a lot of writing. What if f could be applied at all points from 1 to 10,000? Sometimes the three dots are used, but, as we have seen, this leads to all sorts of problems. Thus we are led to introduce a terser notation. We will write

$$f(i : 1 \le i < 9) \tag{1}$$

to indicate that function f is defined only at points i, for $1 \le i < 9$. Thus both (0) and (1) are equivalent.

Variable i is called a *dummy* or *bound variable*. It is meaningful only within the scope of the parentheses. Its name is irrelevant — (1) could equivalently be written

$$f(j : 1 \le j < 9).$$

A variable that is not a dummy is said to be *free*. For example, in

$$g(i : 0 \le i < x) \tag{2}$$

variable i is a dummy and variable x is free. Take care not to give a dummy and a free variable the same name. For example, in (2) we would never rename dummy i to x. If we did we would get

$$g(x : 0 \leq x < x)$$

which is clearly not the same as (2). To avoid such problems we strongly recommend that certain letters (e.g. i, j, and k) be used only as dummies.

Another advantage of this notation is that it is easy to generalize. We allow

$$h(i : R.i)$$

where i is a list of dummies, and $R.i$ is a boolean valued function of these dummies. For example, we would write

$$h(j, k : \ 0 \leq j < 3 \ \ and \ \ k = 5)$$

to indicate that $h.0.5$, $h.1.5$, and $h.2.5$ are the only legal applications of h.

1.9   What next?

Now that we have the basics down, we turn to those formulae that we will use in programming. These formulae are called *predicates* and the set of rules governing their manipulation is called the *predicate calculus*. A *calculus*, according to Webster's, is "any branch of mathematics involving calculation".

Calculations involving predicates will be our main vehicle for the development of programs from their specifications. They will also be our main vehicle for writing specifications in the first place. Recall that we prefer calculation to the endless cycle of guessing, checking, and guessing again. We prefer it for practical reasons. It is also more satisfying.

Thus if we are to develop programs, we had better become adept at calculations involving predicates. We carry out our study in the next two chapters.

Remark   Practicing programmers tend to use predicates for descriptive purposes only — to write down the results of a problem solved "intuitively". Intuition is somewhat limiting:

Exercise: Solve $12345 * 7826$ using intuition *only*.

Quite a difficult problem! Allowing calculation, however, it is trivial, provided that we are familiar with the rules for doing multiplications. The same applies to program development using the predicate calculus. So if you have an "intuitive" familiarity with predicates, it is best forgotten. Instead concentrate on learning the rules for their manipulation. When this too becomes second nature, you will find that many "difficult" problems aren't so difficult after all. □

2

Predicates A — Boolean operators

2.0 Introduction

As already mentioned, the manipulation of predicates will be our main vehicle for program development. As such, manipulating them must become second nature. This comes from practice. Throughout this chapter there are theorems whose proofs are omitted. Although these proofs are exercises at chapter end, we highly recommend attacking them as they appear in the text. They are a lot of fun, and will be of great help in absorbing the material. Attacking theorems whose proofs are included will be of great help too.

Before we begin, we point out that our sole interest in this chapter (and in the next) is in *playing a game with symbols*. Certain sequences of symbols are postulated to be laws. In other words, these sequences are true by definition. Other sequences are theorems, and must be proved. The symbols mean nothing at all, just like the ↑ from the previous chapter. Our aim is to become proficient players of this game. First because it is fun, and second because a proficiency will serve us well later on.

2.1 The equivalence

Our first boolean operator is the *equivalence*, which is written ≡, as in $P \equiv Q$. The equivalence is postulated to be

- associative: $((P \equiv Q) \equiv R) \equiv (P \equiv (Q \equiv R))$
- symmetric: $(P \equiv Q) \equiv (Q \equiv P)$
- and to have unit *true*: $(P \equiv true) \equiv P$

Because the equivalence is associative, we are free to omit the parentheses. From now on we will, allowing us to write this last postulate, for example, as simply

$$P \equiv true \equiv P.$$

⋆   ⋆

Now we prove our first theorem — the reflexivity of the equivalence:

○ The equivalence is reflexive: $X \equiv X$
  Proof: For any boolean expression X, we observe

$$X \equiv X$$
$\equiv$ ⟨ $P \equiv true \equiv P$, written $(P \equiv P) \equiv true$
             (by the symmetry and associativity of $\equiv$)⟩
    $true$

This theorem tells us that any expression of shape $Y \equiv Y$ can be replaced by $true$. For example:

$$Z \equiv Z \equiv Y$$
$\equiv$ ⟨ The equivalence is reflexive: $P \equiv P$ ⟩
    $true \equiv Y$
$\equiv$ ⟨ $true$ is the unit of the equivalence ⟩
    Y

Because this last calculation is quite common, we typically omit its last step, as understood, and write simply

$$Z \equiv Z \equiv Y$$
$\equiv$ ⟨ $P \equiv P$ ⟩
    Y

⋆   ⋆

The equivalence is the alternative for $=$ when dealing with booleans. It was introduced for a very good reason: $\equiv$ is associative, while $=$ is not. For example, $(3 = 3) = true$ is OK, but $3 = (3 = true)$ is not. A secondary reason is that it has a lower binding power than the $=$, so its inclusion helps us avoid parentheses. For example, we can write

$$x \le y \ \ and \ \ y \le x \ \equiv \ x = y$$

instead of

$$x \le y \ \ and \ \ y \le x \ = \ (x = y).$$

2.2 The disjunction

Our next boolean operator is the *disjunction*, which is written $\lor$, as in $P \lor Q$. It is postulated to have higher binding power than the equivalence, and to be

- associative and symmetric
- idempotent: $P \lor P \equiv P$
- distribute over $\equiv$: $P \lor (Q \equiv R) \equiv P \lor Q \equiv P \lor R$

$$\star \qquad\qquad \star$$

○ The disjunction distributes over itself:

$$X \lor (Y \lor Z) \equiv (X \lor Y) \lor (X \lor Z)$$

Proof: For any X, Y, and Z, we observe

$$(X \lor Y) \lor (X \lor Z)$$
$\equiv$ ⟨ Associativity of $\lor$ ⟩
$$X \lor Y \lor X \lor Z$$
$\equiv$ ⟨ Symmetry of $\lor$ ⟩
$$X \lor X \lor Y \lor Z$$
$\equiv$ ⟨ Idempotence of $\lor$, i.e. $P \lor P \equiv P$ ⟩
$$X \lor Y \lor Z$$
$\equiv$ ⟨ Associativity of $\lor$ ⟩
$$X \lor (Y \lor Z)$$

We will normally omit appeals to symmetry and associativity as understood, allowing this theorem to be proved in one step by:

$$(X \lor Y) \lor (X \lor Z)$$
$\equiv$ ⟨ Idempotence of $\lor$ ⟩
$$X \lor (Y \lor Z)$$

○ The disjunction has zero *true*: $X \lor true \equiv true$
Proof: For any X we observe

$$X \lor true$$
$\equiv$ ⟨ $P \equiv P \equiv true$, with $P := Y$ ⟩
$$X \lor (Y \equiv Y)$$
$\equiv$ ⟨ $\lor$ distributes over $\equiv$ ⟩
$$X \lor Y \equiv X \lor Y$$
$\equiv$ ⟨ $P \equiv P$ ⟩
$$true$$

The first step in this proof is a little mysterious. Starting with $X \vee true$ what do we do? We have no formula of this shape, so we must concentrate on its components. In particular we have to find an expression equivalent to one of them. In this case we chose a simple expression equivalent to $true$, namely $Y \equiv Y$. Other choices would do the trick too.

2.3   Intermezzo on some interesting formulae

Using the equivalence and the disjunction, there are three "interesting formulae" we can write in two variables, namely

(a) $P \vee Q \equiv P \equiv Q$
(b) $P \vee Q \equiv P$
(c) $P \vee Q \equiv Q$

Our next three boolean operators, the *conjunction*, the *consequence*, and the *implication*, will be defined using these three formulae.

Formula (a) has a nice symmetry, so we introduce the symmetric looking operator $\wedge$, called the *conjunction*, and define it by

$$P \wedge Q \equiv \text{(a)}$$

Formula (b) is not too symmetric looking, so we introduce the not too symmetric looking operator $\Leftarrow$, called the *consequence*, and define it by

$$P \Leftarrow Q \equiv \text{(b)}$$

Formula (c) is not too symmetric looking either, but it looks a lot like (b). In fact, if we reverse the operands in (b)'s disjunction, we get (c). So we reverse the $\Leftarrow$, introducing the $\Rightarrow$, called the *implication*, and define it by

$$P \Rightarrow Q \equiv \text{(c)}$$

In the next three sections we derive many formulae about these three new operators.

Remark   As a reminder (to certain readers): These formulae have no meaning whatsoever. They are sequences of meaningless symbols. Our sole interest is in manipulating them!   □

2.4 The conjunction

Our first new operator, the *conjunction*, is postulated to have the same binding power as the disjunction, therefore we must be careful in parenthesizing formulae that contain both. The conjunction is defined using our first "interesting formula". In other words, it is postulated to satisfy

- $P \land Q \equiv P \equiv Q \equiv P \lor Q$ (Golden Rule)

This formula, sometimes known as the *Golden Rule*, is a rich one. Because of the associativity and symmetry of the equivalence, it can be parsed as

$$(P \land Q) \equiv (P \equiv Q) \equiv (P \lor Q) \quad \text{or as}$$
$$(P \land Q) \equiv (P \equiv Q \equiv P \lor Q) \quad \text{or as}$$
$$(P \land Q \equiv P \equiv Q) \equiv (P \lor Q) \quad \text{or as}$$
$$(P \equiv Q) \equiv (P \land Q \equiv P \lor Q) \quad \text{and so on.}$$

$\star$ $\star$

○ The conjunction is symmetric: $X \land Y \equiv Y \land X$
Proof: omitted.

○ The conjunction is associative: $X \land (Y \land Z) \equiv (X \land Y) \land Z$
Proof: omitted.

○ The conjunction is idempotent: $X \land X \equiv X$
Proof: For any X we observe

$$X \land X$$
$$\equiv \quad \langle \text{ Golden Rule, parsed } (P \land Q) \equiv (P \equiv Q \equiv P \lor Q) \rangle$$
$$X \equiv X \equiv X \lor X$$
$$\equiv \quad \langle \lor \text{ is idempotent} \rangle$$
$$X \equiv X \equiv X$$
$$\equiv \quad \langle P \equiv P \rangle$$
$$X$$

○ The conjunction has unit *true*: $X \land true \equiv X$
Proof: For any X we observe

$$X \land true$$
$$\equiv \quad \langle \text{ Golden Rule} \rangle$$
$$X \equiv true \equiv X \lor true$$
$$\equiv \quad \langle \lor \text{ has zero } true \rangle$$
$$X \equiv true \equiv true$$
$$\equiv \quad \langle P \equiv P \rangle$$
$$X$$

⋆   ⋆

We have derived some basic formulae about the conjunction, but none about its distribution properties, which tend to be quite useful. We continue with some of these:

○ The conjunction distributes over itself:

$$X \wedge (Y \wedge Z) \equiv (X \wedge Y) \wedge (X \wedge Z)$$

Proof: omitted.

We might guess that the conjunction distributes over the equivalence, in other words that

$$X \wedge (Y \equiv Z) \equiv X \wedge Y \equiv X \wedge Z$$

holds. Let's see:

$$X \wedge Y \equiv X \wedge Z$$
$\equiv$ ⟨ Golden Rule, once per conjunction ⟩
$$X \equiv Y \equiv X \vee Y \equiv X \equiv Z \equiv X \vee Z$$
$\equiv$ ⟨ Rearranging, by the symmetry of $\equiv$ ⟩
$$X \equiv Y \equiv Z \equiv X \vee Y \equiv X \vee Z \equiv X$$
$\equiv$ ⟨ To distribute X out, as in our target:
            the disjunction distributes over the equivalence ⟩
$$X \equiv Y \equiv Z \equiv X \vee (Y \equiv Z) \equiv X$$
$\equiv$ ⟨ Golden Rule, with $P := X$, $Q := (Y \equiv Z)$ ⟩
$$X \wedge (Y \equiv Z) \equiv X$$

Thus we have proved:

○ $X \wedge Y \equiv X \wedge Z \equiv X \wedge (Y \equiv Z) \equiv X$

— a result that tells us, because of the trailing " $\equiv X$", that the conjunction *does not* distribute over the equivalence! The conjunction does, however, distribute over an *even* number of equivalences:

○ $W \wedge (X \equiv Y \equiv Z) \equiv W \wedge X \equiv W \wedge Y \equiv W \wedge Z$
   Proof: omitted.

○ The conjunction distributes over disjunction:

$$X \wedge (Y \vee Z) \equiv (X \wedge Y) \vee (X \wedge Z)$$

Proof: omitted.

o The disjunction distributes over conjunction:

$$X \lor (Y \land Z) \equiv (X \lor Y) \land (X \lor Z)$$

Proof: For any X, Y, and Z we observe

$(X \lor Y) \land (X \lor Z)$
$\equiv$ ⟨ Golden Rule ⟩
$X \lor Y \equiv X \lor Z \equiv X \lor Y \lor X \lor Z$
$\equiv$ ⟨ Idempotence of $\lor$ (∗) ⟩
$X \lor Y \equiv X \lor Z \equiv X \lor Y \lor Z$
$\equiv$ ⟨ The disjunction distributes over the equivalence ⟩
$X \lor (Y \equiv Z \equiv Y \lor Z)$
$\equiv$ ⟨ Golden Rule ⟩
$X \lor (Y \land Z)$

We prove this theorem again, this time starting with the simpler side:

$X \lor (Y \land Z)$
$\equiv$ ⟨ Golden Rule ⟩
$X \lor (Y \equiv Z \equiv Y \lor Z)$
$\equiv$ ⟨ The disjunction distributes over the equivalence ⟩
$X \lor Y \equiv X \lor Z \equiv X \lor Y \lor Z$
$\equiv$ ⟨ Idempotence of $\lor$ (∗) ⟩
$X \lor Y \equiv X \lor Z \equiv X \lor Y \lor X \lor Z$
$\equiv$ ⟨ Golden Rule, with $P := X \lor Y$ and $Q := X \lor Z$ ⟩
$(X \lor Y) \land (X \lor Z)$

Comparing these two proofs, notice that the first was straightforward, while in the second we had to pull a "rabbit out of the hat". In the first proof, at step (∗), we transformed $X \lor X$ into X, a step which was quite natural. In the second proof, we transformed X into $X \lor X$, a step that was a bit mysterious. Such "rabbits" we would like to avoid.

This is another illustration of why it is better to prove an equivalence by starting with the more complicated side. The more complicated side has more manipulative possibilities.

⋆ ⋆

We conclude our treatment of the conjunction with two *Absorption Laws*.

o $X \lor (X \land Y) \equiv X$
Proof: omitted.

o $X \land (X \lor Y) \equiv X$
Proof: For any X and Y we observe

$$X \land (X \lor Y)$$
$$\equiv \qquad \langle \text{Golden Rule, with } P := X \;,\; Q := X \lor Y \rangle$$
$$X \equiv X \lor Y \equiv X \lor (X \lor Y)$$
$$\equiv \qquad \langle \text{Associativity and idempotence of } \lor \rangle$$
$$X \equiv X \lor Y \equiv X \lor Y$$
$$\equiv \qquad \langle P \equiv P \rangle$$
$$X$$

2.5   The implication

The implication is postulated to have higher binding power than the equivalence, but lower binding power than the disjunction (and therefore, the conjunction). It is defined using our third "interesting formula". In other words, it is postulated to satisfy

$$\bullet \; P \Rightarrow Q \equiv P \lor Q \equiv Q \qquad\qquad\qquad \text{(Impl)}$$

⋆   ⋆

We prove some theorems:

○ $X \Rightarrow X$
   Proof: omitted.

○ $X \Rightarrow true$
   Proof: omitted.

○ $X \land Y \Rightarrow X$
   Proof: omitted.

○ $X \Rightarrow X \lor Y$
   Proof: For any X and Y we observe

$$X \Rightarrow X \lor Y$$
$$\equiv \qquad \langle \text{Impl} \rangle$$
$$X \lor X \lor Y \equiv X \lor Y$$
$$\equiv \qquad \langle \text{Idempotence of } \lor \rangle$$
$$X \lor Y \equiv X \lor Y$$
$$\equiv \qquad \langle P \equiv P \rangle$$
$$true$$

○ $true \Rightarrow X \equiv X$
   Proof: omitted.

∘ $X \Rightarrow Y \equiv X \wedge Y \equiv X$
   Proof: For any X and Y we observe

$$X \wedge Y \equiv X$$
$\equiv \qquad$ ⟨ Golden Rule ⟩
$$Y \equiv X \vee Y$$
$\equiv \qquad$ ⟨ Impl ⟩
$$X \Rightarrow Y$$

— a result which shows us how to convert an implication into a formula containing only conjunction and equivalence.

∘ $X \Rightarrow (Y \Rightarrow Z) \equiv X \wedge Y \Rightarrow Z$
   Proof: omitted.

∘ $X \wedge (X \Rightarrow Y) \equiv X \wedge Y$
   Proof: For any X and Y we observe

$$X \wedge (X \Rightarrow Y)$$
$\equiv \qquad$ ⟨ $P \Rightarrow Q \equiv P \wedge Q \equiv P$ ⟩
$$X \wedge (X \wedge Y \equiv X)$$
$\equiv \qquad$ ⟨ $P \wedge (Q \equiv R) \equiv P \wedge Q \equiv P \wedge R \equiv P$ ⟩
$$X \wedge X \wedge Y \equiv X \wedge X \equiv X$$
$\equiv \qquad$ ⟨ Idempotence of $\wedge$, twice ⟩
$$X \wedge Y \equiv X \equiv X$$
$\equiv \qquad$ ⟨ $P \equiv P$ ⟩
$$X \wedge Y$$

∘ The implication is transitive: $(X \Rightarrow Y) \wedge (Y \Rightarrow Z) \Rightarrow (X \Rightarrow Z)$
   Proof: For any X, Y, and Z, we observe

$$(X \Rightarrow Y) \wedge (Y \Rightarrow Z) \Rightarrow (X \Rightarrow Z)$$
$\equiv \qquad$ ⟨ $P \Rightarrow (Q \Rightarrow R) \equiv P \wedge Q \Rightarrow R$, with
$\qquad \qquad P := (X \Rightarrow Y) \wedge (Y \Rightarrow Z)$ ⟩
$$(X \Rightarrow Y) \wedge (Y \Rightarrow Z) \wedge X \Rightarrow Z$$
$\equiv \qquad$ ⟨ Symmetry of $\wedge$ ⟩
$$X \wedge (X \Rightarrow Y) \wedge (Y \Rightarrow Z) \Rightarrow Z$$
$\equiv \qquad$ ⟨ $P \wedge (P \Rightarrow Q) \equiv P \wedge Q$ ⟩
$$X \wedge Y \wedge (Y \Rightarrow Z) \Rightarrow Z$$
$\equiv \qquad$ ⟨ $P \wedge (P \Rightarrow Q) \equiv P \wedge Q$ ⟩
$$X \wedge Y \wedge Z \Rightarrow Z$$
$\equiv \qquad$ ⟨ $P \wedge Q \Rightarrow P$ ⟩
   true

This last proof is good example of the importance of hints. Without the hints a great deal of labor would be forced onto the shoulders of the reader.

With hints, this labor is avoided.

Continuing our investigation of the implication, we find:

o $(X \Rightarrow Y) \vee (Y \Rightarrow Z)$
  Proof: omitted.

o Mutual implication: $(X \Rightarrow Y) \wedge (Y \Rightarrow X) \equiv X \equiv Y$
  Proof: omitted.

This last formulae shows how a mutual implication can be converted into an equivalence.

2.6   The consequence

The consequence is postulated to have the same binding power as the implication. It is defined using our second "interesting formula". In other words, it is postulated to satisfy

$$\bullet \; P \Leftarrow Q \equiv P \vee Q \equiv P \qquad\qquad\qquad \text{(Cons)}$$

$$\star \qquad\qquad\qquad \star$$

o Connection between $\Rightarrow$ and $\Leftarrow$: $(X \Leftarrow Y) \equiv (Y \Rightarrow X)$
  Proof: For any X and Y we observe

$$
\begin{array}{ll}
& X \Leftarrow Y \\
\equiv & \langle \text{ Cons, the only formula containing a } \Leftarrow \rangle \\
& X \vee Y \equiv X \\
\equiv & \langle \; \vee \; \text{is symmetric} \rangle \\
& Y \vee X \equiv X \\
\equiv & \langle \text{Impl} \rangle \\
& Y \Rightarrow X
\end{array}
$$

This result yields a lot of other formulae for free. For example:

$$
\begin{array}{ll}
& X \wedge Y \Rightarrow X \\
\equiv & \langle \text{This last theorem} \rangle \\
& X \Leftarrow X \wedge Y
\end{array}
$$

As a result, we will not explicitly prove other theorems about the consequence.

2.7   The negation

Our next operator, the *negation*, is a unary operator. It is written $\neg$, as in $\neg P$. Our first two operators, the equivalence and the disjunction, were used to define the conjunction, the consequence, and the implication. We will define the negation in terms of the equivalence and the disjunction too.

★   ★

The negation is postulated to have a higher binding power than the disjunction. Therefore it has the highest binding power of any boolean operator. It is connected to the equivalence by the postulate

- $\neg(P \equiv Q) \equiv \neg P \equiv Q$ (Neg)

and is connected to the disjunction by the postulate

- $P \vee \neg P$ (Excluded Middle)

★   ★

We prove some theorems about the negation:

○ $\neg X \equiv Y \equiv X \equiv \neg Y$
    Proof: For any X and Y we observe

$$
\begin{array}{ll}
& \neg X \equiv Y \\
\equiv & \quad \langle \text{Neg} \rangle \\
& \neg(X \equiv Y) \\
\equiv & \quad \langle \text{Neg} \rangle \\
& X \equiv \neg Y
\end{array}
$$

○ $\neg\neg X \equiv X$
    Proof: For any X we observe

$$
\begin{array}{ll}
& \neg\neg X \equiv X \\
\equiv & \quad \langle \neg P \equiv Q \equiv P \equiv \neg Q, \text{ with } P := \neg X \,,\, Q := X \rangle \\
& \neg X \equiv \neg X \\
\equiv & \quad \langle P \equiv P \rangle \\
& \textit{true}
\end{array}
$$

○ $\neg X \vee Y \equiv X \vee Y \equiv Y$
    Proof: omitted.

$$\star \qquad\qquad \star$$

Next we have *De Morgan's Laws*, named after the 19th century mathematician Augustus De Morgan:

o $\neg X \wedge \neg Y \equiv \neg(X \vee Y)$
   Proof: omitted.

o $\neg X \vee \neg Y \equiv \neg(X \wedge Y)$
   Proof: For any X and Y we observe

$$
\begin{aligned}
&\quad \neg X \vee \neg Y \\
\equiv&\quad \langle \neg P \vee Q \equiv P \vee Q \equiv Q \rangle \\
&\quad X \vee \neg Y \equiv \neg Y \\
\equiv&\quad \langle \neg P \vee Q \equiv P \vee Q \equiv Q \rangle \\
&\quad Y \vee X \equiv X \equiv \neg Y \\
\equiv&\quad \langle P \equiv \neg Q \equiv \neg(P \equiv Q), \text{ with } P := Y \vee X \equiv X \rangle \\
&\quad \neg(Y \vee X \equiv X \equiv Y) \\
\equiv&\quad \langle \text{Golden Rule} \rangle \\
&\quad \neg(X \wedge Y)
\end{aligned}
$$

$$\star \qquad\qquad \star$$

Next we have the *Complement Rules*:

o $X \vee (\neg X \wedge Y) \equiv X \vee Y$
   Proof: omitted.

o $X \wedge (\neg X \vee Y) \equiv X \wedge Y$
   Proof: omitted.

$$\star \qquad\qquad \star$$

And now we prove a few results that connect the negation and the implication:

o $\neg X \vee Y \equiv X \Rightarrow Y$
   Proof: For any X and Y we observe

$$
\begin{aligned}
&\quad \neg X \vee Y \\
\equiv&\quad \langle \neg P \vee Q \equiv P \vee Q \equiv Q \rangle \\
&\quad X \vee Y \equiv Y \\
\equiv&\quad \langle \text{Impl} \rangle \\
&\quad X \Rightarrow Y
\end{aligned}
$$

o Contrapositive: $X \Rightarrow Y \equiv \neg Y \Rightarrow \neg X$
   Proof: omitted.

○ Shuffle: $(X \wedge Y \Rightarrow Z) \equiv (X \Rightarrow \neg Y \vee Z)$
  Proof: omitted.

This last result, is called the *Shuffle* because it shows how to shuffle expressions between the sides of an implication. Sometimes it is referred to as *Shunting*.

○ $X \vee \neg true \equiv X$
  Proof: For any X we observe

$$X \vee \neg true$$
$$\equiv \qquad \langle \neg P \vee Q \equiv P \vee Q \equiv Q \rangle$$
$$true \vee X \equiv X$$
$$\equiv \qquad \langle \text{ } true \text{ is the zero of the disjunction} \rangle$$
$$true \equiv X$$
$$\equiv \qquad \langle \text{ } true \text{ is the unit of the equivalence} \rangle$$
$$X$$

This result tells us that $\neg true$ is the unit of the disjunction. The unit of the disjunction deserves its own name, and so we postulate

● $\neg true \equiv false$

With *false* defined we can capture this last result as

○ *false* is the unit of the disjunction: $X \vee false \equiv X$
  Proof: See above.

which we will do from now on.

$$\star \qquad\qquad \star$$

Next we derive some formulae that include *false*:

○ $\neg false \equiv true$
  Proof: omitted.

○ *false* is the zero of the conjunction: $X \wedge false \equiv false$
  Proof: For any X we observe

$$X \wedge false$$
$$\equiv \qquad \langle \text{ Golden Rule} \rangle$$
$$X \vee false \equiv X \equiv false$$
$$\equiv \qquad \langle \text{ } false \text{ is the unit of the disjunction} \rangle$$
$$X \equiv X \equiv false$$
$$\equiv \qquad \langle P \equiv P \rangle$$
$$false$$

o $X \equiv \neg X \equiv false$
   Proof: omitted.

o $false \Rightarrow X$
   Proof: For any X we observe

   $\qquad false \Rightarrow X$
   $\equiv \qquad \langle P \Rightarrow Q \equiv P \vee Q \equiv Q \rangle$
   $\qquad false \vee X \equiv X$
   $\equiv \qquad \langle false$ is the unit of the disjunction $\rangle$
   $\qquad X \equiv X$
   $\equiv \qquad \langle P \equiv P \rangle$
   $\qquad true$

o Contradiction: $X \wedge \neg X \equiv false$
   Proof: omitted.

2.8   The discrepancy

Our final boolean operator is the *discrepancy*, written $\not\equiv$, as in $P \not\equiv Q$. The discrepancy is postulated to have the same binding power as the equivalence. It is also postulated to be

- associative and symmetric

- to associate with the equivalence: $P \equiv (Q \not\equiv R) \equiv (P \equiv Q) \not\equiv R$

- and to satisfy $P \not\equiv Q \equiv \neg (P \equiv Q)$

$$\star \qquad\qquad\qquad \star$$

o $X \not\equiv false \equiv X$
   Proof: omitted.

o The conjunction distributes over the discrepancy:

   $$X \wedge (Y \not\equiv Z) \equiv X \wedge Y \not\equiv X \wedge Z$$

   Proof: omitted.

This last result is interesting in that the conjunction distributes over the discrepancy, but not over the equivalence.

2.9   Summary of binding powers

highest:	$\neg$		
	$\vee$	and	$\wedge$
	$\Rightarrow$	and	$\Leftarrow$
lowest:	$\equiv$	and	$\not\equiv$

2.10   Final comments

An accountant arrives at a value by calculation, not by guessing. As programmers, we will arrive at programs by calculation too, not by guessing. The calculations of an accountant involve the manipulation of numbers. The calculations of programmers involve the manipulation of predicates.

It was in grade school that we learned the rules for manipulating numbers. At first we had to get the rules into our heads. The problems were difficult. With practice the rules went from our heads to our fingertips. Once difficult problems became easy.

Analogously, we must get the manipulation of predicates into our fingertips. This too requires lots of practice. At first problems will seem difficult. With practice they become easy.

To this end we *strongly* recommend lots of practice in the form of exercises. These exercises can be a lot of fun. Try to keep your calculations as short and clear as possible. Concentrate on the shapes of the formulae, where you need to go, and on the rules that might get you there.[0]

2.11   Exercises

Ex 2.0   Prove the following:

   (a) The conjunction is symmetric: $X \wedge Y \equiv Y \wedge X$
   (b) The conjunction distributes over itself:
        $X \wedge (Y \wedge Z) \equiv (X \wedge Y) \wedge (X \wedge Z)$
   (c) The conjunction distributes over disjunction:
        $X \wedge (Y \vee Z) \equiv (X \wedge Y) \vee (X \wedge Z)$

---

[0]It has been strongly recommended, by a number of students, that the best practice consists in proving every theorem in the chapter. They also mention that this is a lot of fun!

(d) Absorption: $X \lor (X \land Y) \equiv X$

□

Ex 2.1   Prove the following:

(a) $X \Rightarrow X$

(b) $X \Rightarrow true$

(c) $X \land Y \Rightarrow X$

(d) $true \Rightarrow X \equiv X$

(e) $X \Rightarrow (Y \Rightarrow Z) \equiv X \land Y \Rightarrow Z$

(f) $(X \Rightarrow Y) \lor (Y \Rightarrow Z)$

(g) Mutual implication: $(X \Rightarrow Y) \land (Y \Rightarrow X) \equiv X \equiv Y$

(h) The implication distributes over the equivalence:
$$X \Rightarrow (Y \equiv Z) \equiv X \Rightarrow Y \equiv X \Rightarrow Z$$

(i) $(X \Rightarrow (Y \equiv Z)) \Rightarrow (X \land Y \Rightarrow Z)$

□

Ex 2.2   Prove the following:

(a) $\neg X \lor Y \equiv X \lor Y \equiv Y$

(b) De Morgan: $\neg X \land \neg Y \equiv \neg(X \lor Y)$

(c) Complement: $X \lor (\neg X \land Y) \equiv X \lor Y$

(d) Complement: $X \land (\neg X \lor Y) \equiv X \land Y$

(e) Contrapositive: $X \Rightarrow Y \equiv \neg Y \Rightarrow \neg X$

(f) Shuffle: $(X \land Y \Rightarrow Z) \equiv (X \Rightarrow \neg Y \lor Z)$

(g) $X \equiv \neg X \equiv false$

(h) Contradiction: $X \land \neg X \equiv false$

□

Ex 2.3   Prove the following:

(a) $X \not\equiv false \equiv X$

(b) The conjunction distributes over the discrepancy:
$$X \land (Y \not\equiv Z) \equiv X \land Y \not\equiv X \land Z$$

(c) $X \equiv (X \not\equiv Y) \equiv \neg Y$

□

Ex 2.4   Prove the following:

    (a) The conjunction is associative: $X \wedge (Y \wedge Z) \equiv (X \wedge Y) \wedge Z$

    (b) $(X \Rightarrow Z) \vee (Y \Rightarrow Z) \equiv X \wedge Y \Rightarrow Z$

    (c) $X \Rightarrow Y \equiv Y \Rightarrow X \equiv X \equiv Y$

    (d) $X \wedge (X \Rightarrow Y) \equiv X \wedge Y$

    (e) $X \vee (X \Rightarrow Y)$

    (f) $Y \vee (X \Rightarrow Y) \equiv X \Rightarrow Y$

    (g) $X \vee Y \Rightarrow X \wedge Y \equiv X \equiv Y$

□

3

Predicates B — Quantified expressions

3.0   How to write quantified expressions

For symmetric and associative binary[0] operators op we write the quantified version of op as

$$(\underline{OP}\, i \,:\, R \,:\, T) \tag{0}$$

Expression (0) is called a *quantified expression*, or a *quantification* for short. Its type is the same as the type of op: if op is an arithmetic operator, then (0) is an arithmetic expression, if op is a boolean operator, then (0) is a boolean expression, and so on. The components of (0) are defined as follows:

- $\underline{OP}$ is called a *quantifier*. Its underlying operator is op. It is formed by capitalizing and underlining op.

- i is a list of dummies. The parentheses indicate the scope of the dummies. In other words, the dummies are defined only within the parentheses.

- R is called the *range*. It is a boolean expression, and is typically a function of the dummies. We have some conventions. We usually omit a range of *true*:

  $$(\underline{OP}\, i \,::\, T) \;\; = \;\; (\underline{OP}\, i \,:\, true \,:\, T)\,,$$

  and when we say that the range of

  $$(\underline{OP}\, i \,:\, R.i \,:\, T)$$

---

[0]Recall that a binary operator is an operator that takes two operands, for example $P \wedge Q$ or $P \, min \, Q$.

is *empty*, we mean that

$$R.i \equiv false \quad \text{for all } i.$$

By way of abbreviation, we often indicate an empty range by writing simply

$$(\underline{OP}\, i : false : T).$$

- T is called the *term*. It has same type as op: for $+$ it is an arithmetic expression, for $\vee$ it is a boolean expression, and so on. It is usually a function of the dummies.

$$\star \qquad \qquad \star$$

For example, max is a symmetric and associative binary operator. Therefore there is a quantified version of max. It is written

$$(\underline{MAX}\, i : R : T).$$

This is an arithmetic expression because max is an arithmetic operator. The range, R, must be a boolean expression, as is the case for all quantified expressions. The term, T, must be an arithmetic expression because max is an arithmetic operator.

Ex 3.0   Why can't there be a quantified version of division?   □

Remark   As a reminder, our sole interest in this chapter is the uninterpreted manipulation of these sequences of (meaningless) symbols!   □

3.1   Laws for quantified expressions

For the remainder of this chapter the letter Z is a function that does not depend on the dummies, and other letters are, in general, functions of the dummies. In other words, the expression

$$(\underline{OP}\, i : R : Z \; op \; T)$$

is short for

$(\underline{OP}\, i \,:\, R.i \,:\, Z \; op \; T.i\,)\,.$

This shorthand will make our formulae easier to read.

★   ★

Quantified expressions are postulated to satisfy the following laws:

- *term rule*:

$$(\underline{OP}\, i \,:\, R \,:\, P \; op \; Q\,) \;=\; (\underline{OP}\, i \,:\, R \,:\, P\,) \; op \; (\underline{OP}\, i \,:\, R \,:\, Q\,)\,.$$

The term rule allows two quantified expressions with the same range to be made into one. In hints we refer to *joining the term* and *splitting the term*.

Examples: On account of the term rule, we can always write

$$
\begin{aligned}
& (\underline{MAX}\, i \,:\, R \,:\, P \; max \; Q\,) \\
=\quad & \langle \text{Splitting the term} \rangle \\
& (\underline{MAX}\, i \,:\, R \,:\, P\,) \; max \; (\underline{MAX}\, i \,:\, R \,:\, Q\,)
\end{aligned}
$$

and

$$
\begin{aligned}
& (\underline{MAX}\, i \,:\, R \,:\, P\,) \; max \; (\underline{MAX}\, i \,:\, R \,:\, Q\,) \\
=\quad & \langle \text{Joining the term} \rangle \\
& (\underline{MAX}\, i \,:\, R \,:\, P \; max \; Q\,)
\end{aligned}
$$

- *range rule*:

$$(\underline{OP}\, i \,:\, P \vee Q \,:\, T\,) \;=\; (\underline{OP}\, i \,:\, P \,:\, T\,) \; op \; (\underline{OP}\, i \,:\, Q \,:\, T\,),$$

provided that:

- *op* is idempotent[1] or
- $P.i \not\equiv Q.i$ for all i.

The range rule allows two quantified expressions with the same term to be made into one. In hints we refer to *joining the range* and *splitting the range*. Note that it always holds for quantified versions of idempotent operators.

Example: *max* is idempotent, so we can write

---

[1] Recall that operator *op* is idempotent if it satisfies $P \; op \; P = P$, for any P. Examples include $\wedge$, $\vee$, *max*, and *min*.

$$(\underline{\text{MAX}}\,i : P \vee Q : T)$$
$$= \quad \langle\,\text{Splitting the range}\,\rangle$$
$$(\underline{\text{MAX}}\,i : P : T)\ \ max\ \ (\underline{\text{MAX}}\,i : Q : T)$$

- *distributivity*:

$$(\underline{\text{OP}}\,i : R : Z \odot T)\ =\ Z \odot (\underline{\text{OP}}\,i : R : T),$$

provided that:

- $\odot$ distributes over *op* and
- the range is non-empty.

Example: $+$ distributes over *max*, so $+$ distributes over a $\underline{\text{MAX}}$ with a non-empty range. In other words, we can write

$$(\underline{\text{MAX}}\,i : R : Z + T)$$
$$= \quad \langle\,\text{Distributivity, provided that the range is non-empty}\,\rangle$$
$$Z + (\underline{\text{MAX}}\,i : R : T)$$

- *empty range rule*:

$$(\underline{\text{OP}}\,i : false : T)\ =\ \text{unit of } op,$$

provided that:

- *op* has a unit.

Example: $-inf$ is the unit of *max*, so we can write

$$(\underline{\text{MAX}}\,i : false : T)$$
$$= \quad \langle\,\text{Empty range rule}\,\rangle$$
$$-inf$$

- *constant term rule*:

$$(\underline{\text{OP}}\,i : R : Z)\ =\ Z,$$

provided that:

- *op* is idempotent and
- the range is non-empty.

Example: *max* is idempotent, so we can write

$$(\underline{\text{MAX}}\, i \,:\, R \,:\, Z\,)$$
$$=\qquad \langle\, \text{Constant term rule, provided that the}$$
$$\text{range is non-empty}\,\rangle$$
$$Z$$

⋆   ⋆

We also have postulates that have nothing to do with *op*:

- *dummy transformation rule*:

$$(\underline{\text{OP}}\, i \,:\, R.i \,:\, T.i\,) \;\;=\;\; (\underline{\text{OP}}\, j \,:\, R.(f.j) \,:\, T.(f.j))\,,$$

  provided that:

  - Function f is invertible   and
  - j does not appear in $R.i$ or $T.i$.

Function f is *invertible* if $i \neq j \;\equiv\; f.i \neq f.j$, i.e. it cannot have the same value at two distinct points. An invertible function is sometimes called a *one-to-one correspondence* and is sometimes called a *bijection*.

The reason why j cannot occur in R (or T) is the same as the reason we had to be careful in renaming dummies when we talked about function application. If j was named in R, it would turn into a dummy.

- *nesting rule*:

$$(\underline{\text{OP}}\, i \,:\, P.i \,:\, (\underline{\text{OP}}\, j \,:\, Q.i.j \,:\, T.i.j\,)) \;\;=$$
$$(\underline{\text{OP}}\, i,j \,:\, P.i \,\wedge\, Q.i.j \,:\, T.i.j\,)$$

The nesting rule provides a way to remove quantified expressions from the term, and vice-versa. In hints we refer to *nesting* and *unnesting*.

- *1-point rule*:

$$(\underline{\text{OP}}\, i \,:\, i = Z \,:\, T.i\,) \;\;=\;\; T.Z\,,$$

  provided that:

  - $T.Z$ is defined.

From these postulates we prove a few theorems:

- Using dummy transformation for the case that f is the identity function (i.e. $f.j = j$), yields the theorem:

$$(\underline{OP}\, i \,:\, R.i \,:\, T.i) \;=\; (\underline{OP}\, j \,:\, R.j \,:\, T.j),$$

  provided that:
  - j is not named in R or T.

Proof:

$$
\begin{aligned}
&(\underline{OP}\, j \,:\, R.j \,:\, T.j) \\
=\quad &\langle\, \text{Let } f.j = j \,\rangle \\
&(\underline{OP}\, j \,:\, R.(f.j) \,:\, T.(f.j)) \\
=\quad &\langle\, f \text{ is invertible. Further assuming that } j \text{ is not named} \\
&\qquad \text{in } R \text{ or } T, \text{ we apply dummy transformation} \,\rangle \\
&(\underline{OP}\, i \,:\, R.i \,:\, T.i)
\end{aligned}
$$

This theorem states that dummies can be renamed, with the usual caveat that the names cannot already be in use. In hints we refer to *renaming the dummy*.

- We can generalize distributivity to

$$(\underline{OP}\, i \,:\, R \,:\, Z \odot T) \;=\; Z \odot (\underline{OP}\, i \,:\, R \,:\, T),$$

  provided that:
  - $\odot$ distributes over op and
  - either the range is non-empty or the unit of op is the zero of $\odot$.

  Proof: As this is postulated to hold for the non-empty range, we restrict the proof to the case of the empty range:

$$
\begin{aligned}
&(\underline{OP}\, i \,:\, \textit{false} \,:\, Z \odot T) \;=\; Z \odot (\underline{OP}\, i \,:\, \textit{false} \,:\, T) \\
\equiv\quad &\langle\, \text{Empty range rule, twice ; let } U = \text{unit of } op \,\rangle \\
&U \;=\; Z \odot U \\
\equiv\quad &\langle\, U \text{ is the zero of } \odot \,\rangle \\
&U \;=\; U \\
\equiv\quad &\langle\, = \text{ is reflexive} \,\rangle \\
&\textit{true}
\end{aligned}
$$

We refer to this law as *generalized distributivity.*

Remark   In this case we converted the entire expression to *true.* Had we converted one side of the equality to the other, we would have written less.   □

★   ★

The quantifier associated with an operator is formed by capitalizing and underlining it. Historically, however, the quantified versions of the following operators have been given special symbols:

op	OP
∧	∀
∨	∃
+	Σ
*	Π

With the basics down, we will proceed by examining specific instances of quantified expressions. In particular we will examine the quantified versions of ∧, ∨, +, *max* and *min*. A few of these have additional postulates, which will be presented along the way.

We begin with the quantified version of the conjunction.

★   ★

Ex 3.1   Prove the following:

(a) $(\underline{OP}\, i, j : i = Z \,\wedge\, R.i.j : T.i.j\,) \;=\; (\underline{OP}\, j : R.Z.j : T.Z.j\,).$

(b) $(\underline{OP}\, i : R : Z\,) \;=\; Z,$

provided that:

- Z is the unit of *op*   and
- *op* is idempotent.

Theorem (a) is called the *dummy elimination rule.*[2]   □

---

[2]Due to Mark Schneider and Ted Czotter.

3.2   Universal quantification

Universal quantification is the name given to the quantified version of $\wedge$. It is written

$$(\forall i : R : T).$$

Applying our list of laws, we find:

- *term rule*:

  $$(\forall i : R : P \wedge Q) \;\equiv\; (\forall i : R : P) \wedge (\forall i : R : Q).$$

- *range rule*:   Because the conjunction is idempotent, we have

  $$(\forall i : P \vee Q : T) \;\equiv\; (\forall i : P : T) \wedge (\forall i : Q : T)$$

- *The conjunction distributes over $\forall$ with non-empty range*:   Because the conjunction distributes over itself, by distributivity we have

  $$(\forall i : R : Z \wedge T) \;\equiv\; Z \wedge (\forall i : R : T),$$

  provided that:
    - the range is non-empty.

- *The disjunction distributes over $\forall$*:   Because the

    disjunction distributes over the conjunction, and the
    unit of conjunction is the zero of disjunction (both *true*),

  by generalized distributivity we have

  $$(\forall i : R : Z \vee T) \;\equiv\; Z \vee (\forall i : R : T).$$

- *empty range rule*:   Since *true* is the unit of the conjunction, we have

  $$(\forall i : false : T) \;\equiv\; true.$$

- *constant term rule*:   Since the conjunction is idempotent, we have

$$(\forall i : R : Z) \equiv Z,$$

provided that:

- the range is non-empty.

$$\star \qquad\qquad \star$$

We give one proof about the universal quantification, namely that implication distributes over it:

$$(\forall i : R : Z \Rightarrow T) \equiv Z \Rightarrow (\forall i : R : T).$$

Proof: We arbitrarily start with the righthand side to find

$$Z \Rightarrow (\forall i : R : T)$$
$$\equiv \qquad \langle \text{ Our target has } Z \text{ inside of the quantification. The only}$$
operator that distributes over the universal quantification,
even for the empty range, is the disjunction, so we will
rewrite the implication using a disjunction. Of our many
choices, we choose a rewriting that contains *only* a
disjunction, namely: $P \Rightarrow Q \equiv \neg P \vee Q \rangle$
$$\neg Z \vee (\forall i : R : T)$$
$$\equiv \qquad \langle \vee \text{ distributes over the universal quantification } \rangle$$
$$(\forall i : R : \neg Z \vee T)$$
$$\equiv \qquad \langle \neg P \vee Q \equiv P \Rightarrow Q \rangle$$
$$(\forall i : R : Z \Rightarrow T)$$

This completes the proof that the implication distributes over the universal quantification.

$$\star \qquad\qquad \star$$

We close by introducing the additional postulate:

- $(\forall i : R : T) \equiv (\forall i :: \neg R \vee T).$ \hfill (Trading)

This postulate is useful because it shows how to move expressions between the range and term. In fact, the name *trading* is short for "trading between the range and term".

Remark   A law of this kind is only possible when the range and term are of the same type. Because the range is always a boolean, it can only come up when the term is too. For this reason, there can be no analogous law for quantified versions of arithmetic operators.   □

⋆   ⋆

Ex 3.2   Prove the following:

$$\text{(a) } (\forall i : R \wedge S : T) \equiv (\forall i : R : S \Rightarrow T)$$
$$\text{(b) } (\forall i :: f.i) \Rightarrow f.x$$

Theorem (a) is a form of *trading* that uses the implication, and (b) is known as the *rule of instantiation*.   □

3.3   Existential quantification

Existential quantification is the name given to the quantified version of $\vee$. It is written

$$(\exists i : R : T).$$

Applying our list of laws, we find:

- *term rule*:

$$(\exists i : R : P \vee Q) \equiv (\exists i : R : P) \vee (\exists i : R : Q).$$

- *range rule*:   Because the disjunction is idempotent, we have

$$(\exists i : P \vee Q : T) \equiv (\exists i : P : T) \vee (\exists i : Q : T).$$

- *The disjunction distributes over $\exists$ with non-empty range*:   Since the disjunction distributes over itself, by distributivity we have

$$(\exists i : R : Z \vee T) \equiv Z \vee (\exists i : R : T),$$

    provided that:

    - the range is non-empty.

- *The conjunction distributes over $\exists$:*   Because the

  conjunction distributes over the disjunction, and the
  unit of disjunction is the zero of conjunction (both *false*),

  by generalized distributivity we have

  $$(\exists i : R : Z \wedge T) \;\equiv\; Z \wedge (\exists i : R : T).$$

- *empty range rule:*   Since *false* is the unit of the disjunction, we have

  $$(\exists i : false : T) \;\equiv\; false.$$

- *constant term rule:*   Since the disjunction is idempotent, we have

  $$(\exists i : R : Z) \;\equiv\; Z,$$

  provided that:
  - the range is non-empty.

★   ★

Existential quantification enjoys the additional postulate

- $(\exists i : R : T) \;\equiv\; \neg(\forall i : R : \neg T),$ \hfill (De Morgan)

which is known as *Generalized De Morgan*, or *De Morgan* for short. Its usefulness derives from the fact that it connects universal and existential quantification.

★   ★

Ex 3.3   Prove the following:

  (a) $\neg(\exists i : R : \neg T) \;\equiv\; (\forall i : R : T)$
  (b) $f.x \;\Rightarrow\; (\exists i :: f.i)$
  (c) $(\exists i : R : T) \;\equiv\; (\exists i :: R \wedge T)$

Law (a) is the dual to Generalized De Morgan. Law (b) is the *rule of instantiation* for existential quantification. Law (c) is *trading* for existential quantification. (Hint on (c): As only one prior law allows movement between the range and the term, expect to use it.)   □

3.4   Some arithmetic quantifications

Here we examine the quantified versions of some arithmetic operators. Recall that the terms are arithmetic expressions.

SUMMATION, MAXIMIZATION, AND MINIMIZATION

Summation is the name given to the quantified version of $+$. It is written

$$(\Sigma i : R : T).$$

We omit its laws, but be careful with the range and constant term rules, as $+$ is not idempotent.

Ex 3.4   List the laws for Σ. $\square$

$\star$ $\star$

Maximization is the name given to the quantified version of max. It is written

$$(\underline{MAX}\, i : R : T).$$

$\star$ $\star$

Minimization is the name given to the quantified version of min. It is written

$$(\underline{MIN}\, i : R : T).$$

The usual laws apply, plus the following, a postulate that connects minimization and maximization:

- $(\underline{MIN}\, i : R : -T) \;=\; -(\underline{MAX}\, i : R : T).$

Ex 3.5   List the laws for $\underline{MIN}$. $\square$

NUMERICAL QUANTIFICATION

Numerical quantification is written

$$(\underline{N} i : R : T).$$

Numerical quantification is not defined in terms of its underlying operator as other quantifications are. Instead it is defined in terms of the summation quantification using the postulate

- $(\underline{N} i : R : T) = (\Sigma i : R \wedge T : 1),$

where T is a boolean expression. Its other laws are derived from this definition. Numerical quantification is introduced because it will be useful later on.

We derive one law for numerical quantification, namely its 1-point rule:

$$(\underline{N} i : i = Z : T)$$
$$= \quad \langle \text{ Definition of } \underline{N} \rangle$$
$$(\Sigma i : i = Z \wedge T : 1)$$

Now, if $T \equiv false$, then the range is empty. Application of the empty range rule for Σ yields 0. If $T \equiv true$, then the range is $i = Z$. Application of the 1-point rule yields 1. As this situation comes up in calculations, we introduce notation to smooth its use. In particular, we define

$$n.x = 0 \quad \text{if } x \equiv false \quad \text{or}$$
$$\qquad 1 \quad \text{if } x \equiv true.$$

With this new notation, the 1-point rule for numerical quantification can be expressed as

$$(\underline{N} i : i = Z : T.i) = n.(T.Z),$$

which is quite succinct. In terms of "n" we sometimes appeal to the additional postulate:

- $(\underline{N} i : R : T) = (\Sigma i : R : n.T).$

$$\star \qquad\qquad \star$$

Ex 3.6   For numerical quantification, derive the following laws:

    (a) range rule.
    (b) empty range rule.

☐

Ex 3.7   Prove: $(\Sigma i : R \wedge T : Z) = Z * (\underline{N}i : R : T)$.   ☐

3.5   Other quantified expressions

Because we have a rich set of laws for quantified expressions, and because we have a uniform way of writing quantifiers from their underlying operators, we can easily introduce quantified versions of other symmetric and associative binary operators. We will do so as the need arises.

Ex 3.8   Set-union is a symmetric and associative binary operator denoted by $\cup$. Its unit is the empty set, denoted by $\emptyset$, and it is idempotent, i.e. $P \cup P = P$. Set-intersection is a symmetric and associative binary operator denoted by $\cap$. Its zero is $\emptyset$, and it is idempotent. It distributes over $\cup$, and $\cup$ distributes over it.

    (a) Invent a quantified version of $\cup$ and list its laws.
    (b) Invent a quantified version of $\cap$ and list its laws.

☐

Ex 3.9   Invent a quantified version of $*$ and list its laws.   ☐

3.6   Additional exercises

The following exercises are highly recommended. They are the kind we encounter when developing programs.

Ex 3.10   Given the validity of

    (a) $x = (\Sigma i : R.i : f.i)$
    (b) $R.i \not\equiv i = N$ for any i

calculate a quantifier-free expression equivalent to

$$(\Sigma i : R.i \ \lor \ i = N : f.i).$$

The solution should take the usual form:

$$(\Sigma i : R.i \ \lor \ i = N : f.i)$$
$$= \quad \langle \text{hint} \rangle$$
$$\cdots$$
$$= \quad \langle \text{hint} \rangle$$

an expression that does not contain a quantifier

☐

Ex 3.11 Given the validity of

(a) $x = (\underline{MAX} i, j : R.i.j \ \land \ j < N + 1 : f.i.j)$
(b) $y = (\underline{MAX} i : R.i.(N + 1) : f.i.(N + 1))$

calculate a quantifier-free expression equivalent to:

$$(\underline{MAX} i, j : R.i.j \ \land \ (j < N + 1 \ \lor \ j = N + 1) : f.i.j) .$$

☐

Ex 3.12 Given the validity of

(a) $x = (\underline{MAX} i : R.i.N : f.i.N)$
(b) $R.y.(z + 1) \equiv R.y.z \ \lor \ y = z + 1$ for any y and z
(c) $f.y.y = 0$ for any y
(d) $f.y.(z + 1) = f.y.z + g.z$ for any y and z
(e) $R.y.z \not\equiv false$ for any y and z

calculate a quantifier-free expression equivalent to

$$(\underline{MAX} i : R.i.(N + 1) : f.i.(N + 1)).$$

☐

Ex 3.13 Given the validity of

(a) $x \equiv (\forall i, j : R.i.j \ \land \ j < N : f.i \Rightarrow f.j)$
(b) $y \equiv (\forall i : R.i.N : \neg f.i)$

calculate a quantifier-free expression equivalent to

$$(\forall i, j : R.i.j \ \land \ (j < N \ \lor \ j = N) : f.i \Rightarrow f.j).$$

☐

4

Specifications

4.0 Introduction

What do we do when asked to construct a "customer database". At first glance the problem seems straightforward enough. Upon closer inspection many questions arise: what characterizes a customer?, what functions must be provided?, and so on. Given to ten different people, ten different solutions will appear, and it is entirely likely that none will provide what was desired. The problem, of course, is that "customer database" is much too imprecise.

What do we do when asked to determine the customer with the second largest outstanding balance. The problem seems simple enough until we realize that there may be no such customer. Indeed, all customers might have the same balance (for example, all could be 0), or the second largest balance could be shared by a number of customers. Again, the informal problem statement is much too imprecise.

We intend to make problems precise by composing *functional specifications* or simply *specifications* for them. A specification is an equation of a certain shape. Programming is the activity of solving a specification for its unknown. Its unknown is called a *program*.

So before we can develop programs, we must learn to compose specifications. A specification, as we shall see, contains predicates. These predicates capture the meaning of the given problem. Our predicates have no meaning, and so we begin our study of specifications by assigning meaning to our predicates. Afterwards we introduce notation for specifications. We then look at a number of examples.

4.1 Assigning meaning to our predicates

We begin by assigning meanings to the boolean operators:

Expression	Pronounced	is *true* if
$P \equiv Q$	*P equivales Q*	exactly an even number of its operands are *false*
$P \lor Q$	*P or Q*	at least one of its operands is
$P \land Q$	*P and Q*	all of its operands are
$P \Rightarrow Q$	*P implies Q*	either Q is *true* or P is *false*
$P \Leftarrow Q$	*P follows from Q*	either P is *true* or Q is *false*
$\neg P$	*not P*	P is false
$P \not\equiv Q$	*P differs from Q*	exactly an odd number of its operands are *true*

A boolean expression not equal to *true* is equal to *false*.

⋆   ⋆

We go on to quantified expressions:

- The value of the universal quantification

$$(\forall i : R.i : T.i)$$

is that of the "conjunction of the $T.i$, for i satisfying $R.i$".

Example:

    ○ $(\forall i : 0 \leq i \land i < 3 : T.i) \equiv T.0 \land T.1 \land T.2$

Proof:

$$\begin{aligned}
&(\forall i : 0 \leq i \land i < 3 : T.i) \\
\equiv \quad &\langle 0 \leq i \land i < 3 \equiv i = 0 \lor i = 1 \lor i = 2 \rangle \\
&(\forall i : i = 0 \lor i = 1 \lor i = 2 : T.i) \\
\equiv \quad &\langle \text{Split range, twice} \rangle \\
&(\forall i : i = 0 : T.i) \land \\
&(\forall i : i = 1 : T.i) \land \\
&(\forall i : i = 2 : T.i) \\
\equiv \quad &\langle \text{1-point rule, thrice} \rangle \\
&T.0 \land T.1 \land T.2
\end{aligned}$$

Another example:

    ○ $(\forall i : 0 \leq i \land i < 0 : T.i) \equiv true$

Proof:

$$(\forall i : 0 \le i \wedge i < 0 : T.i)$$
$$\equiv \qquad \langle i < 0 \equiv \neg(0 \le i) \rangle$$
$$(\forall i : 0 \le i \wedge \neg(0 \le i) : T.i)$$
$$\equiv \qquad \langle \text{Contradiction, i.e. } P \wedge \neg P \equiv \textit{false} \rangle$$
$$(\forall i : \textit{false} : T.i)$$
$$\equiv \qquad \langle \text{Empty-range rule for universal quantification} \rangle$$
$$\textit{true}$$

Thus the conjunction of 0 values equals *true*, by the empty range rule for $\forall$.

The $\forall$ is pronounced *for all*. Thus we might assert the truth of

$$(\forall i : R.i : T.i)$$

by saying: "for all i satisfying $R.i$, $T.i$ holds".

- The value of the existential quantification

  $$(\exists i : R.i : T.i)$$

  is that of the "disjunction of the $T.i$, for i satisfying $R.i$". By its empty range rule, the disjunction of zero values is *false*.

  Examples:

  $$(\exists i : 0 \le i \wedge i < 3 : T.i) \equiv T.0 \vee T.1 \vee T.2$$
  $$(\exists i : 0 \le i \wedge i < 0 : T.i) \equiv \textit{false}$$

  The $\exists$ is pronounced *there exists*.

- The value of the summation

  $$(\Sigma i : R.i : T.i)$$

  is that of the "sum of the $T.i$, for i satisfying $R.i$". By its empty range rule, the sum of zero values is 0.

  Examples:

  $$(\Sigma i : 0 \le i \wedge i < 3 : T.i) = T.0 + T.1 + T.2$$
  $$(\Sigma i : 0 \le i \wedge i < 0 : T.i) = 0$$

  The Σ is pronounced *sum of*.

- The value of the maximization

    $$(\underline{MAX}\, i\, :\, R.i\, :\, T.i\,)$$

    is that of the "maximum of the $T.i$, for i satisfying $R.i$". By its empty range rule, the maximum of zero values is $-inf$.

    Examples:

    $$\begin{aligned}
    (\underline{MAX}\, i\, :\, 0 \le i \,\wedge\, i < 3\, :\, T.i\,) &= T.0\ max\ T.1\ max\ T.2 \\
    (\underline{MAX}\, i\, :\, 0 \le i \,\wedge\, i < 0\, :\, T.i\,) &= -inf
    \end{aligned}$$

    The $\underline{MAX}$ is pronounced *maximum of*.

- The value of the minimization

    $$(\underline{MIN}\, i\, :\, R.i\, :\, T.i\,)$$

    is that of the "minimum of the $T.i$, for i satisfying $R.i$". By its empty range rule, the minimum of zero values is $+inf$.

    Examples:

    $$\begin{aligned}
    (\underline{MIN}\, i\, :\, 0 \le i \,\wedge\, i < 3\, :\, T.i\,) &= T.0\ min\ T.1\ min\ T.2 \\
    (\underline{MIN}\, i\, :\, 0 \le i \,\wedge\, i < 0\, :\, T.i\,) &= +inf
    \end{aligned}$$

    The $\underline{MIN}$ is pronounced *minimum of*.

- The value of the numerical quantification

    $$(\underline{N}\, i\, :\, R.i\, :\, T.i\,)$$

    is that of the "number of true $T.i$, for i satisfying $R.i$". By its empty range rule, the number of zero true values is 0.

    Examples:

    $$\begin{aligned}
    (\underline{N}\, i\, :\, 0 \le i \,\wedge\, i < 3\, :\, T.i\,) &= \text{n.}(T.0) + \text{n.}(T.1) + \text{n.}(T.2) \\
    (\underline{N}\, i\, :\, 0 \le i \,\wedge\, i < 0\, :\, T.i\,) &= 0
    \end{aligned}$$

    The $\underline{N}$ is pronounced *number of*.

Remark   We sometimes abbreviate a formula like $0 \le i \,\wedge\, i < j$ as $0 \le i < j$. □

4.2 Towards writing specifications

THE HOARE TRIPLE AS A NOTATION FOR SPECIFICATIONS

A *Hoare triple* is the boolean expression

$$\{Q\}\ S\ \{R\}$$

where Q and R are boolean expressions, and where S is a mechanism we leave undefined for now. The Hoare triple is defined to have higher binding power than function application.

Informally, the value of $\{Q\}\ S\ \{R\}$ is given by

$$\{Q\}\ S\ \{R\}\ \equiv\ \text{truth of ``mechanism } S \text{ begun with } Q \text{ satisfied}$$
$$\text{is guaranteed to terminate with } R$$
$$\text{satisfied''}.$$

Q and R are called the *precondition* and *postcondition* of S, respectively, and together constitute the *functional specification*, or simply *specification* of S.[0]

EQUATIONS

Consider the equation

$$x^2 + b * x = 0$$

Is this a quadratic equation or a linear equation? This depends on the unknown. If x is the unknown it is a quadratic equation. If b is the unknown it is a linear equation. To be clear, we will write the quadratic equation as

---

[0]The Hoare triple is named after C.A.R. Hoare who, in a landmark paper in 1969 entitled "An axiomatic basis for computer programming", proposed the slightly different notation $Q\ \{S\}\ R$. His definition differs too. In particular $Q\ \{S\}\ R$ holds if S, beginning with Q satisfied, is guaranteed to establish R, *if it terminates*. This is known as *partial correctness*. The notation $\{Q\}\ S\ \{R\}$ denotes *total correctness*, which is partial correctness plus termination. Hoare's paper is reproduced in a number of places, including D. Gries (ed.), *Programming Methodology*, Springer-Verlag 1978, and C.A.R. Hoare and C.B. Jones (ed.), *Essays in Computing Science*, Prentice-Hall 1989.

$$x: \ x^2 + b * x = 0$$

and the linear equation as

$$b: \ x^2 + b * x = 0$$

In other words, we will write boolean equation $f.u$ in unknown u as

$$u: \ f.u$$

In general, u is a list of unknowns.

WHAT IS PROGRAMMING?

Programming is solving the equation

$$S: \ \{Q\} \ S \ \{R\}$$

In other words, find a mechanism that satisfies a given functional specification.

Such a mechanism (i.e. S) is called a *program*. The allowable shapes of programs will be discussed later, as will what it means for a program to satisfy a specification.

WHAT IS THE UNKNOWN?

Consider the Hoare triple

$$\{Q\} \ S \ \{x = y\}$$

which informally states that program S, beginning with Q satisfied, must terminate with $x = y$ satisfied.

There are a number of ways that $x = y$ can be satisfied:

(a) Set x to the value of y.
(b) Set y to the value of x.
(c) Set both x and y to the same value. Any value will do.

Usually only one of the three is intended. We need to be explicit as to which. To accomplish this we will write our postconditions as equations. We will write the three specifications, corresponding to these three choices, as:

(a) $\{Q\}\ S\ \{x:\ x = y\}$
(b) $\{Q\}\ S\ \{y:\ x = y\}$
(c) $\{Q\}\ S\ \{x, y:\ x = y\}$

In each instance only variables to the left of the colons can be meddled with. The others are constants and, as such, cannot be changed. We will go even further, omitting the S altogether, and write simply

$$\{Q\}\ x:\ x = y$$

for (a). This we view as the specification of a program that, beginning with Q satisfied, establishes $x = y$ by only meddling with x. In particular, y is a constant.

ADDING DECLARATIONS

The remaining problem with the specification

$$\{Q\}\ x:\ x = y$$

is what is x's type? Is x an integer, a list, a boolean, or is it a polygon? To be clear we expand our notation for functional specifications. If x and y are integers, we will write this specification as

$$\underline{\text{var}}\ x, y : int\ \{Q\}\ ;\ x:\ x = y$$

This states that x and y are variables of type integer (*int* is short for integer). The semicolon is simply a separator, as in English. The new part, "$\underline{\text{var}}\ x, y : int$", is called the *declaration of x and y*. Its sole function is to indicate the types of x and y.

If x and y were booleans, instead of integers, we would write

$$\underline{\text{var}}\ x, y : bool\ \{Q\}\ ;\ x:\ x \equiv y$$

Remark   For clarity, we usually write specifications on multiple lines, for
example:

> <u>var</u> $x, y : bool$ $\{Q\}$
> ; $x :$ $x \equiv y$

□

4.3   Examples of specifications

(0) The specification of a program that sets[1] integer variable x equal to
7:

> <u>var</u> $x : int$ $\{true\}$
> ; $x :$ $x = 7$

Since *true* always equals *true*, the precondition of *true* means that the x
can have *any* initial value. We note here that we will often omit mention
of a precondition of *true*. For example, in

> <u>var</u> $x, y : int$ $\{y > 0\}$
> ; $x, y :$ R

x can have any initial value while y must initially exceed 0.

(1) Given natural a and b, set z to their product:

> <u>var</u> $a, b, z : int$ $\{a \geq 0 \land b \geq 0\}$
> ; $z :$ $z = a * b$

(2) Set z to the absolute value of x:

> <u>var</u> $x, z : int$
> ; $z :$ $z = |x|$

---

[1]The word "sets" has unfortunate connotations. We mean that the program
terminates with the postcondition satisfied. What we should say is that the program terminates with $x = 7$ satisfied.

(3) Set z to its own absolute value:

> $\underline{\text{var}} \; z : int \;\; \{z = Z\}$
> $; z : \;\; z = |Z|$

This example deserves some attention. By "set z to its own absolute value", we really mean that z is to be set to the absolute value of its *initial value*. We characterized this initial value via the precondition $z = Z$. In other words, the precondition states that the initial value of z is Z. (We know that Z is simply a name for a value, and not a variable, because Z does not appear in a declaration).

(4) Swap the (initial) values of integers x and y:

> $\underline{\text{var}} \; x, y : int \;\; \{x = X \wedge y = Y\}$
> $; x, y : \;\; x = Y \wedge y = X$

★   ★

Ex 4.0   Specify a program that

> (a) Sets z to the maximum of integers x and y.
> (b) Sets x to the maximum of integers x and y.

□

★   ★

(5) Set q and r to the quotient and remainder of integer division of $x \geq 0$ by $y > 0$:

> $\underline{\text{var}} \; x, y, q, r : int \;\; \{x \geq 0 \wedge y > 0\}$
> $; q, r : \;\; q * y + r = x \wedge 0 \leq r \wedge r < y$

Then first conjunct states that the quotient times the denominator plus the reminder equals the numerator. The last two conjuncts bound the remainder: the remainder is at least 0 and is less than the denominator.

Sometimes we declare variables on separate lines, separated by semicolons:

$$\underline{\text{var}}\ x : int\ \{x \geq 0\}$$
$$;\underline{\text{var}}\ y : int\ \{y > 0\}$$
$$;\underline{\text{var}}\ q, r : int$$
$$;q, r :\ q * y + r = x\ \land\ 0 \leq r\ \land\ r < y$$

In this case the precondition is the conjunction of $x \geq 0$ and $y > 0$.

(6) Set x to the integer square-root of $N \geq 0$. (The integer square-root of N is the largest integer whose square is at most N):

$$\underline{\text{var}}\ N : int\ \{N \geq 0\}$$
$$;\underline{\text{var}}\ x : int$$
$$;x :\ x \leq \sqrt{N}\ \land\ \sqrt{N} < x + 1$$

(7) Given integer $N > 0$, set x to the largest integer that is a power of 2 and is at most N:

$$\underline{\text{var}}\ N : int\ \{N > 0\}$$
$$;\underline{\text{var}}\ x : int$$
$$;x :\ (\exists i : 0 \leq i : x = 2^i)\ \land\ x \leq N\ \land\ N < 2 * x$$

The first conjunct states that x is a power of 2. The second states that x is at most N, while the third states that the next power of 2 exceeds N.

⋆   ⋆

Ex 4.1   Specify a program that sets x to the number of positive divisors of positive integer N. Feel free to use the arithmetic operator *mod*, (informally) defined by

$$X\ mod\ Y\ =\ \text{remainder when } X \text{ is divided by } Y.$$

□

4.4 Intermezzo on the array

An array is a function. We allow the declaration

$$\underline{\text{var}}\ f(i : x \leq i < y) : bool \qquad\qquad (0)$$

provided that $x \leq y$. This declares f to be a boolean-valued function that takes as argument any integer i satisfying $x \leq i < y$. If "*bool*" was replaced by "*int*", f would be an integer-valued function. Using (0), we introduce the following terminology:

- ($f.k$ is an *element* of f) $\equiv$ $x \leq k < y$.

- We say that f has $y - x$ elements, or length $y - x$. The restriction $x \leq y$ constrains arrays to at least length 0. An array with 0 elements is called *empty*. We define the function $\#.f$ to be the length of f . We usually omit the period and write simply $\#f$.

- We say that value v *occurs in*, is *contained in*, or is simply *in* f if some element of f equals v .

- The function *bag.f* is defined to be the (unordered) collection of elements of f , i.e. the elements of f thrown in a bag.

- We sometimes appeal to the notion of an *array section*:

  $f(k : i \leq k < j)$ is an array section $\equiv$ $x \leq i \leq j \leq y$.

  We say that this section has length $j - i$. An array section with length exceeding 0 is called non-empty.

We sometimes abbreviate common array declarations:

- We sometimes abbreviate
  <u>var</u> $f(i : 0 \leq i < N) : int$ as   <u>var</u> $f(0..N - 1) : int$.

- We often abbreviate
  <u>var</u> $f(i : 0 \leq i < \#f) : int$ $\{\#f \geq 0\}$ as   <u>var</u> $f : array\ of\ int$.

4.5 More examples of specifications

(8) Given integer x and integer array b, set boolean p to the truth of "x occurs in b":

  <u>var</u> $b : array\ of\ int$
  ; <u>var</u> $x : int$
  ; <u>var</u> $p : bool$
  ; $p: \ p \ \equiv \ (\exists i : 0 \leq i < \#b : b.i = x)$

(9) Set x to the maximum value in integer array b:

> var b : *array of int*
> ; var x : *int*
> ; x : $x = (\text{MAX}\, i : 0 \le i < \#b : b.i)$

When b is empty (i.e. $\#b = 0$), this specification is satisfied by $x = -inf$ (by the empty range rule for MAX). An informal problem statement would probably say nothing in this case. Writing the specification forces us to be precise.

(10) Set x to the maximum value in non-empty integer array b:

> var b : *array of int* $\{\#b > 0\}$
> ; var x : *int*
> ; x : $x = (\text{MAX}\, i : 0 \le i < \#b : b.i)$

Notice that the specification says nothing should b be empty. If it did it would be the specification of a different problem!

(11) Set x to 0 if array b is empty, otherwise set x to b's maximum value:

> var b : *array of int*
> ; var x : *int*
> ; x : $(\#b = 0 \ \wedge \ x = 0) \ \vee$
> $(\#b > 0 \ \wedge \ x = (\text{MAX}\, i : 0 \le i < \#b : b.i))$

Since $\#b$ is a constant, when $\#b = 0$ the only way to establish the postcondition is to establish its first disjunct, and when $\#b > 0$ the only way to establish the postcondition is to establish its second disjunct. The only way to establish the first is to set $x = 0$, and the only way to establish the second is to set x to the maximum value in b.

★   ★

Ex 4.2   Specify a program that

    (a) Determines the sum of the elements in a given integer array.

    (b) Determines the number of occurences of X in a given array.

(c) Given boolean array b containing a *true*, sets integer x to the smallest z such that $b.z$ holds.

(d) Given boolean array b containing a *true*, sets integer x to the largest z such that $b.z$ holds.

(e) Determines the number of distinct values in a given integer array.

(f) Determines the majority in array b, given that there is one. A *majority* in an array containing N elements is a value that occurs more than N *div* 2 times.

(g) Given that there is one, determines the second largest value in a given integer array.

□

4.6   Intermezzo on ascending functions

For function f, we define

- $(f \text{ is increasing}) \equiv (\forall i, j :: i < j \equiv f.i < f.j)$

- $(f \text{ is ascending}) \equiv (\forall i, j :: i < j \Leftarrow f.i < f.j)$

- $(f \text{ is decreasing}) \equiv (\forall i, j :: i < j \equiv f.i > f.j)$

- $(f \text{ is descending}) \equiv (\forall i, j :: i < j \Leftarrow f.i > f.j)$

One useful theorem is

○ $(f \text{ is ascending}) \equiv (\forall i, j : i \leq j : f.i \leq f.j)$

Proof:

$$(\forall x, y : x \leq y : f.x \leq f.y)$$
$\equiv \qquad \langle \text{Trading, to get a range of } true \rangle$
$$(\forall x, y :: x \leq y \Rightarrow f.x \leq f.y)$$
$\equiv \qquad \langle \text{Contrapositive, to get a consequence} \rangle$
$$(\forall x, y :: \neg(x \leq y) \Leftarrow \neg(f.x \leq f.y))$$
$\equiv \qquad \langle \neg(a \leq b) = a > b, \text{ twice} \rangle$
$$(\forall x, y :: x > y \Leftarrow f.x > f.y)$$
$\equiv \qquad \langle \text{Rename dummies: } x, y := j, i \rangle$
$$(\forall i, j :: j > i \Leftarrow f.j > f.i)$$
$\equiv \qquad \langle \text{Definition of ascending} \rangle$
f is ascending

⋆   ⋆

Informally, ascending (and descending) sequences can contain duplicates, while increasing (and decreasing) sequences cannot. Thus

　　2, 4, 7　　　　is increasing, and
　　2, 4, 4, 7　　is ascending.

Introducing the positive terminology "ascending" (and "descending") allows us to discard the conventional, but cumbersome, "non-decreasing", or even worse, "monotonically non-decreasing".

⋆   ⋆

Ex 4.3　　Prove the following:

　　(a)　$(f$ is decreasing$)\ \Rightarrow\ (\forall i, j : i < j : f.i > f.j)$

　　(b)　An increasing function is ascending:

　　　　　　$(f$ is ascending$)\ \Leftarrow\ (f$ is increasing$)$

□

4.7　Even more examples of specifications

(12)　Given integer array b, set boolean z to the truth of "b is ascending":

　　$\underline{\text{var}}\ b : array\ of\ int$
　　$;\underline{\text{var}}\ z : bool$
　　$;z :\ z\ \equiv\ (\forall i, j : 0 \le i < \#b\ \wedge\ 0 \le j < \#b : i < j\ \Leftarrow\ b.i < b.j)$

Remark　　The bounds on i (and j) guarantee that $b.i$ (and $b.j$) are defined. For instance, $b.i$ is defined only if $0 \le i < \#b$. In other words, we must guarantee that $b.i$ is an element of array b.　□

An alternative specification, inspired by our recent theorem, is

　　$\underline{\text{var}}\ b : array\ of\ int$
　　$;\underline{\text{var}}\ z : bool$
　　$;z :\ z\ \equiv\ (\forall i, j : 0 \le i \le j < \#b : b.i \le b.j)$

Notice that an empty array is ascending. This follows from the empty range rule for universal quantification: for $\#b = 0$, the range is empty, and so the quantification equals *true*.

(13) Sort integer array b into ascending order:

$$\underline{\text{var}}\ b : array\ of\ int\ \{bag.b = B\}$$
$$;b:\ bag.b = B\ \wedge\ (\forall i, j\ :\ 0 \leq i \leq j < \#b\ :\ b.i \leq b.j\,)$$

The conjunct $bag.b = B$ appears in both the pre- and postconditions. Its appearance guarantees that b when sorted is the same bunch of values as it was initially. (After all, a simple way to make b ascending is to set all its elements to 5 (say) — clearly not what was intended).

★   ★

Ex 4.4 Find a different specification for this last problem. Prove that your postcondition is equivalent to the definition of "ascending". □

★   ★

(14) A *plateau* is an array section of equal values. Set z to the length of the longest plateau in integer array b:

$$\underline{\text{var}}\ b : array\ of\ int$$
$$;\underline{\text{var}}\ z : int$$
$$;z:\ z = (\underline{\text{MAX}}\,x, y\ :\ 0 \leq x \leq y \leq \#b\ \wedge\ f.x.y\ :\ y - x\,)$$

where

$$f.x.y = (\forall i, j\ :\ x \leq i < y\ \wedge\ x \leq j < y\ :\ b.i = b.j\,).$$

Had f not been introduced, there would have been a quantification in the range, and the specification would have been unwieldy. Introducing f kept the specification both managable and readable. We tend to do this with longer specifications.

★   ★

A non-trivial specification can be developed methodically. To illustrate this we develop the postcondition of this last example:

length of the longest plateau in b
$=$ $\langle$ This is the maximum of plateau lengths, so use $\underline{\text{MAX}}$ $\rangle$
$(\underline{\text{MAX}}\,p :\; p$ a plateau in b : length of p)
$=$ $\langle$ A plateau is an array section of equal values $\rangle$
$(\underline{\text{MAX}}\,p :\; p$ is a section of b $\wedge$
                    p contains equal values : length of p)
$=$ $\langle$ Denote section $b(i : x \le i < y)$ by the pair (x,y) $\rangle$
$(\underline{\text{MAX}}\,x,y :\; (x,y)$ is a section of b $\wedge$
                         (x,y) contains equal values : length of (x,y))
$=$ $\langle$ To save writing, let $f.x.y \equiv$ "(x,y) contains equal values" $\rangle$
$(\underline{\text{MAX}}\,x,y :\; (x,y)$ is a section of b $\wedge$ $f.x.y$: length of (x,y))
$=$ $\langle$ Length of $(x,y) = y - x$ $\rangle$
$(\underline{\text{MAX}}\,x,y :(x,y)$ is a section of b $\wedge$ $f.x.y:\; y - x$)
$=$ $\langle$ (x,y) is a section of b $\equiv$ $0 \le x \le y \le \#b$ $\rangle$
$(\underline{\text{MAX}}\,x,y :\; 0 \le x \le y \le \#b \;\wedge\; f.x.y :\; y - x$)

The development of $f.x.y$ is a separate sequence of steps and is omitted here.

★   ★

Ex 4.5   Specify a program that

   (a) Determines the length of the longest ascending section in a given integer array.

   (b) Determines the maximum section sum in a given integer array. A section's *section sum* is the sum of the section's elements.

   (c) Determines the length of the longest section containing at most two distinct values in a given array.

   (d) Determines the length of the longest alternating section in a given boolean array. An *alternating section* is a section in which no pair of adjacent elements have the same value.

   (e) Determines the length of the longest smooth section in a given integer array. A *smooth section* is a section in which no two elements differ in value by more than 1.

□

4.8   Other notations for functional specifications

There are a number of alternative notations for functional specifications. When suitable, we borrow from them. We contrast two by appealing to the example

$$\underline{\text{var}}\ x, y : int\ \ \{Q\}$$
$$;x:\ \ x = y$$

• Dijkstra and Feijen[2] distinguish the variables that can be meddled with from the variables that cannot be meddled with by the use of an outer and an inner scope. The variables declared in the outer scope cannot be meddled with, while the variables declared in the inner scope can be. They would cast our example as

$$|[\underline{\text{var}}\ y : int$$
$$\ \ |[\underline{\text{var}}\ x : int\ \ \{Q\}$$
$$\ \ ;S$$
$$\ \ \ \{x = y\}$$
$$\ \ ]|$$
$$]|$$

• Gries[3] might cast our example as

Given fixed integer y and that Q holds, establish $x = y$.

The adjective "fixed" means that y cannot be meddled with, i.e. is a constant.

4.9   Comments on specifications

One thing that should be clear from these examples is that an informal problem statement, even for very simple problems, is likely to be ambiguous. This phenomenom is magnified as problems become more involved.

Informal problem statements, often called *requirements*, give the programmer great freedom, often too much freedom. Many programmers end up solving problems that were not intended. Programmers end up solving a whole series of problems until they finally find the one that was intended, or give up entirely.

---

[2]Edsger W. Dijkstra and W.H.J. Feijen, *A Method of Programming*, Addison-Wesley 1988.

[3]David Gries, *The Science of Programming*, Springer-Verlag 1981.

Much more effective is to translate the requirements into a specification. In the course of composing a specification, questions will arise. When these are resolved the specification will match the client's intentions.

Thus a well-organized project is a sequence of phases. First the requirements are translated into a specification. Then, from the specification, a solution to the specification is developed. This solution is called a program. The requirements can be ignored when the program is developed, since the program is developed solely from the specification. The two phases provide a nice separation of concerns.

One way to obtain a program is to guess it. But why write a formal specification if we are going to introduce uncertainty when we develop the program? And so, we have another reason for writing a specification: We intend to let it guide us during the development of the program. In particular we will appeal to the shapes of its pre- and postconditions.

Before we do so, however, we must see what shapes our programs can have.

NOTES

• Even a formal specification can be ambiguous or inconsistent, and may not match the intentions of the client. But with a formal specification this is less likely. Composing a specification isn't an easy job, lots of practice is required.

• Sometimes the client's intentions change after the specification has been written. This is often used as an argument against writing the specification at all. But without the specification, we do not know what program to write, and experience shows that most of these changes are due to a vague notion of the problem in the first place. Composing a specification forces us to get rid of this vagueness.

• In industry these days, the terms "requirement" and "specification" are often used interchangably. Further, what is usually called a specification has little in common with what we would consider to be one. Don't be confused: Just because it says "specification" doesn't mean it is one. The industry uses terminology very loosely!

• There is another prevelant problem in industry: Many projects, especially important ones, are "specified" not by programmers, but by managers (or by "systems analysts") who do not understand the issues involved. Teams of programmers are assembled to solve these vaguely posed problems. They must iterate through solutions, getting feedback along the way, until they happen to hit upon something deemed acceptable. Such iterative efforts are very common, and are a major contribution to the enormous costs of software to industry.[4]

---

[4]Because programmers do not know what program to write, there is no way to estimate the labor involved. As a result these projects almost always go over budget, often substantially. Since whatever happens to exist at this point is often far from what is desired (assuming that anyone remembers!), either the current effort is declared a "success", the gap to be filled by "future enhancements", or it suddenly becomes a "prototype", in which case the effort was valuable since "a great deal was learned". This Orwellian state of affairs is, to a very large extent, the result of a non-existent or inadequate specification.

Good project managers, on the other hand, avoid these situations by making sure that the specifications are composed by capable programmers.

5

The shapes of programs

5.0 Introduction

The activity of programming is the activity of solving a specification for its unknown, where this unknown is called a *program*. Programs are formulae of a certain shape.

The ability to write down a number does not make an accountant. An accountant has the additional ability, acquired by education and practice, to arrive at a number that solves a given problem.

Similarly, the ability to write down a program does not make a programmer. A programmer has the additional ability, acquired by education and practice, to arrive at a program that solves a given specification.

Thus in addition to knowing the shapes programs can have, a programmer must be able to find a program that satisfies a given specification. Such a program is called *correct*. The activity of programming is the activity of finding correct programs for given specifications.

We begin this chapter by listing the legal shapes of programs. Then we define what is meant by a program being correct. In the course of doing so we prove a number of theorems that will serve us well when we begin our study of programming.

5.1 The shapes of programs

- Our first program is called *skip* and is written

    skip

- Our second program is called *abort* and is written

    abort

- Our third program is called a *composition* and is written

    $S; T$

    where S and T are programs. The semicolon " ; " is called the *composition operator* because it allows two programs to be composed into a longer program. Sometimes we write a composition on two lines as

    $S;$ or more often as S
    T $;T$.

- Next we have the *multiple assignment*, or *assignment* for short, which is written

    $x := E$

    where x is a list of distinct variable names and E is an equal-lengthed list of expressions. List x cannot include array names. Elements in these lists are separated by commas, and the two lists are pairwise of the same type, e.g. if the first variable in x is of type integer, then the first expression in E must be an integer expression, and so on.

    We will not specify the allowable shapes of expressions. We allow the usual ones from mathematics. Thus 6 and $x + 6$ are examples of expressions of type integer, and $P \wedge Q$ is an expression of type boolean. With integer variable x and boolean variable b, three assignments we can write are

    $$x := x + 7 \qquad b := true \qquad x, b := x + 7, true \quad .$$

    Remark   In most famous programming languages only a single variable name is allowed in variable list x. This restriction is quite unfortunate, as we shall see.   □

- Our next program is the *alternation* which is written

    $\underline{\text{if}} \ B.0 \qquad \rightarrow \quad S.0$
    $\square \ B.1 \qquad \rightarrow \quad S.1$
    $\cdots$
    $\square \ B.(n-1) \ \rightarrow \ S.(n-1)$
    $\underline{\text{fi}}$

where the B's are boolean expressions called *guards*, and the S's are programs called *commands*. Each construct "$B \rightarrow S$" is called a *guarded command*. An alternation is a list of guarded commands, separated by boxes (☐), beginning with an if and ending with a fi. We often take the liberty of writing alternations with small numbers of guarded commands on a single line, for example:

if $B0 \rightarrow S0$ ☐ $B1 \rightarrow S1$ fi .

- Our last program is the *repetition* which is written

do $B.0$ $\rightarrow$ $S.0$
☐ $B.1$ $\rightarrow$ $S.1$
$\cdots$
☐ $B.(n-1)$ $\rightarrow$ $S.(n-1)$
od

Thus a repetition is a list of guarded commands that begins with a do and ends with an od. Just as with the alternation, we often take the liberty of writing a repetition on a single line. For example, we might write a repetition with a single guarded command as

do $B \rightarrow S$ od .

These are the shapes that programs can have.

5.2   When is a program correct?

When asked to write a program, we are not interested in writing *any* program. We are interested in writing a program that is correct, i.e. that satisfies its specification. Thus we must define what is meant when we say that a program satisfies its specification.

Given program S having precondition Q and postcondition R, we define

- $\{Q\}\, S\, \{R\} \quad \equiv \quad Q \Rightarrow (wp.S).R \qquad$ (Definition of the Hoare triple)

where $wp.S$ is a function that will be defined shortly. We will take this as the *Definition of the Hoare triple*. Until this point the Hoare triple was defined informally.

With program S having precondition Q and postcondition R, we combine this definition with our informal notion of the Hoare triple, to find that

(Program S satisfies its specification) $\equiv$ $Q \Rightarrow (wp.S).R$.

Thus we have defined what is meant by a program satisfying its specification!

Remark   Since function application binds to the left, from now on we will write $(wp.S).R$ as $wp.S.R$. □

Remark   There are a few observations to be made. The first is that the notion of program correctness is now on firm ground. In particular, it is now tied to the predicate calculus. As soon as we learn how to evaluate $wp.S$, we will be able to *calculate* whether program S is correct with respect to its specification. It is correct if $Q \Rightarrow wp.S.R$ holds.

The second observation is that because $Q \Rightarrow wp.S.R$ is a boolean expression, the correctness of a program (with respect to its specification) is now a boolean proposition. In other words, a program is either correct or it is not! □

⋆   ⋆

Without knowing anything else about our soon to be defined function $wp.S$, we can prove a result that will serve us well later:

○ $\{wp.S.R\}\ S\ \{R\}$ ($wp.S.R$ is always a precondition)

Proof: For any S and R we observe

$$\{wp.S.R\}\ S\ \{R\}$$
$\equiv$ ⟨ Definition of the Hoare triple ⟩
$$wp.S.R \Rightarrow wp.S.R$$
$\equiv$ ⟨ $P \Rightarrow P$ ⟩
$$true$$

— a result that tells us that $wp.S.R$ is always a precondition for program S having postcondition R.

⋆   ⋆

All that remains is to define our as yet undefined function $wp.S$. When we have defined $wp.S$ for all programs S, we will be able to determine whether a program meets its specification. We will do so shortly, but first will digress a bit, to examine $wp.S$ in some detail.

5.3   A bit about $wp.S$

For given program S, $wp.S.R$ is a function from a predicate,[0] namely R, to a predicate, namely $wp.S.R$. For this reason $wp.S$ is sometimes called a *predicate transformer*.

The predicate transformer $wp.S$ is postulated to satisfy:[1]

Law	Name
$wp.S.false \equiv false$	Excluded miracle
$wp.S.(X \wedge Y) \equiv wp.S.X \wedge wp.S.Y$	Conjunctivity

From Conjunctivity and Leibniz's rule (that a function applied to equal arguments yields equal values), i.e.

$$(P \equiv Q) \Rightarrow (f.P \equiv f.Q) \qquad \text{(Leibniz's rule)}$$

we can prove

∘ $(X \Rightarrow Y) \Rightarrow (wp.S.X \Rightarrow wp.S.Y)$ \qquad ($wp.S$ is monotonic)

Proof:

$$
\begin{array}{ll}
& wp.S.X \ \Rightarrow\ wp.S.Y \\
\equiv & \quad \langle\, P \Rightarrow Q \equiv P \wedge Q \equiv P \,\rangle \\
& wp.S.X \ \wedge\ wp.S.Y \ \equiv\ wp.S.X \\
\equiv & \quad \langle\, \text{Conjunctivity} \,\rangle \\
& wp.S.(X \wedge Y) \ \equiv\ wp.S.X \\
\Leftarrow & \quad \langle\, \text{Leibniz's rule} \,\rangle \\
& X \wedge Y \ \equiv\ X \\
\equiv & \quad \langle\, P \Rightarrow Q \equiv P \wedge Q \equiv P \,\rangle \\
& X \Rightarrow Y
\end{array}
$$

---

[0]Specifically, a boolean expression.

[1]The predicate transformer $wp.S$ is due to E.W. Dijkstra. The name wp is mnemonic for *weakest precondition* because $wp.S.R$ is defined as the (unique) weakest solution to the equation $Q: \{Q\} \, S \, \{R\}$. A weakest solution to a boolean equation is a solution that is implied by all solutions. In this case, for any solution Q, $Q \Rightarrow wp.S.R$ holds. We introduced $wp.S$ to define what is meant by program correctness. There exist definitions of program correctness that do not use $wp.S$, but $wp.S$ has an added benefit — it is an enormous help in the development of programs.

We use the monotonicity of $wp.S$, in turn, to prove:

> ◦ $\{Q\}\ S\ \{R\}\ \Leftarrow\ \{Q\}\ S\ \{A\}\ \wedge\ (A\ \Rightarrow\ R)$ \qquad (Postcondition Rule)
>
> Proof:

$$\begin{aligned}
& \{Q\}\ S\ \{A\}\ \wedge\ (A\ \Rightarrow\ R) \\
\equiv\quad & \langle\,\text{Definition of the Hoare triple, the only possible step}\,\rangle \\
& (Q\ \Rightarrow\ wp.S.A)\ \wedge\ (A\ \Rightarrow\ R) \\
\Rightarrow\quad & \langle\,\text{Monotonicity of } wp.S\ (*)\,\rangle \\
& (Q\ \Rightarrow\ wp.S.A)\ \wedge\ (wp.S.A\ \Rightarrow\ wp.S.R) \\
\Rightarrow\quad & \langle\,\text{Transitivity of } \Rightarrow\ \rangle \\
& Q\ \Rightarrow\ wp.S.R \\
\equiv\quad & \langle\,\text{Definition of the Hoare triple}\,\rangle \\
& \{Q\}\ S\ \{R\}
\end{aligned}$$

The Postcondition Rule will be helpful when we develop loops.

Remark   The validity of the step marked $(*)$ is discussed in the next chapter. □

★   ★

We conclude with a definition, that of the equivalence of programs. For programs S and T

> • $S = T\ \equiv\ (\text{For all } R\colon wp.S.R\ \equiv\ wp.T.R)$ \quad (Program equivalence)

Thus programs S and T are equivalent when $wp.S.R\ \equiv\ wp.T.R$, for all R.

★   ★

Ex 5.0   Using the definition of the Hoare triple and properties of $wp.S$, prove:

> (a) $\{Q\}\ S\ \{R\}\ \Leftarrow\ (Q\ \Rightarrow\ A)\ \wedge\ \{A\}\ S\ \{R\}$
> (b) $\{Q0\ \wedge\ Q1\}\ S\ \{R0\ \wedge\ R1\}\ \Leftarrow\ \{Q0\}\ S\ \{R0\}\ \wedge\ \{Q1\}\ S\ \{R1\}$
> (c) $\{Q0\ \vee\ Q1\}\ S\ \{R0\ \vee\ R1\}\ \Leftarrow\ \{Q0\}\ S\ \{R0\}\ \wedge\ \{Q1\}\ S\ \{R1\}$

□

5.4 Defining *wp.S* for all programs *S*

Before our digression, we observed that once we have defined *wp.S* for all programs *S*, then we have a way to determine whether a program satisfies its specification, namely by the equivalence

$$\{Q\}\ S\ \{R\}\ \equiv\ Q\ \Rightarrow\ wp.S.R$$

— which we took as the definition of the Hoare triple.

Now we proceed to define, for all our programs *S*, *wp.S*. In addition to the definitions, we will also prove a few theorems that will be useful when we develop programs. We begin with the *skip* and *abort*.

5.4.0 THE *skip* AND THE *abort*

The *skip* is postulated to satisfy

- $wp.skip.R\ \equiv\ R$ (Definition of *skip*)

In terms of Hoare triples we can prove

- $\{Q\}\ skip\ \{R\}\ \equiv\ Q\ \Rightarrow\ R$

  Proof:

  $$\begin{aligned}
  &\{Q\}\ skip\ \{R\} \\
  \equiv\quad &\langle\ \text{Definition of the Hoare triple}\ \rangle \\
  &Q\ \Rightarrow\ wp.skip.R \\
  \equiv\quad &\langle\ \text{Definition of }skip\ \rangle \\
  &Q\ \Rightarrow\ R
  \end{aligned}$$

This theorem gives us insight into how a *skip* can be executed. Assuming that $\{Q\}\ skip\ \{R\}$ holds, we see that $Q \Rightarrow R$ holds, which in turn tells us that R holds in any state in which Q holds. Since R is the postcondition and Q is the precondition, we see that the postcondition holds in any state in which the precondition does. Therefore the simplest way to execute a *skip* is to do nothing.

⋆   ⋆

The *abort* is postulated to satisfy

- $wp.abort.R \equiv false$ (Definition of $abort$)

In terms of Hoare triples we have

○ $\{Q\}\ abort\ \{R\} \equiv (Q \equiv false)$

   Proof:

$$\begin{array}{ll}
 & \{Q\}\ abort\ \{R\} \\
\equiv & \quad \langle\ \text{Definition of the Hoare triple}\ \rangle \\
 & Q \Rightarrow wp.abort.R \\
\equiv & \quad \langle\ \text{Definition of}\ abort\ \rangle \\
 & Q \Rightarrow false \\
\equiv & \quad \langle\ P \Rightarrow false \equiv P \equiv false\ \rangle \\
 & Q \equiv false
\end{array}$$

Therefore, an $abort$ will only establish its postcondition if its precondition equals $false$. Since $false$ is satisfied in no state (i.e. can never equal $true$), an $abort$ can never establish its postcondition. As a result, we consider a program containing an $abort$ to be erroneous.

5.4.1   THE COMPOSITION

The *composition* is postulated to satisfy

- $wp.(S;T).R \equiv wp.S.(wp.T.R)$ (Definition of composition)

In terms of Hoare triples we have

○ $\{Q\}\ S;T\ \{R\} \Leftarrow \{Q\}\ S\ \{H\} \land \{H\}\ T\ \{R\}$

   Proof: For any H we have

$$\begin{array}{ll}
 & \{Q\}\ S\ \{H\} \land \{H\}\ T\ \{R\} \\
\equiv & \quad \langle\ \text{Definition of the Hoare triple, twice}\ \rangle \\
 & (Q \Rightarrow wp.S.H) \land (H \Rightarrow wp.T.R) \\
\Rightarrow & \quad \langle\ \text{Monotonicity of}\ wp.S\ \rangle \\
 & (Q \Rightarrow wp.S.H) \land (wp.S.H \Rightarrow wp.S.(wp.T.R)) \\
\Rightarrow & \quad \langle\ \text{Transitivity of}\ \Rightarrow\ \rangle \\
 & Q \Rightarrow wp.S.(wp.T.R) \\
\equiv & \quad \langle\ \text{Definition of composition}\ \rangle \\
 & Q \Rightarrow wp.(S;T).R \\
\equiv & \quad \langle\ \text{Definition of the Hoare triple}\ \rangle \\
 & \{Q\}\ S;T\ \{R\}
\end{array}$$

Thus $\{Q\}\ S; T\ \{R\}$ follows from the existence of some expression H satisfying

$$\{Q\}\ S\ \{H\} \ \wedge \ \{H\}\ T\ \{R\}$$

This result gives us insight into how a composition can be executed. Since S starting in a state satisfying Q will establish H, and since T starting in a state satisfying H will establish R, then $S; T$ starting in a state satisfying Q can establish R by first executing S, and when S terminates, executing T.

⋆　　　　⋆

Ex 5.1　Using the definition of program equivalence, prove that:

　　(a) *skip* is the unit of composition, i.e.:

$$S;\ skip = S \ \text{ and } \ skip;\ S = S.$$

　　(b) *abort* is the zero of composition, i.e.:

$$S;\ abort = abort \ \text{ and } \ abort;\ S = abort.$$

□

5.4.2　THE ASSIGNMENT

Before we define the assignment, we pause to introduce the notion of *textual substitution*, a notion we will need to define $wp.(x := E).R$.

⋆　　　　⋆

The formula

$$R(x := E) \hspace{4cm} \text{(textual substitution)}$$

is obtained from R by simultaneously replacing all occurrences of x in R by E. If a variable in E would become a dummy, then rename the dummy in R before the substitution. In general, x and E are lists of the same length.

Examples:

With $R \equiv i \leq j$, we have

- $R(i := i + 1) = i + 1 \leq j$
- $R(i, j := i + 1, i + j) = i + 1 \leq i + j$
- $R(x := 3) = R$, since x does not occur in R.

With $R \equiv x < y \ \wedge \ (\forall j :: f.j < y)$, we have

- $R(y := y + 1) = x < y + 1 \ \wedge \ (\forall j :: f.j < y + 1)$
- $R(y := y + j) = x < y + j \ \wedge \ (\forall k :: f.k < y + j)$

In this last example, because E contained a j, the dummy j was renamed before the substitution. The omitted steps appear below:

$$R(y := y + j)$$
$$\equiv \qquad \langle \text{Definition of } R \rangle$$
$$(x < y \ \wedge \ (\forall j :: f.j < y))(y := y + j)$$
$$\equiv \qquad \langle \ j \text{ is a dummy in the quantification, so rename it } k \rangle$$
$$(x < y \ \wedge \ (\forall k :: f.k < y))(y := y + j)$$
$$\equiv \qquad \langle \text{Perform the textual substitution} \rangle$$
$$x < y + j \ \wedge \ (\forall k :: f.k < y + j)$$

Remark   Sometimes textual substitution is written instead as R_E^x or as $(x := E).R$.   □

$$\star \qquad\qquad\qquad \star$$

The *assignment* is postulated to satisfy

- $wp.(x := E).R \ \equiv \ def.E \ \wedge \ R(x := E)$

First we discuss $def.E$, which is defined to be equivalent to the statement "E can be evaluated". For example,

$$def.(x \ div \ y) \ \equiv \ y \neq 0,$$

i.e. $x \ div \ y$ can only be evaluated when $y \neq 0$. Another example is the so-called "array subscript out-of-range": With array $b(k : 0 \leq k < N)$:

$$def.(b.i) \ \equiv \ 0 \leq i < N.$$

In other words, $b.i$ can only be evaluated when $0 \leq i < N$.

Because we have not formally defined the allowable expressions E, we cannot define $def.E$, except in this informal way. We usually omit it from the definition of assignment, as understood, and define the assignment as simply:

- $wp.(x := E).R \equiv R(x := E)$ (Definition of assignment)

Examples:

(a) With integer variable x:

$$wp.(x := 6 * x + 15).(x = 57)$$
$$\equiv \quad \langle\, \text{Definition of assignment}\,\rangle$$
$$(x = 57)(x := 6 * x + 15)$$
$$\equiv \quad \langle\, \text{Definition of textual substitution}\,\rangle$$
$$6 * x + 15 = 57$$
$$\equiv \quad \langle\, \text{Arithmetic}\,\rangle$$
$$x = 7$$

(b) With integer variables x and y;

$$wp.(x, y := x + 1, x + y).(x = y)$$
$$\equiv \quad \langle\, \text{Definition of assignment}\,\rangle$$
$$(x = y)(x, y := x + 1, x + y)$$
$$\equiv \quad \langle\, \text{Definition of textual substitution}\,\rangle$$
$$x + 1 = x + y$$
$$\equiv \quad \langle\, \text{Arithmetic}\,\rangle$$
$$1 = y$$

(c) With integer variables x and y:

$$wp.(x := x + 1 \ ; \ y := x + y).(x = y)$$
$$\equiv \quad \langle\, \text{Definition of composition}\,\rangle$$
$$wp.(x := x + 1).(wp.(y := x + y).(x = y))$$
$$\equiv \quad \langle\, \text{Definition of assignment}\,\rangle$$
$$wp.(x := x + 1).((x = y)(y := x + y))$$
$$\equiv \quad \langle\, \text{Definition of textual substitution}\,\rangle$$
$$wp.(x := x + 1).(x = x + y)$$
$$\equiv \quad \langle\, \text{Arithmetic}\,\rangle$$
$$wp.(x := x + 1).(0 = y)$$
$$\equiv \quad \langle\, \text{Definition of assignment}\,\rangle$$
$$(0 = y)(x := x + 1)$$
$$\equiv \quad \langle\, \text{Definition of textual substitution}\,\rangle$$
$$0 = y$$

Recalling that $wp.S.R$ is always a precondition of program S having post-condition R, it is because of these examples that we can assert:

(a) $\{x = 7\}\ x := 6 * x + 15\ \{x = 57\}$

(b) $\{1 = y\}\ x, y := x + 1, x + y\ \{x = y\}$

(c) $\{0 = y\}\ x := x + 1\ ;\ y := x + y\ \{x = y\}$

⋆   ⋆

The assignment $x := E$ can be executed by first evaluating the expressions in E, and then assigning them, in any order, to the variables in x.

⋆   ⋆

Ex 5.2   Compute and simplify $wp.S.R$ for the following:

	S	R
(a)	$x := 5$	$x = 5$
(b)	$x := 5$	$x \neq 5$
(c)	$x := (x - y) * (x + y)$	$x + y^2 = 0$
(d)	$q, r := q + 1, r - y$	$q * y + r = x$
(e)	$x := (x \equiv y)$	
	$;y := (x \equiv y)$	
	$;x := (x \equiv y)$	$(x \equiv Y) \wedge (y \equiv X)$
(f)	$x, y := y, x$	$(x \equiv Y) \wedge (y \equiv X)$

□

Ex 5.3   Using the definition of program equivalence, prove:

$$(x := x) = skip.$$

□

5.4.3   THE ALTERNATION

With the abbreviation IF for the alternation

<u>if</u> $B.0$ → $S.0$
□ $B.1$ → $S.1$

. . .

□ $B.(n-1)$ → $S.(n-1)$
<u>fi</u>

IF is postulated to satisfy

- $wp.\text{IF}.R \ \equiv$ (Definition of IF)

$$BB \ \wedge \ (\forall i : 0 \leq i < n : B.i \ \Rightarrow \ wp.(S.i).R\,)$$

where

$$BB \ \equiv \ (\exists i : 0 \leq i < n : B.i\,).$$

Remark Interpreting BB we see that it is *true* in any state in which at least one guard holds, and is *false* otherwise.   □

★   ★

Towards decreasing the labor involved in evaluating $wp.\text{IF}.R$, observe that BB is the disjunction of the guards. Therefore BB can be evaluated by evaluating

$$B.0 \ \vee \ B.1 \ \vee \ \ldots \ \vee \ B.(n-1).$$

Observe also that the universal quantification can be evaluated by evaluating the conjunction of

$$B.i \ \Rightarrow \ wp.(S.i).R \quad \text{for } 0 \leq i < n.$$

For example, with program IF2 given by

    <u>if</u> $B0 \ \rightarrow \ S0$
    ▯ $B1 \ \rightarrow \ S1$
    <u>fi</u>

using

    (0) $B0 \ \vee \ B1$
    (1) $B0 \ \Rightarrow \ wp.S0.R$
    (2) $B1 \ \Rightarrow \ wp.S1.R$

we see that

$wp.\text{IF2}.R \equiv (0) \wedge (1) \wedge (2).$

In other words, to evaluate $wp.\text{IF2}.R$, first evaluate each of (0), (1), and (2), and then compute their conjunction.

★   ★

Ex 5.4 Compute and simplify $wp.S.R$ for the following

	S	R
(a)	$\underline{\text{if}}\ a > b \ \rightarrow\ skip\ \square\ b > a \ \rightarrow\ skip\ \underline{\text{fi}}$	$true$
(b)	$\underline{\text{if}}\ true \ \rightarrow\ x := 2\ \square\ true \ \rightarrow\ x := -2\ \underline{\text{fi}}$	$x = 2$

□

Ex 5.5 Prove that an alternation with 0 guarded commands is equivalent to an *abort*. □

★   ★

From the definition of the alternation we prove two useful theorems:

∘ $\{Q\}\ \text{IF}\ \{R\} \equiv$ (IF-Theorem)

$$(Q \Rightarrow BB) \wedge (\forall i : 0 \leq i < n : \{Q \wedge B.i\}\ S.i\ \{R\})$$

Proof: Taking the liberty of not writing the range of the $\forall$, we have

$\qquad (Q \Rightarrow BB) \wedge (\forall i :: \{Q \wedge B.i\}\ S.i\ \{R\})$
$\equiv \qquad \langle\,\text{Definition of the Hoare triple (our only choice)}\,\rangle$
$\qquad (Q \Rightarrow BB) \wedge (\forall i :: Q \wedge B.i \Rightarrow wp.(S.i).R)$
$\equiv \qquad \langle\,\text{Towards distributing }Q\text{ out of the quantification:}$
$\qquad\qquad X \wedge Y \Rightarrow Z \equiv X \Rightarrow (Y \Rightarrow Z)\,\rangle$
$\qquad (Q \Rightarrow BB) \wedge (\forall i :: Q \Rightarrow (B.i \Rightarrow wp.(S.i).R))$
$\equiv \qquad \langle\,\text{``}Q \Rightarrow\text{'' distributes over }\forall\,\rangle$
$\qquad (Q \Rightarrow BB) \wedge (Q \Rightarrow (\forall i :: B.i \Rightarrow wp.(S.i).R))$
$\equiv \qquad \langle\,(X \Rightarrow Y) \wedge (X \Rightarrow Z) \equiv X \Rightarrow Y \wedge Z\,\rangle$
$\qquad Q \Rightarrow (BB \wedge (\forall i :: B.i \Rightarrow wp.(S.i).R))$
$\equiv \qquad \langle\,\text{Definition of IF}\,\rangle$
$\qquad Q \Rightarrow wp.\text{IF}.R$
$\equiv \qquad \langle\,\text{Definition of the Hoare triple}\,\rangle$
$\qquad \{Q\}\ \text{IF}\ \{R\}$

o $\neg BB \implies$ IF $=$ *abort*

Proof:

$$
\begin{aligned}
& \text{IF} = abort \\
\equiv\quad & \langle\,\text{Definition of program equivalence}\,\rangle \\
& wp.\text{IF}.R \equiv wp.abort.R \\
\equiv\quad & \langle\,\text{Definition of } abort\,\rangle \\
& wp.\text{IF}.R \equiv false \\
\equiv\quad & \langle\, P \equiv false \equiv \neg P\,\rangle \\
& \neg wp.\text{IF}.R \\
\equiv\quad & \langle\,\text{Definition of IF}\,\rangle \\
& \neg(BB \;\wedge\; (\forall i : 0 \le i \le n : B.i \implies wp.(S.i).R)) \\
\equiv\quad & \langle\,\text{De Morgan}\,\rangle \\
& \neg BB \;\vee\; \neg(\forall i : 0 \le i \le n : B.i \implies wp.(S.i).R) \\
\Leftarrow\quad & \langle\, P \vee Q \Leftarrow P\,\rangle \\
& \neg BB
\end{aligned}
$$

$\star$ $\qquad\qquad$ $\star$

These theorems give us insight into how an IF might be executed. The first tells us that $\{Q\}$ IF $\{R\}$ is as valid as the conjunction of

(a) In the initial state there is a true guard (i.e. $Q \implies BB$ holds), and

(b) $\{Q \wedge B\}\, S\, \{R\}$ holds for every guarded command $B \to S$.

On account of (b), we see that each command must establish R, whenever its guard holds in the initial state. Since R is the postcondition of the IF, we see that an IF can establish its postcondition by executing *any* (but only one) command whose guard holds initially.

The fact that *any* command whose guard holds initially can be selected for execution is known as *non-determinism*. For example, in:

```
if true → S0
[] true → S1
fi
```

either, but only one, of $S0$ or $S1$ may be selected for execution. If this IF is executed several times, one alternative may never be selected for execution, while the other may always be selected. It does not matter — (b) requires that either establishes the IF's postcondition. Thus the order of the guarded commands is irrelevant, which is why the list of guarded commands is more accurately called a *guarded command set*.

Remark   The question might arise as to why non-determinism is admitted. The answer is that it greatly eases program development, as we shall see.   □

But what if no guard holds initially? The second theorem says that if no guard holds (i.e. $\neg BB$ holds), then the IF is equivalent to an *abort*. Because an *abort* cannot be executed, such an IF cannot either. As a result, we consider such an IF to be erroneous.

⋆   ⋆

Ex 5.6   Prove that it is never necessary to write an IF with a single guarded command, i.e. prove:

$$\{Q\}\ S\ \{R\}\ \Leftarrow\ \{Q\}\ \underline{if}\ B \to S\ \underline{fi}\ \{R\}$$

— in other words, if the second program is valid, then so is the first. And both have the same specification.   □

Ex 5.7   Prove that the two programs:

$$X:\ \underline{if}\ B0 \to S0; T\ \square\ B1 \to S1; T\ \underline{fi}$$
$$Y:\ \underline{if}\ B0 \to S0\ \ \ \ \square\ B1 \to S1\ \ \ \ \underline{fi}\ ;\ T$$

are equivalent — i.e. prove: $wp.X.R \equiv wp.Y.R$ for any R. (Notice that this shows one way in which programs can distribute over an alternation.)   □

5.4.4   THE REPETITION

The *repetition*, or *loop*, is written

$$\underline{do}\ B.0\ \ \ \ \ \ \to\ S.0$$
$$\square\ \ \ \ B.1\ \ \ \ \ \ \to\ S.1$$
$$\cdots$$
$$\square\ \ \ \ B.(n-1)\ \to\ S.(n-1)$$
$$\underline{od}$$

In order to simplify the presentation of its definition, we constrain ourselves to a repetition with a single guarded command, namely:

$$\underline{do}\ B \to S\ \underline{od}$$

Later we will come back to the general case.

⋆   ⋆

The definition of the repetition in terms of wp is not useful for our purposes, and would serve only to delay us. From its omitted definition, however, an exceedingly useful result can be proved. It is known as the *Invariance Theorem*:

- $\{P\} \; \underline{do} \; B \;\rightarrow\; S \; \underline{od} \; \{P \wedge \neg B\}$ (Invariance Theorem)

    $\Leftarrow$ the conjunction of

$$\{P \wedge B\} \, S \, \{P\} \qquad\qquad\qquad \text{(Invariance)}$$
$$\{P \wedge B \wedge t = T\} \, S \, \{t < T\} \qquad \text{(Progress)}$$
$$P \wedge t \leq 0 \;\Rightarrow\; \neg B \qquad\qquad \text{(Boundedness)}$$

    for some integer function t.

We begin our examination of the Invariance Theorem by ignoring the conjuncts called *Boundedness* and *Progress*, constraining ourselves to considering:

$$\{P\} \; \underline{do} \; B \;\rightarrow\; S \; \underline{od} \; \{P \wedge \neg B\} \quad \Leftarrow \quad \{P \wedge B\} \, S \, \{P\}$$
$$(0) \qquad\qquad\qquad\qquad\qquad\quad (1)$$

Ignoring B for a moment, (1) states that if loop body S begins in a state satisfying P, it will terminate in a state satisfying P. In other words, the loop body S maintains the truth of P invariantly. It is for this reason that P is called an *invariant of the repetition*, a *loop invariant*, or simply an *invariant*.

Next take B into account in order to gain some insight about how a repetition might be executed. Given that P holds initially (by (0)), and given that S maintains P providing that B holds initially (by (1)), a repetition can be executed by repeatedly executing S until B does not hold. When B does not hold, the postcondition of (0), namely $P \wedge \neg B$, will.

But what if B always holds? The repetition will forever execute S, and will never establish $P \wedge \neg B$. The guarantee that B doesn't hold forever is called the *Requirement of Termination*, a requirement satisfied when we take the hitherto ignored requirements of *Boundedness* and *Progress* into account.

Boundedness requires that B is false when integer function t is small enough — in particular when $t \leq 0$. *Progress* requires that (each execution of) S decreases t: t's final value is less than its initial value. (The T denotes t's initial value.)

The minimal decrease of an integer function is by 1. Therefore no matter what t's initial value is, if it is decreased enough times, $t \leq 0$ will eventually hold. Thus if B isn't falsified before $t \leq 0$, it will be when $t \leq 0$ holds. In either case termination is guaranteed!

Remark Each execution of loop body S is called a *repetition* (or an *iteration*). Because termination is guaranteed when $t \leq 0$, we see that the (initial) value of t gives an upper-bound on the (total) number of repetitions. For example, if initially $t = 10$, then there will be at most 10 repetitions. □

It is because of Boundedness that t is sometimes called a *bound function*. It is because of Progress that t is sometimes called a *variant function*. Progress requires that t varies, in particular that it decreases.[2]

★   ★

Ex 5.8 Prove that Boundedness can also be written as

$$P \wedge B \Rightarrow t > 0$$

a result which which shows that Boundedness can be guaranteed by guaranteeing that $t > 0$ (i.e. that t is bounded from below by 0) is maintained as long as the guard holds. □

★   ★

Now we return to the general case, the repetition with any number of guarded commands, namely:

<u>do</u> $B.0$ → $S.0$
▯ $B.1$ → $S.1$
· · ·
▯ $B.(n-1)$ → $S.(n-1)$
<u>od</u>

---

[2]We could also guarantee termination by requiring an increase of t, where a large enough increase guarantees the falsity of the guard. In other words, where progress is made by an increase of t, and where that increase is bounded from above. The Invariance Theorem, as we have presented it, is actually a restricted version of the full theorem. For a statement and proof of the full theorem, see Edsger W. Dijkstra and A.J.M. van Gasteren, A simple fixpoint argument without the restriction to continuity, *Acta Informatica 23* 1986, 1-7.

— a program we denote by DO. DO is postulated to be equivalent to the following repetition, a repetition with single guarded command:

$$
\begin{aligned}
&\underline{\text{do}}\ BB\ \rightarrow \\
&\quad \underline{\text{if}}\ B.0 \qquad\ \ \rightarrow\ S.0 \\
&\quad \Box\ \ B.1 \qquad\ \ \rightarrow\ S.1 \\
&\quad \cdots \\
&\quad \Box\ \ B.(n-1)\ \ \rightarrow\ S.(n-1) \\
&\quad \underline{\text{fi}} \\
&\underline{\text{od}}
\end{aligned}
$$

where BB equals the disjunction of the guards, i.e.

$$BB \equiv (\exists i : 0 \leq i < n : B.i).$$

Combining our operational notion of a single guarded command repetition with that of the IF we see how a (many guarded command) repetition can be executed: For as long as a guard is true, execute *any* command associated with a true guard. Thus the repetition is non-deterministic too. Notice that all guards are false upon termination.

The Invariance Theorem in this case is the obvious generalization:

- $\{P\}$ DO $\{P \wedge \neg BB\}$ (Invariance Theorem for DO)

  $\Leftarrow$ the conjunction of

  - $(\forall i : 0 \leq i < n : \{P \wedge B.i\}\ S.i\ \{P\})$
  - $(\forall i : 0 \leq i < n : \{P \wedge B.i \wedge t = T\}\ S.i\ \{t < T\})$
  - $P \wedge t \leq 0 \Rightarrow \neg BB$

for some integer function t.

In other words, when the invariant is maintained by every guarded command that may be selected (that has a true guard), i.e. when

$$\{P \wedge B \wedge t = T\}\ S\ \{P\}$$

holds for every guarded command $B \rightarrow S$, and when progress is made by every guarded command that may be selected, i.e. when

$$\{P \wedge B \wedge t = T\}\ S\ \{t < T\}$$

holds for every guarded command $B \rightarrow S$, and when $t \leq 0$ guarantees the falsity of all the guards, i.e. when

$$P \wedge t \leq 0 \;\Rightarrow\; \neg BB$$

holds, then

$$\{P\} \; DO \; \{P \wedge \neg BB\}$$

holds as well. This is a repetition that terminates with the invariant true and all guards false.

$$\star \qquad\qquad \star$$

Ex 5.9   Prove that Boundedness for the Invariance Theorem for DO can be written as

$$(\forall i : 0 \leq i < n : P \wedge t \leq 0 \;\Rightarrow\; \neg B.i)$$

a result which which shows that Boundedness can be guaranteed by guaranteeing that it holds for each guarded command in isolation. □

Ex 5.10   Prove that a repetition with 0 guarded commands can be replaced with a *skip*.   □

Ex 5.11   Prove that the Invariance Theorem for DO follows from:

- the equivalence between DO and a single guarded command loop,
- the Invariance Theorem for a single guarded command loop, and
- the definition of the IF.

□

6

Intermezzo on calculations

In the next chapter we embark on our study of programming. What we will find is that most of it boils down to calculation and, as such, an effective programmer must first be an effective calculator.

With the aim of keeping our future calculations clear and succinct, we pause for further investigation of the calculation format. This little investigation will serve us well when we begin our study of programming.

On avoiding excessive writing

One way to prove $P \equiv Q$ is via two proofs: one of $P \equiv X$, and the other of $X \equiv Q$, where X is some intermediate expression. Notice that X is duplicated — it appears once in each proof. Next look at how this would be rendered in the calculation format:

$$
\begin{array}{ll}
& P \\
\equiv & \langle \text{ hint why } P \equiv X \rangle \\
& X \\
\equiv & \langle \text{ hint why } X \equiv Q \rangle \\
& Q
\end{array}
$$

Notice that X is not duplicated — a great improvement, especially if X is a long expression, or if there are a number of intermediate expressions (as is often the case).

⋆   ⋆

Had the implication been disallowed from the lefthand column of calculations, a proof of $P \Rightarrow Q$ might be organized as:

$$
\begin{array}{ll}
& P \\
\equiv & \langle \text{ hint why } P \equiv P \wedge Q \rangle \\
& P \wedge Q
\end{array}
$$

which is a proof of $P \Rightarrow Q$ on account of $P \Rightarrow Q \equiv P \equiv P \wedge Q$.

To further appreciate the improvement afforded by allowing the implication into the lefthand column, consider a proof of $P \Rightarrow Q$ that uses intermediate expression X:

$$
\begin{array}{ll}
& P \\
\Rightarrow & \quad \langle \text{ hint why } P \Rightarrow X \rangle \\
& X \\
\Rightarrow & \quad \langle \text{ hint why } X \Rightarrow Q \rangle \\
& Q
\end{array}
$$

This is a proof of $P \Rightarrow Q$ via a proof of $(P \Rightarrow X) \wedge (X \Rightarrow Q)$ which, by the transitivity of implication, implies $P \Rightarrow Q$. Allowing only equality into the lefthand column, we would have to write:

$$
\begin{array}{ll}
& P \\
\equiv & \quad \langle \text{ hint why } P \equiv P \wedge X \rangle \\
& P \wedge X \\
\equiv & \quad \langle \text{ hint why } X \equiv X \wedge Q \rangle \\
& P \wedge X \wedge Q \\
\equiv & \quad \langle \text{ hint why } P \equiv P \wedge X \rangle \\
& P \wedge Q
\end{array}
$$

Notice that this proof is longer and wider, and the second half is an undoing of the first half. For further appreciation of the improvement afforded by allowing the implication into the lefthand column of calculations, prove $P \Rightarrow Q$ using *three* intermediate expressions!

★   ★

Ex 6.0 Prove: $(X \equiv X \Rightarrow Y) \Rightarrow Y$ when the implication

   (a) *is not* allowed in the lefthand column of calculations.

   (b) *is* allowed in the lefthand column of calculations.

   □

What a calculation really means

Each step in a calculation has shape

$$
\begin{array}{ll}
& P \\
op & \quad \langle \text{ hint } H \rangle \\
& Q
\end{array}
$$

where *op* is some operator. A step is defined to be another way to express that $(P \ op \ Q)$ holds under the assumption of H. In other words, it is simply an alternative way to render $H \Rightarrow (P \ op \ Q)$.

A calculation is simply an alternative way to render the conjunction of the renderings of its steps. Therefore, the calculation

$$
\begin{array}{ll}
P & \\
op & \langle \ H0 \ \rangle \\
\quad X & \\
op & \langle \ H1 \ \rangle \\
\quad Q &
\end{array}
$$

is simply an alternative way to write

$$(H0 \ \Rightarrow \ (P \ op \ X)) \ \wedge \ (H1 \ \Rightarrow \ (X \ op \ Q)).$$

On proving consequences (and implications)

In programming, as we shall see, we often prove formulae like $wp.S.R \Leftarrow P$. In general, a proof of $Q \ \Leftarrow \ P$ can take a number of shapes, for example:

$$
\begin{array}{ll}
\quad Q & \\
\Leftarrow & \langle \ \text{hint why } Q \ \Leftarrow \ P \ \rangle \\
\quad P &
\end{array}
$$

or

$$
\begin{array}{ll}
\quad Q & \\
\equiv & \langle \ \text{Assuming } P \ \rangle \\
\quad true &
\end{array}
$$

This last calculation, according to the definition of a step, is simply another way to write

$$P \ \Rightarrow \ (Q \ \equiv \ true),$$

which, by simple predicate calculus, is equivalent to

$$Q \ \Leftarrow \ P,$$

which is what we were after. In other words, we have the option of organizing a proof of $Q \ \Leftarrow \ P$ into a calculation having the following shape:

$$Q$$
$\equiv$ ⟨ Assuming P ⟩
    $true$

*   *

Often P is a conjunction, i.e. we wish to prove

$$P0 \land P1 \Rightarrow Q. \tag{0}$$

One way to organize this is as

$$P1$$
$\Rightarrow$ ⟨ Assuming $P0$ ⟩
    Q

which, by the definition of a step, is simply a rendering of

$$P0 \Rightarrow (P1 \Rightarrow Q) \tag{1}$$

which, by simple predicate calculus (see exercise below), is equivalent to (0), which is what we were after. Note also that

$$P1$$
$\equiv$ ⟨ Assuming $P0$ ⟩
    Q

does the same job. This is an alternative rendering of

$$P0 \Rightarrow (P1 \equiv Q) \tag{2}$$

which, by simple predicate calculus, implies (0). In other words, if (2) holds then so does (0), and therefore a proof of (2) is also a proof of (0). Next we show that the following calculation is yet another way to do the job:

$$Q$$
$\equiv$ ⟨ Assuming $P0$ ⟩
    X
$\equiv$ ⟨ Assuming $P1$ ⟩
    $true$

Towards showing that this is yet another way to organize a proof of (0), first notice that this calculation is simply an alternative way to write

$$(P0 \Rightarrow (Q \equiv X)) \;\wedge\; (P1 \Rightarrow (X \equiv \mathit{true})) \qquad (3)$$

We can show that it is an alternative way to organize a proof of (0) if we can show that (0) holds if (3) does, in other words, if we can prove that

$$(3) \Rightarrow (0). \qquad (4)$$

Proof of (4):

$$\quad (3)$$
$$\equiv \qquad \langle\, \text{Definition of (3)} \,\rangle$$
$$\quad ((P0 \Rightarrow (Q \equiv X)) \;\wedge\; (P1 \Rightarrow (X \equiv \mathit{true}))$$
$$\equiv \qquad \langle\, \text{So as not to drag the } X \equiv \mathit{true} \text{ along, } \ldots \,\rangle$$
$$\quad ((P0 \Rightarrow (Q \equiv X)) \;\wedge\; (P1 \Rightarrow X)$$
$$\Rightarrow \qquad \langle\, \text{See exercise below} \,\rangle$$
$$\quad (P0 \wedge X \Rightarrow Q) \;\wedge\; (P1 \Rightarrow X)$$
$$\equiv \qquad \langle\, \text{Observe that the } X \text{ must somehow be eliminated. This}$$

can be accomplished by getting X to the righthand side of the first implication, and to the lefthand side of the second, and then appealing to the transitivity of the implication to eliminate it. Continuing with this aim, apply Shuffle, a number of times. $\rangle$

$$\quad (P0 \wedge \neg Q \Rightarrow \neg X) \;\wedge\; (\neg X \Rightarrow \neg P1)$$
$$\Rightarrow \qquad \langle\, \text{Transitivity of } \Rightarrow \,\rangle$$
$$\quad P0 \wedge \neg Q \Rightarrow \neg P1$$
$$\equiv \qquad \langle\, \text{Shuffle, twice} \,\rangle$$
$$\quad P0 \wedge P1 \Rightarrow Q$$
$$\equiv \qquad \langle\, \text{Definition of (0)} \,\rangle$$
$$\quad (0)$$

which proves that a calculation of shape

$$\quad Q$$
$$\equiv \qquad \langle\, \text{Assuming } P0 \,\rangle$$
$$\quad X$$
$$\equiv \qquad \langle\, \text{Assuming } P1 \,\rangle$$
$$\quad \mathit{true}$$

is yet another way to organize a proof of $P0 \wedge P1 \Rightarrow Q$. A calculation of this shape is often to be preferred because it allows each conjunct on the lefthand side of the implication to be introduced separately.

$$\star \qquad\qquad \star$$
$$\star$$

Ex 6.1   Prove the following:

     (a)   (1) ≡ (0)
     (b)   (2) ⇒ (0)

□

Ex 6.2   The second step of the last calculation was an appeal to

$$(P0 \Rightarrow (Q \equiv X)) \Rightarrow (P0 \wedge X \Rightarrow Q)$$

Prove this.   □

Ex 6.3   In the proof of the Postcondition Rule (from the last chapter), we had a step of shape

$$\begin{array}{ll} & X \wedge Y \\ \Rightarrow & \langle\, Y \Rightarrow Z \,\rangle \\ & X \wedge Z \end{array}$$

Using the definition of a step, prove that a step of this shape is always valid.   □

A few other ways to prove a premise

There are other ways to prove a premise. Because of the validity of the following three formulae

     (a) $P \equiv true \equiv P$
     (b) $P \equiv true \Rightarrow P$
     (c) $P \equiv \neg P \Rightarrow false$

premise P can be proved by proving any of

     (a) $true \equiv P$
     (b) $true \Rightarrow P$
     (c) $\neg P \Rightarrow false$

A proof of shape (c), which we can organize as

$$\neg P$$
$$\Rightarrow \qquad \langle\, \text{hint}\, \rangle$$
$$false$$

is commonly called a "proof by contradiction".

★   ★

Finally, we point out that a proof of $P \equiv Q$ is also a proof of $P \Rightarrow Q$. That this is so follows from the validity of

$$(P \equiv Q) \Rightarrow (P \Rightarrow Q) \tag{5}$$

★   ★

Ex 6.4   Prove (5).   □

On Leibniz's rule

Leibniz's rule, or *Leibniz* for short, is the law we write as

$$x = y \Rightarrow f.x = f.y$$

or for booleans as

$$(x \equiv y) \Rightarrow (f.x \equiv f.y).$$

Leibniz expresses that equality is preserved by function application, that is, that a function applied to equal arguments yields equal values. It is a great help in shortening our calculations. For example, when asked to prove

$$E = b \Rightarrow a \ max \ E = a \ max \ b$$

we might write

$$a \ max \ E = a \ max \ b$$
$$= \qquad \langle\, \text{Assume } E = b \,\rangle$$
$$a \ max \ b = a \ max \ b$$
$$= \qquad \langle\, P = P \,\rangle$$
$$true$$

Using Leibniz we can write simply

$$a \; max \; E = a \; max \; b$$
$$\Leftarrow \qquad \langle \, \text{Leibniz} \, \rangle$$
$$E = b$$

Notice the improvement, even in this little example.

⋆   ⋆

Now that we have a few ways to keep our calculations succinct, we are ready to turn to our main topic: the calculations of programs from their specifications.

7

Developing loopless programs

7.0 Introduction

The activity of programming is the activity of solving a specification for its unknown. A specification's unknown is called a program. This chapter marks the beginning of our study of programming. Here we constrain ourselves to the development of programs that contain no loops. In subsequent chapters we study the development of loops. For now we concentrate on the assignment and the IF. We will discover that the development of assignments and IFs are mainly matters of straightforward calculation!

7.1 Calculating expressions in assignments

Consider solving for (unknown) E in

$$\{true\}\ x := E\ \{x = 4\}$$

We calculate:

$$\{true\}\ x := E\ \{x = 4\}$$
$$=\qquad \langle\, \text{Definition of the Hoare triple (our only possibility)} \,\rangle$$
$$true\ \Rightarrow\ wp.(x := E).(x = 4)$$
$$=\qquad \langle\, true\ \Rightarrow\ P\ \equiv\ P \,\rangle$$
$$wp.(x := E).(x = 4)$$
$$=\qquad \langle\, \text{Definition of the assignment} \,\rangle$$
$$E = 4$$

What we have derived is

$$\{true\}\ x := 4\ \{x = 4\,\}.$$

We see that an unknown expression in an assignment can be found by calculation. As we intend to rely heavily on these kinds of calculations, we turn our attention towards making them succinct.

★   ★

We start by noticing that the first step in the calculation was an appeal to
the definition of the Hoare triple, namely:

$$\{Q\} \ S \ \{R\} \ \equiv \ Q \ \Rightarrow \ wp.S.R.$$

Therefore we can always shorten a proof of $\{Q\} \ S \ \{R\}$ to one of $Q \ \Rightarrow \ wp.S.R$. In the last chapter we saw a number of ways to organize such a
proof. We learned that we can organize a proof of $Q \ \Rightarrow \ wp.S.R$ into

$$
\begin{array}{ll}
Q & \\
\Rightarrow & \langle \text{hint why } Q \ \Rightarrow \ wp.S.R \rangle \\
wp.S.R &
\end{array}
$$

or alternatively into

$$
\begin{array}{ll}
wp.S.R & \\
\Leftarrow & \langle \text{hint why } wp.S.R \ \Leftarrow \ Q \rangle \\
Q &
\end{array}
$$

or even into

$$
\begin{array}{ll}
wp.S.R & \\
\equiv & \langle Q \rangle \\
true &
\end{array}
$$

These last two are often to be preferred since $wp.S.R$ typically has more
manipulative possibilities. (Consider, in this last case, transforming *true*
into $wp.S.R$!) In the last chapter we also saw that a proof of

$$Q0 \ \wedge \ Q1 \ \Rightarrow \ wp.S.R$$

can be organized as

$$
\begin{array}{ll}
wp.S.R & \\
\equiv & \langle Q0 \rangle \\
\ldots & \\
\equiv & \langle Q1 \rangle \\
true &
\end{array}
$$

This format has the advantage that each conjunct of Q can be used separately, allowing us to be more precise in expressing the requirements of
each step.

⋆ ⋆

We turn to some examples. Solving for E in

$$\{0 \leq x \ \wedge \ 0 < y\} \ q, r := E, x \ \{0 \leq r \ \wedge \ q * y + r = x\}$$

boils down, on account of the definition of the Hoare triple, to solving for E in

$$0 \leq x \ \wedge \ 0 < y \ \Rightarrow \ wp.(q, r := E, x).(0 \leq r \ \wedge \ q * y + r = x).$$

Since the lefthand side of the implication is a conjunction, we can solve for E using a calculation of the following shape:

$$wp.(q, r := E, x).(0 \leq r \ \wedge \ q * y + r = x)$$
$\equiv$ $\langle \ 0 \leq x \ \rangle$
    $\ldots$
$\equiv$ $\langle \ 0 < y \ \rangle$
    $E = ?$

What we find is that

$$wp.(q, r := E, x).(0 \leq r \ \wedge \ q * y + r = x)$$
$\equiv$ $\langle$ Definition of assignment $\rangle$
    $0 \leq x \ \wedge \ E * y + x = x$
$\equiv$ $\langle$ Arithmetic $\rangle$
    $0 \leq x \ \wedge \ E * y = 0$
$\equiv$ $\langle 0 \leq x \rangle$
    $E * y = 0$
$\equiv$ $\langle 0 < y$, hence $0 \neq y$; by division $\rangle$
    $E = 0$

In other words, we have derived

$$\{0 \leq x \ \wedge \ 0 < y\} \ q, r := 0, x \ \{0 \leq r \ \wedge \ q * y + r = x\}.$$

⋆ ⋆

For another example, to solve for E in

$$\{q = a * c \ \wedge \ w = c^2\} \ a, q := a + c, E \ \{q = a * c\}$$

we calculate

$$wp.(a, q := a + c, E).(q = a * c)$$
$$\equiv \qquad \langle \text{ Definition of assignment } \rangle$$
$$E = (a + c) * c$$

Thus we have solved for E. Notice, however, that the precondition never entered into the calculation. If we take the precondition into account, perhaps we can simplify E a bit. We continue with this aim:

$$(a + c) * c$$
$$= \qquad \langle \text{ Arithmetic } \rangle$$
$$a * c + c^2$$
$$= \qquad \langle \text{ From the precondition: } \quad q = a * c \text{ and } w = c^2 \rangle$$
$$q + w$$

What we have derived is

$$\{q = a * c \ \wedge \ w = c^2\} \ a, q := a + c, q + w \ \{q = a * c\}.$$

★　　　　　　　★

These examples leave us with the following:

> | Heuristic | To determine an unknown expression in an assignment, calculate.

Just as in doing arithmetic, we have the freedom to choose the most effective way to organize our calculations.

Remark   That we can solve for unknown expressions by simple calculation means that problems that once required all sorts of clever insight can now be solved in an entirely straightforward way.   □

★　　　　　　★
★

Ex 7.0   Solve for E in the following:

       (a) $\{true\} \ n, r := n + 1, E \ \{r = n^2\}$
       (b) $\{r = n^2\} \ n, r := n + 1, E \ \{r = n^2\}$
       (c) $\{r = n^2 \ \wedge \ s = 2 * n\} \ n, r := n + 1, E \ \{r = n^2\}$

□

Ex 7.1   Solve for E in the following:

(a) $\{true\}\ n, s := 0, E\ \{s = (\Sigma i\ :\ 0 \le i\ \wedge\ i < n\ :\ f.i)\}$
(b) $\{true\}\ n, s := 1, E\ \{s = (\Sigma i\ :\ 0 \le i\ \wedge\ i < n\ :\ f.i)\}$

□

7.2   Developing IFs

Our insight into the development of the alternation:

$$
\begin{array}{lll}
\underline{\text{if }} B.0 & \rightarrow & S.0 \\
{[\!]}\ B.1 & \rightarrow & S.1 \\
\cdots \\
{[\!]}\ B.(n-1) & \rightarrow & S.(n-1) \\
\underline{\text{fi}}
\end{array}
$$

— a program we abbreviate by IF, comes from a theorem we have already seen, namely:

$\{Q\}$ IF $\{R\}$ $\equiv$ the conjunction of   (IF-Theorem)

(a) $Q \Rightarrow BB$
(b) $\{Q \wedge B\}\ S\ \{R\}$ for all guarded commands $B \rightarrow S$

where

$$BB \equiv (\exists i\ :\ 0 \le i < n\ :\ B.i).$$

SOLVING FOR GUARDS

By conjunct (b) of the IF-Theorem, each guarded command $B \rightarrow S$ must satisfy

$$\{Q \wedge B\}\ S\ \{R\}\tag{0}$$

As a result, solving for a guard boils down to solving for B in (0). For example, to solve for G in

$$
\begin{array}{l}
\{x > 0\} \\
\underline{\text{if }} G \rightarrow y := y - x\ \underline{\text{fi}} \\
\{R:\ x > 0\ \wedge\ y > 0\}
\end{array}
$$

we must solve for G in

$$\{x > 0 \ \wedge \ G\} \ y := y - x \ \{R\}.$$

This, in turn, boils down to solving for G in

$$x > 0 \ \wedge \ G \ \Rightarrow \ wp.(y := y - x).(R).$$

Organizing our calculation as

$$wp.(y := y - x).R$$
$$\equiv \qquad \langle \, x > 0 \, \rangle$$
$$G$$

we find that

$$wp.(y := y - x).R$$
$$\equiv \qquad \langle \, \text{Definitions of } R \text{ and assignment} \, \rangle$$
$$x > 0 \ \wedge \ y - x > 0$$
$$\equiv \qquad \langle \, \text{Arithmetic} \, \rangle$$
$$x > 0 \ \wedge \ y > x$$
$$\equiv \qquad \langle \, \text{From the precondition: } x > 0 \, \rangle$$
$$y > x$$

Thus the unknown guard is $y > x$. Not only can we calculate for unknown expressions in assignments, we can calculate for unknown guards in IFs too! Indeed:

| Heuristic | To determine an unknown guard in an IF, calculate.

Remark   We mention that we haven't taken conjunct (a) of the IF- Theorem into account yet. This we save until the next section.   □

$$\star \qquad\qquad\qquad \star$$

Ex 7.2   With P given by $a^2 \leq x \ \wedge \ x < b^2$, solve for B in

$$\{P\} \ \underline{\text{if}} \ B \ \rightarrow \ a := m \ \underline{\text{fi}} \ \{P\}$$

□

Ex 7.3   With P given by $x > 0 \land y > 0$, solve for guards $B0$ and $B1$
in

$$\{P \land x \neq y\}$$
$$\underline{\text{if}} \; B0 \; \rightarrow \; x := x - y$$
$$\square \; B1 \; \rightarrow \; y := y - x$$
$$\underline{\text{fi}}$$
$$\{P\}$$

First solve for $B0$, then solve for $B1$.   □

DEVELOPING IFS FROM SCRATCH

By conjunct (b) of the IF-Theorem, each guarded command $B \rightarrow S$ must satisfy

$$\{Q \land B\} \, S \, \{R\} \tag{b}$$

We are free to invent as many guarded commands $B \rightarrow S$ as we like, provided that each satisfies (b). But when have we invented enough? The answer to this question is in conjunct (a) of the IF-Theorem:

$$Q \; \Rightarrow \; BB \tag{a}$$

We have invented enough when (a) holds. Informally (a) requires that some guard holds initially. For example, assume that we have developed

$$\{Q \land B0\} \, S0 \, \{R\} \quad \text{and}$$
$$\{Q \land B1\} \, S1 \, \{R\} \quad \text{and}$$
$$\{Q \land B2\} \, S2 \, \{R\} \, .$$

Assume also that $Q \Rightarrow BB$ holds, i.e. assume that

$$Q \; \Rightarrow \; (B0 \lor B1 \lor B2)$$

holds. Therefore requirements (a) and (b) of the IF-Theorem are fulfilled, allowing us to construct the following IF:

$\{Q\}$
<u>if</u> $B0 \rightarrow S0$
$\square$ $B1 \rightarrow S1$
$\square$ $B2 \rightarrow S2$
<u>fi</u>
$\{R\}$

The development of IF's is summarized by the following:

> | Heuristic | $\{Q\}$ IF $\{R\}$ is developed by inventing guarded com-
> mands $B \rightarrow S$ which satisfy conjunct (b) of the IF-
> Theorem. Enough have been invented when conjunct
> (a) of the IF-Theorem is satisfied, at which point they
> can be assembled into an IF.

$\star$ $\star$

For example, we are asked to solve for S in $\{Q\}$ S $\{R\}$ when given

$Q:\ x = X \ \wedge \ y = Y$
$R:\ (x = X \ \vee \ x = Y) \ \wedge \ x \geq X \ \wedge \ x \geq Y$

and where X and Y denote the initial values of x and y, repectively, and consequently cannot appear in program S.

Interpreting this specification, we see that we are asked to set x to the maximum of x's and y's initial values. The obvious solution, $x := x \ max \ y$, we disallow here.

We begin our development by observing that there are only two ways to establish the first conjunct of R, namely:

$x := x$ or
$x := y$

The first establishes R's first conjunct by establishing $x = X$, and the second does the job by establishing $x = Y$. Since both establish R's first conjunct, either is a good candidate for S. Seeing no reason to prefer one over the other, we arbitrarily propose for S:

$S:\ x := y$

We calculate:

$$wp.(x := y).R$$
$$\equiv \quad \langle \text{ Definitions of } R \text{ and assignment } \rangle$$
$$(y = X \ \vee \ y = Y) \ \wedge \ y \geq X \ \wedge \ y \geq Y$$
$$\equiv \quad \langle \text{ From precondition } Q: \ y = Y \ \rangle$$
$$(y = X \ \vee \ true) \ \wedge \ y \geq X \ \wedge \ true$$
$$\equiv \quad \langle \text{ Predicate calculus } \rangle$$
$$y \geq X$$
$$\equiv \quad \langle \text{ From precondition } Q: \ x = X \ (\text{to eliminate the } X) \rangle$$
$$y \geq x$$

What we have derived is

$$\{Q \ \wedge \ y \geq x\} \ x := y \ \{R\} .$$

Because $x := y$ establishes R only if $y \geq x$ holds initially, $x := y$ is not a solution for S. Thus we are led to try our second candidate:

$$S: \ x := x$$

We calculate:

$$wp.(x := x).R$$
$$= \quad \langle \text{ Similar steps as before } \rangle$$
$$x \geq y$$

What we have derived is

$$\{Q \ \wedge \ x \geq y\} \ x := x \ \{R\} .$$

Because $x := x$ establishes R only if $x \geq y$ holds initially, $x := x$ is not a solution for S. Since there are no other ways to establish R's first conjunct, is there a way out?

We observe that the two programs we have derived, namely

$$\{Q \ \wedge \ y \geq x\} \ x := y \ \{R\} \tag{0}$$
$$\{Q \ \wedge \ x \geq y\} \ x := x \ \{R\} \tag{1}$$

both satisfy conjunct (b) of the IF-Theorem. If conjunct (a), in this case

$$Q \Rightarrow (y \geq x \ \lor \ x \geq y) \tag{2}$$

also holds, then we can assemble (0) and (1) into the following solution for S:

$$\{Q\}$$
$$S: \ \underline{if} \ y \geq x \ \rightarrow \ x := y$$
$$\quad \ \square \ x \geq y \ \rightarrow \ x := x$$
$$\quad \ \underline{fi}$$
$$\{R\}$$

We check (2):

$$\quad \ y \geq x \ \lor \ x \geq y$$
$$\equiv \qquad \langle \, \text{Obvious} \, \rangle$$
$$\quad \ true$$
$$\Leftarrow \qquad \langle \, true \ \Leftarrow \ P \, \rangle$$
$$\quad \ Q$$

It does, and so we are finished. We have developed a solution for S.

Remark   We usually do not put so much effort into a program as trivial as this one. The thoroughness was mainly for illustrative purposes.
□

Notice the non-determinism in the solution. When $x = y$, it does not matter which guarded command is selected: either establishes the postcondition. The power of non-determinism is that guarded commands can be developed in isolation — the precondition of one command is totally independent of that of another.

★   ★

Remark   This is not the case with the typical if-statement, which is usually rendered as something like:

$$\underline{if} \ B \ \underline{then} \ S$$
$$\qquad \ \underline{else} \ \ T$$
$$\underline{fi}$$

Notice that T *cannot* be developed in isolation — its precondition depends on the choice of guard for S. In particular, its (invisible) guard is the negation of S's guard. Things get very bad when these ifs are nested:

$$\underline{\text{if }} B \wedge C \underline{\text{ then }} S$$
$$\underline{\text{else }} \underline{\text{if }} D \vee \neg B \underline{\text{ then }} U$$
$$\underline{\text{else }} V$$
$$\underline{\text{fi}}$$
$$\underline{\text{fi}}$$

Notice how the precondition of V depends on that of U, which, in turn, depends on that of S. Thus V cannot be developed in isolation. Its development must follow the development of S and U. $\square$

★ ★

Ex 7.4 Why was the assignment $x := x$, or equivalently *skip*, necessary to our solution? In other words why wasn't

$$\underline{\text{if }} y \geq x \ \rightarrow \ x := y \ \underline{\text{fi}}$$

a solution for S? $\square$

ON RESTRICTING NON-DETERMINISM

To build an IF, we assemble programs satisfying

$$\{Q \wedge B\} \ S \ \{R\} \tag{0}$$

into guarded commands of the shape

$$B \rightarrow S. \tag{1}$$

Because of the theoremhood of

$$\{X \wedge Z\} \ S \ \{Y\} \ \Leftarrow \ \{X\} \ S \ \{Y\} \tag{2}$$

if (0) holds, then so does

$$\{Q \wedge B \wedge C\} \ S \ \{R\}$$

for any C. As a result, if we can write guarded command (1), we can also write

$$B \wedge C \to S.$$

without invalidating conjunct (b) of the IF-Theorem. Thus strengthening a guard (i.e. adding a conjunct) will *never* invalidate conjunct (b) of the IF-Theorem. It may however invalidate conjunct (a), namely that some guard holds initially. On this last count we must be careful.

⋆   ⋆

We give an example. From the (postulated) validity of

$\{Q\}$
<u>if</u> $B0 \to S0$
$\square$ $B1 \to S1$
<u>fi</u>
$\{R\}$

we will prove the validity of

$\{Q\}$
<u>if</u> $B0 \qquad\qquad \to S0$
$\square$ $B1 \wedge \neg B0 \to S1$
<u>fi</u>
$\{R\}$

From the validity of the first program, and the fact that strengthening a guard does not violate conjunct (b) of the IF-Theorem, the second program is correct, insofar as conjunct (b) of the IF-Theorem is concerned. So we must turn our attention to conjunct (a), and try to prove that if conjunct (a) holds for the first program, that it also holds for the second. We calculate:

$\qquad Q \Rightarrow (B0 \vee (B1 \wedge \neg B0))$
$\equiv \qquad$ ⟨ Complement: $X \vee (Y \wedge \neg X) \equiv X \vee Y$ ⟩
$\qquad Q \Rightarrow (B0 \vee B1)$
$\equiv \qquad$ ⟨ $Q \Rightarrow (B0 \vee B1)$ holds, by the validity
$\qquad\qquad$ of the first program ⟩
$\qquad$ *true*

Thus, from the validity of the first program, we have demonstrated the validity of the second.

We can always eliminate non-determinism in this way. But why (ever) eliminate non-determinism? Well, sometimes one alternative is preferrable for efficiency reasons, in which case we would like to exclude other (less efficient) alternatives whenever possible. There are other reasons as well, as we shall see.

$\star$ $\star$

Ex 7.5 Prove (2). □

8

Developing loops — an introduction

Our insight into developing loops comes from the Invariance Theorem:

$$\{P\} \underline{do}\ B \rightarrow S\ \underline{od}\ \{P \wedge \neg B\} \tag{0}$$

$\Leftarrow$ the conjunction of

$$\{P \wedge B\}\ S\ \{P\} \tag{a}$$
$$\{P \wedge B \wedge t = T\}\ S\ \{t < T\} \tag{b}$$
$$P \wedge t \leq 0 \Rightarrow \neg B \tag{c}$$

where P is a predicate called a loop invariant, and t is an integer function called the bound function. Conjunct (a) is the requirement of Invariance, conjunct (b) is the requirement of Progress, and conjunct (c) is the requirement of Boundedness.

ALLOWING FOR ARBITRARY PRE- AND POSTCONDITIONS

In (0), both the precondition and the postcondition have special shapes. In general we are given an arbitrary precondition, say Q, and an arbitrary postcondition, say R, and are asked to solve for the program. We begin our investigation of the loop by adding requirements that allow for arbitrary pre- and postconditions.

First we deal with the postcondition: Because of the Postcondition Rule, which we have already seen, if both

$$\{P\} \underline{do}\ B \rightarrow S\ \underline{od}\ \{P \wedge \neg B\} \quad \text{and}$$
$$P \wedge \neg B \Rightarrow R$$

hold, then so does

$$\{P\} \underline{do}\ B \rightarrow S\ \underline{od}\ \{R\} \tag{1}$$

— a program with postcondition R, as desired. In other words, if R is our postcondition, we simply choose invariant P and guard B to satisfy

$$P \wedge \neg B \Rightarrow R.$$

That was easy!

Now the precondition: If we have Q for our precondition, we simply build another program $S0$, say, that has precondition Q and postcondition P, and then compose it with repetition (1) into:

$$\{Q\}\ S0\ \{P\}\ ;\ \{P\}\ \underline{do}\ B \rightarrow S\ \underline{od}\ \{R\} \tag{2}$$

— a program with precondition Q and postcondition R, as desired.

All that remains to complete (2) is the development of the loop body S. This is where the Invariance Theorem comes in. It is the Invariance Theorem that gives us the requirements for S.

On developing the loop body

Conjuncts (a) and (b) of the Invariance Theorem says that S, the loop body, must satisfy both

$$\{P \wedge B\}\ S\ \{P\} \tag{a}$$
$$\{P \wedge B \wedge t = T\}\ S\ \{t < T\} \tag{b}$$

At this point guard B and invariant P have already been chosen. Thus specification (a) is complete. To complete specification (b), we need t, the bound function. And so our next step is to choose an appropriate bound function.

Well, how do we choose it? By conjunct (c) of the Invariance Theorem we see that t's decrease must eventually falsify B. Thus we choose t to satisfy conjunct (c): we choose a bound function whose repeated decrease is guaranteed to eventually falsify the guard.

For example, if we have $B \equiv n \neq 10$, where n is initially 0, say, then B will eventually be falsified if $10 - n$ is decreased. Thus we would choose for our bound function $t = 10 - n$. Decreasing t will eventually falsify B.

Now that specification (b) is complete, we are left with our final step, namely the development of program S to satisfy (a) and (b).

In (a) and (b) we see the general requirement for a loop body: Under the initial truth of invariant and guard, the loop body must "maintain the invariant and decrease the bound function".

SUMMARY OF THE STEPS FOR LOOP DEVELOPMENT

In general, a loop has the shape:

$\{Q\}$
$S0$
$\{P, \text{the invariant}\}$
$;\underline{\text{do }} B \rightarrow S \underline{\text{ od}}$
$\{P \land \neg B, \text{ hence } R\}$

Initially Q, the precondition, and R, the postcondition, are given. The rest, namely invariant P, guard B, and loop body S must be developed. The steps are as follows:

> Step 0 Choose invariant P and guard B to satisfy $P \land \neg B \Rightarrow R$. This guarantees that R holds upon termination.

> Step 1 Find a way to establish the invariant initially. More precisely, develop program $S0$ to satisfy $\{Q\} S0 \{P\}$. This guarantees that the invariant holds prior to the repetition.

At this point all that remains is the development of loop body S which, by the Invariance Theorem, must satisfy both of

$$\{P \land B\} S \{P\} \tag{a}$$
$$\{P \land B \land t = T\} S \{t < T\} \tag{b}$$

Noticing that all the components in these specifications have been determined, with the sole exception of t, the bound function, our next step is to

> Step 2 Choose a bound function t that satisfies (c), namely $P \land t \le 0 \Rightarrow \neg B$. In other words, choose a bound function whose decrease is guaranteed to falsify the guard. This will guarantee that the loop body won't be executed forever.

All that remains is to develop loop body S. Thus our final step is to

| Step 3 | Develop loop body S to satisfy (a) and (b). In other words, develop a program S that, under the initial truth of the invariant and guard, maintains the invariant and decreases the bound function. |

These are the steps for developing a loop. At this point they are unfamiliar. With a little practice they are certain to become second nature.

CLOSING (OR PERHAPS, OPENING!) COMMENTS

Scanning the steps for developing a loop notice that almost everything hinges on the choice of P, the invariant, which was chosen to satisfy

$$P \wedge \neg B \Rightarrow R. \tag{$*$}$$

There are a few observations we can make. First, the choice of the invariant depends on the shape of the postcondition: P (and B) are chosen from R to satisfy $(*)$. Second, even though P (and B) satisfy $(*)$, they may prove inadequate when subsequent steps are encountered. For example, we may find no way to establish our invariant initially (at step 1), or may find it impossible to develop a loop body that maintains it (at step 3).

There are often a number of ways that an invariant (and guard) can be chosen to satisfy $(*)$, and usually at least one invariant will do the trick.[0] How do we choose? Well, because of the importance of this problem, a number of heuristics have been devised for finding satisfactory invariants from postconditions. These heuristics have fanciful names like "deleting a conjunct" and "replacing constants by fresh variables". The choice depends on the shape of the postcondition. We will examine these heuristics, beginning with the technique of deleting a conjunct. Our examinations will be by way of example.

Our first examples may appear trivial. Bear with them, as they are intended to be illustrative. It is important to master the material presented, and this only comes from practice. In fact we strongly recommend trying each example as it is posed, and then reading the development after you have solved it. With practice you will find that problems that once seemed extraordinarily difficult can be solved with confidence, ease, and with elegance.

---

[0]In fact, often several will.

9

Loops A — On deleting a conjunct

9.0 Introduction

The first step in developing a loop is to choose an invariant (and a guard). In particular, given postcondition R, invariant P and guard B must be chosen to satisfy

$$P \wedge \neg B \Rightarrow R. \tag{0}$$

If R happens to be a conjunction, then this is easy. Choose for P one of the conjuncts, and choose for B the negation of the other. For example, if we are given:

$$R: \ X \wedge Y$$

we could choose either

$$P: \ X$$
$$B: \ \neg Y$$

or

$$P: \ Y$$
$$B: \ \neg X.$$

As far as (0) is concerned, either choice is acceptable: (0) holds in either case.

Looking ahead at the other steps in the development of a loop, however, the choice of invariant might make a big difference. For example, an invariant has to be truthified initially, and a bad choice might make this difficult or even impossible. In fact, a good heuristic is to arrive at an invariant by deleting from the postcondition the conjunct that is most difficult to truthify initially, if there is one.

In summary, an invariant can be found from a postcondition that is a conjunction by deleting a conjunct from the postcondition. The guard then is the negation of the deleted conjunct.

Remark   If the postcondition is not a conjunction, it can often be made into one, as we shall see.   □

9.1   An example — Integer-division

The quotient q and remainder r of integer-division of $x \geq 0$ by $y > 0$ are defined by:

$$R : \; 0 \leq r \;\wedge\; r < y \;\wedge\; q * y + r = x \,.$$

We are asked to solve

> $\underline{\text{var}}\; x, y : int \quad \{Q : \; 0 \leq x \,\wedge\, 0 < y\}$
> $;\underline{\text{var}}\; q, r : int$
> $;q, r : \; R$

Because the problem is integer-division, we disallow division in the solution.

CHOOSING AN INVARIANT AND GUARD

Choosing an invariant boils down to deleting a conjunct from R. Which do we delete? The last is the only one that names q. Further it defines a relationship between all the variables. For these reasons we will not delete it. Of the remaining two we arbitrarily[0] delete the second. Choosing the negation of the deleted conjunct for the guard, we arrive at

> invariant: $0 \leq r \,\wedge\, q * y + r = x$ and
> guard: $r \geq y \,.$

_____

[0]Well, not arbitrarily; see exercise 9.1.

Together these lead to the following (partial) program:

$$\{Q:\ 0 \leq x \ \wedge \ 0 < y\}$$
$$S0$$
$$\{inv\ P:\ 0 \leq r \ \wedge \ q*y+r=x\}$$
$$;\underline{\text{do}}\ r \geq y\ \rightarrow\ S\ \underline{\text{od}}$$
$$\{P\ \wedge\ r < y,\ hence\ R\}$$

All that remains is to develop $S0$ and S.

ESTABLISHING THE INVARIANT

Program $S0$ must establish the invariant initially. In other words, it must satisfy

$$\{Q:\ 0 \leq x \ \wedge \ 0 < y\}\ S0\ \{P:\ 0 \leq r \ \wedge \ q*y+r=x\}.$$

The following is clearly a solution:

$$S0:\ q,r := 0,x$$

(See why?) But, for illustrative purposes, we derive this assignment:

Since q and r are named in P, but not in Q, clearly

$$S0 = q,r := E,F \quad \text{for some } E \text{ and } F.$$

We solve for E and F in the usual manner:

$$wp.(q,r := E,F).P$$
$\equiv$ ⟨ Definitions of P and assignment ⟩
$$0 \leq F \ \wedge \ E*y+F = x$$
$\equiv$ ⟨ Choose $E = 0$, to eliminate the multiplication
         and therefore any potential division. ⟩
$$0 \leq F \ \wedge \ F = x$$
$\equiv$ ⟨ Choose $F = x$, to truthify second conjunct ⟩
$$0 \leq x$$
$\equiv$ ⟨ Using Q, in particular $0 \leq x$ ⟩
$$true$$

What remains is the development of S, the loop body, which must maintain the invariant and must decrease some suitably chosen bound function.

Choosing a bound function

A large enough decrease of the bound function must falsify the guard, in this case $r \geq y$. This can be accomplished by either decreasing r or by increasing y. Since y is a constant in the specification, we are forced to decrease r. Thus for our bound function we choose:

> *bound t* : r

Now we are ready to develop S.

Developing the loop body

The loop body, S, must

- decrease t: This can be accomplished by $r := r - k$, for some $k > 0$.

- maintain P: S must satisfy $\{P \wedge r \geq y\}\ S\ \{P\}$.

Combining these requirements with the observation that r and q are the only variables named in P, for S we envision:

$$\{P \wedge r \geq y\}\ r, q := r - k, E\ \{P\} \quad \text{for some } k > 0 \text{ and } E.$$

We solve for k and E in the usual manner:

$$
\begin{aligned}
& wp.(r, q := r - k, E).P \\
\equiv\ & \quad \langle\, \text{Definitions of } P \text{ and assignment} \,\rangle \\
& r \geq k\ \wedge\ E * y + r - k = x \\
\equiv\ & \quad \langle\, \text{From the precondition: } P, \text{ in particular } q * y + r = x \,\rangle \\
& r \geq k\ \wedge\ E * y + r - k = q * y + r \\
\equiv\ & \quad \langle\, \text{Arithmetic} \,\rangle \\
& r \geq k\ \wedge\ E = q + k/y
\end{aligned}
$$

Since division is not an admissible operation, we must choose for k a value that eliminates the division. This, in turn, can be accomplished by choosing some multiple of y. Since k must be greater than 0, we must choose a positive multiple. Continuing:

$$r \geq k \ \wedge \ E = q + k/y$$
$$\equiv \qquad \langle \text{ Choose } k = y \text{, the smallest positive multiple of } y \rangle$$
$$r \geq y \ \wedge \ E = q + 1$$
$$\equiv \qquad \langle \text{ From the precondition: } r \geq y \rangle$$
$$E = q + 1$$

From this calculation we have arrived at

$$S : \ r, q := r - y, q + 1 \, .$$

This completes the development.

ASSEMBLING THE PIECES

Our annotated solution to $q, r : R$ is

$$\{Q : \ 0 \leq x \ \wedge \ 0 < y\}$$
$$q, r := 0, x$$
$$\{inv \ P : \ 0 \leq r \ \wedge \ q * y + r = x\}$$
$$; \underline{\text{do }} r \geq y \ \rightarrow \ r, q := r - y, q + 1 \ \underline{\text{od}}$$
$$\{P \ \wedge \ r < y, \ hence \ R\}$$

★   ★

Ex 9.0 Without using division, find a different way to establish invariant P, if you can. □

Ex 9.1 Try solving this problem anew, this time choosing the following invariant:

$$P : \ r < y \ \wedge \ q * y + r = x \, .$$

Where in the development do you run into trouble? □

9.2 An example — The linear search (and its billions of uses)

Given boolean function f, and given that f holds at some natural point, i.e. that there exists some X that satisfies

$$0 \leq X \ \wedge \ f.X \,,$$

we are asked to determine the (number of the) smallest natural point at which f holds. More precisely, we are asked to establish

$$R: \ 0 \leq x \ \wedge \ f.x \ \wedge \ (\forall i : 0 \leq i \ \wedge \ i < x : \neg f.i) \,.$$

The first conjunct of R states that x must be natural, the second states that $f.x$ holds, and the third states that f does not hold at any (natural) point less than x.

Remark   Viewing f as an equation, this problem can be characterized as that of determining the smallest natural solution of f, given that there is one.   □

CHOOSING AN INVARIANT

We head for an invariant by deleting a conjunct from R. We argue negatively: if we *do not* delete $f.x$, then $f.x$ will have to be truthified when the invariant is established. To initially truthify $f.x$ we would have to a priori know a solution to f, which we do not. Thus we choose $f.x$ for deletion to arrive at invariant

$$P: \ 0 \leq x \ \wedge \ (\forall i : 0 \leq i \ \wedge \ i < x : \neg f.i) \,.$$

Because we intend to refer to the two conjuncts of P individually, we name them:

$$P0: \ 0 \leq x$$
$$P1: \ (\forall i : 0 \leq i \ \wedge \ i < x : \neg f.i)$$

Since $P \equiv P0 \wedge P1$, we can forget about P, and maintain the equivalent $P0 \wedge P1$. In other words, we will take $P0$ and $P1$ as our invariants.

For the guard we choose $\neg f.x$, the negation of the deleted conjunct.

ESTABLISHING THE INVARIANTS

Since x is the only variable named in the invariants, establishing the invariants boils down to finding an assignment to x that truthifies them initially. Towards discovering what this assignment should be, we focus our attention on truthifying $P1$, since $P1$ is the more complicated expression.

Recalling that a universal quantification equals *true* for an empty range, we can make $P1$'s range empty using the assignment $x := 0$.

Since $x := 0$ also happens to truthify $P0$, this assignment is sufficient to establish the invariants. At this point our program is:

$$x := 0$$
$$\{inv: \ P0 \ \wedge \ P1\}$$
$$; \underline{\text{do}} \ \neg f.x \ \rightarrow \ S \ \underline{\text{od}}$$
$$\{P \ \wedge \ f.x, \ \text{hence } R\}$$

What remains is the development of S, the loop body. Before developing S, however, we must choose a suitable bound function.

CHOOSING A BOUND FUNCTION

A large enough decrease of the bound function must falsify the guard, in this case $\neg f.x$. In other words, it must truthify $f.x$. Since all we know about f is that it holds at point X (for some natural X), we can truthify $f.x$ by decreasing

$$bound \ t: \ \ X - x \, .$$

Since X is simply a name for a value, we see that the only way to decrease t is to increase x.

DEVELOPING THE LOOP BODY

Loop body S must decrease t, which boils down to increasing x. As far as a decrease of t is concerned, for S we propose

$$S: \ \ x := x + k \ \ \ \text{for some } k > 0 \, .$$

S must also maintain the invariants. All that remains is to choose a k that accomplishes this. We observe that

o $P0$ is maintained by *any* increase of x, hence any choice for k.

○ On account of the guard, $P1$ is maintained by an increase of x by 1.

Combining these observations, we see that $k = 1$ does the job. This completes the development.

Remark   Alternatively, k could have been found by solving:

$$\{P0 \wedge P1 \wedge \neg f.x\} \; x := x + k \; \{P0 \wedge P1\} \quad \text{for some } k > 0.$$

Our last two observations eliminated the need for this calculation. Notice, however, that we *always* have the option to calculate.   □

⋆   ⋆

The resulting program is known as the *Linear Search*. In summary, given boolean function f, and given that f holds at some natural point, the Linear Search:

$$x := 0 \; ; \; \underline{\text{do}} \; \neg f.x \; \rightarrow \; x := x + 1 \; \underline{\text{od}}$$

sets x to the smallest natural point at which f holds.

Remark   The Linear Search's precondition tells us that f must hold at some natural point. Another program, called the *Bounded Linear Search*, does not have this requirement. That one we save for later. □

SOME OF THE BILLIONS AND BILLIONS OF APPLICATIONS OF THE LINEAR SEARCH

It is important to recognize when the Linear Search can be applied. Many programmers do not, and end up reinventing the wheel over and over.

> | Heuristic | To determine the smallest natural point at which
> boolean function f holds, given that it holds at some
> natural point, apply the Linear Search.

(a) Given integer M, we are asked to determine the smallest natural x such that $M \leq 2^x$.

Towards applying the Linear Search, we see that we are asked to determine the smallest natural point at which boolean function f holds, when f is given by

$$f.x \equiv M \le 2^x .$$

Because f is guaranteed to hold for some $x \ge 0$, i.e. is guaranteed to hold at some natural point, we can apply the Linear Search. The solution is simply the Linear Search with

$$f.x \quad \text{replaced by} \quad M \le 2^x .$$

This completes the development.

Remark   The complete program text is

$$x := 0 \; ; \; \underline{do} \; \neg(M \le 2^x) \; \rightarrow \; x := x + 1 \; \underline{od}$$

If desired, the guard can be simplified, a simplification which yields:

$$x := 0 \; ; \; \underline{do} \; M > 2^x \; \rightarrow \; x := x + 1 \; \underline{od}$$

For the remaining examples we will not bother to show the program texts.   □

(b) Given positive M, we are asked to determine the *largest* natural x such that $2^x \le M$.

In order to apply the Linear Search, we must transform this problem into one of determining the *smallest* natural point at which some boolean function holds. An equivalent formulation is to determine the smallest natural point at which boolean function f holds, when f is given by

$$f.x \equiv M < 2^{x+1} .$$

Because M is positive, f is guaranteed to hold at some natural point. Therefore we can apply the Linear Search. The solution is simply the Linear Search with

$$f.x \quad \text{replaced by} \quad M < 2^{x+1} .$$

This completes the development.

(c) We are given integer N and positive integer function $G(i : 0 \leq i)$. Viewing G as a curve, we are asked to find the smallest initial section of G such that the area under this section exceeds N.

Towards applying the Linear Search, what we are after is the smallest natural point at which boolean function f holds, when f is given by

$$f.x \equiv (\Sigma i : 0 \leq i < x : G.i) > N .$$

Because G is everywhere positive, f is guaranteed to hold at some natural point. Therefore we can apply the Linear Search. The solution is simply the Linear Search with

$$f.x \quad \text{replaced by} \quad (\Sigma j : 0 \leq j < x : G.j) > N .$$

This completes the development.[1]

$\star$ $\star$

$\star$

Ex 9.2   Given functions G and H, point x is a *crossing point* when $G.x = H.x$. Given that there one, determine the smallest natural crossing point. Apply the Linear Search.   □

Ex 9.3   Person A can meet at moment $x \geq 0$ if $A.x$ holds. Person B can meet at moment $x \geq 0$ if $B.x$ holds. Given that there is one, determine the earliest moment at which both A and B can meet. Apply the Linear Search.   □

Ex 9.4   The number of rabbits on an island at month $x \geq 0$ is $R.x$. The rabbit population is *stable* at month x when the number of rabbits at month x equals the number of rabbits at month $(x + 1)$. Given that the rabbits are stable in some month, determine the first such month. Apply the Linear Search.   □

Ex 9.5   Given integer $N \geq 0$, develop a program that determines the largest integer at most $\sqrt{N}$. Apply the Linear Search. After completing the development, eliminate the square-root from your program.   □

---

[1]In this case the program has a quantification (in the guard). It is possible to remove it, but more on that later.

Ex 9.6   Solve:

> <u>var</u> $Y, Z : real$ $\{0 \leq Y \;\wedge\; 0 < Z\}$
> ; <u>var</u> $x : int$
> ; $x :\; x \leq Y/Z \;\wedge\; Y/Z < x + 1$

Apply the Linear Search. After completing the development, eliminate the division from your program. Multiplication of integers by reals is allowed.   □

★   ★
★

Remark   In our development of the Linear Search, we see that t is decreased each repetition. What we failed to show is that t cannot be decreased forever. For the interested reader, we give that proof here.

What we must show is that the Boundedness requirement is met, which in this case is

$$P0 \;\wedge\; P1 \;\wedge\; \neg f.x \;\Rightarrow\; t > 0 .$$

Starting with the most complicated expression we have, namely $P1$, we find that

$$
\begin{aligned}
&\quad P1 \\
\equiv&\quad \langle \text{Definition of } P1\,;\, \text{trading} \rangle \\
&\quad (\forall i :: 0 \leq i \;\wedge\; i < x \;\Rightarrow\; \neg f.i) \\
\Rightarrow&\quad \langle \text{Rule of instantiation, with } i := X \rangle \\
&\quad 0 \leq X \;\wedge\; X < x \;\Rightarrow\; \neg f.X \\
\equiv&\quad \langle \text{Shuffle, to isolate the precondition} \rangle \\
&\quad 0 \leq X \;\wedge\; f.X \;\Rightarrow\; X \geq x \\
\equiv&\quad \langle \text{Using the precondition, namely } 0 \leq X \;\wedge\; f.X \rangle \\
&\quad true \;\Rightarrow\; X \geq x \\
\equiv&\quad \langle \text{Predicate calculus} \rangle \\
&\quad X \geq x \\
\equiv&\quad \langle f.X \text{ and } \neg f.x, \text{ hence } X \neq x \rangle \\
&\quad X > x \\
\equiv&\quad \langle \text{Arithmetic}\,;\, \text{definition of } t \rangle \\
&\quad t > 0
\end{aligned}
$$

This completes the proof that the Linear Search terminates.   □

9.3   An example — 3-tuple sort (and avoiding avoidable case-analyses)

We are asked to solve:

$\underline{\text{var }} b(0..2) : int \quad \{Q : \ bag.b = B\}$
$; b : \ R$

given

$R : \ b.0 \leq b.1 \ \wedge \ b.1 \leq b.2 \ \wedge \ bag.b = B.$

Remark   This is the specification of a program to make b ascending. Given Q, the last conjunct of R states that b must contain its initial values. Therefore this is a sorting problem, albeit a little one.   □

Choosing an invariant and guard

The conjunct $bag.b = B$ states that b must remain the same bag of values. We will not delete it because it carries too much information. Deleting only one of the other conjuncts would destroy symmetry,[2] so we delete both to arrive at:

$\{Q : \ bag.b = B\}$
$S0$
$\{inv \ P : \ bag.b = B\}$
$; \underline{\text{do }} b.0 > b.1 \ \vee \ b.1 > b.2 \ \rightarrow \ S \ \underline{\text{od}}$
$\{P \ \wedge \ b.0 \leq b.1 \ \wedge \ b.1 \leq b.2, \ hence \ R\}$

Establishing the invariant

$S0$ must satisfy

$\{Q\} \ S0 \ \{P\}$

Since $Q \ \equiv \ P$, we choose $S0 = skip$, and so $S0$ can be omitted.

---

[2] Why choose one over the other?

CHOOSING A BOUND FUNCTION

To make progress, we can decrease the "out-of-orderedness" of b. This is expressed by the bound function:

> *bound* t: Number of out-of-order b-element pairs.[3]

THE LOOP BODY

Loop body S must satisfy

$$\circ \quad \{P \wedge (b0 > b1 \ \vee \ b1 > b2)\} \ S \ \{P\} \qquad\qquad (0)$$

— namely it must not destroy the values in b, and additionally must

$$\circ \quad \text{decrease } t, \text{ the number of out-of-order } b\text{-element pairs.} \qquad (1)$$

To satisfy (0), we constrain S to "swaps" of b-element pairs. To additionally satisfy (1) we further constrain S to swaps of out-of-order b-element pairs. Thus for S we arrive at:

> $\underline{\text{if }} b.0 > b.1 \ \rightarrow \ b : swap\,(0,1)$
> $\square \ \ b.1 > b.2 \ \rightarrow \ b : swap\,(1,2)$
> $\underline{\text{fi}}$

where $b : swap\,(x,y)$ swaps the values of $b.x$ and $b.y$. Noticing that the IF is not an *abort* — by its precondition, $b.0 > b.1 \ \vee \ b.1 > b.2$, at least one guard holds — we see that the development is complete.

Remark   By the equivalence between a many and a single guarded command repetition, this program can be nicely captured as

> $\underline{\text{do }} b.0 > b.1 \ \rightarrow \ b : swap\,(0,1)$
> $\square \ \ \ b.1 > b.2 \ \rightarrow \ b : swap\,(1,2)$
> $\underline{\text{od}}$

□

---

[3]This can be expressed formally as $(\underline{N}\,i,j \ : \ 0 \le i < j < 3 \ : \ b.i > b.j\,)$.

ON AVOIDING AVOIDABLE CASE-ANALYSES

We wrote S as:

> if $b.0 > b.1 \rightarrow b : swap\,(0,1)$
> ▯ $b.1 > b.2 \rightarrow b : swap\,(1,2)$
> fi

instead of as

> if $b.0 > b.1 \rightarrow b : swap\,(0,1)$
> ▯ $b.0 > b.2 \rightarrow b : swap\,(0,2)$
> ▯ $b.1 > b.2 \rightarrow b : swap\,(1,2)$
> fi

One reason is that our solution is the simplest one that preserves symmetry. There is another reason. Consider the generalization from $3-$ to $N-$tuple sort. Our solution generalizes to an IF with $N - 1$ alternatives, or cases. This second solution generalizes to one case per pair of b-elements, or $\frac{1}{2} * N * (N - 1)$ cases. The first grows linearly with N. The second grows quadratically. For $5-$tuple sort we get:

> if $b.0 > b.1 \rightarrow b : swap\,(0,1)$
> ▯ $b.1 > b.2 \rightarrow b : swap\,(1,2)$
> ▯ $b.2 > b.3 \rightarrow b : swap\,(2,3)$
> ▯ $b.3 > b.4 \rightarrow b : swap\,(3,4)$
> fi

instead of

> if $b.0 > b.1 \rightarrow b : swap\,(0,1)$
> ▯ $b.0 > b.2 \rightarrow b : swap\,(0,2)$
> ▯ $b.0 > b.3 \rightarrow b : swap\,(0,3)$
> ▯ $b.0 > b.4 \rightarrow b : swap\,(0,4)$
> ▯ $b.1 > b.2 \rightarrow b : swap\,(1,2)$
> ▯ $b.1 > b.3 \rightarrow b : swap\,(1,3)$
> ▯ $b.1 > b.4 \rightarrow b : swap\,(1,4)$
> ▯ $b.2 > b.3 \rightarrow b : swap\,(2,3)$
> ▯ $b.2 > b.4 \rightarrow b : swap\,(2,4)$
> ▯ $b.3 > b.4 \rightarrow b : swap\,(3,4)$
> fi

For selected values of N we find:

N	Number of Cases	
	Original Solution	Second Solution
3	2	3
4	3	6
5	4	10
10	9	45
20	19	190
100	99	4950

The fast increase in cases, shown in the righthand column, is known as *case explosion*. The avoidance of case explosion provides an excellent heuristic. More generally we propose:

| Heuristic | Avoid avoidable case-analyses.

A very common example of an avoidable case-analysis is

$$\textbf{if} \quad B \; \rightarrow \; x := \textit{true}$$
$$\square \; \neg B \; \rightarrow \; x := \textit{false}$$
$$\textbf{fi}$$

which can be replaced by

$$x := B \,,$$

a program with no case-analysis! For another example, recall the usual definition of the absolute value, namely

$$|X| \;=\; \textbf{if } X \geq 0 \; \rightarrow \quad X$$
$$\square \; X \leq 0 \; \rightarrow \; -X$$
$$\textbf{fi}$$

and then compare it to

$$|X| \;=\; X \; \textit{max} \; -X \,,$$

which also has no case-analysis. Programmers not familiar with the equivalence often appeal to mutual implication.[4] Programmers not familiar with the equivalence also have a tendency to write expressions like

$$(X \wedge Y) \vee (\neg X \wedge \neg Y) \qquad\qquad (*)$$

which, by simple predicate calculus, is equivalent to the much simpler

$$X \equiv Y.$$

Expressions like (*) are often forced onto the users of so-called "database" or "query" languages. Stripping away the details, what these languages provide is a new type, the set (of records), along with operations on this type, in much the same way as the type "integer" comes with operations like addition and multiplication.

A common operation provided by these "query" languages is the "selection" operation, an operation which selects all records that satisfy a given predicate. Many of these languages do not allow the equivalence in these predicates. As a result, a programmer is forced to select all employees (say) that have improper salaries via a predicate like

$$(is\text{-}manager \wedge \neg has\text{-}manager\text{-}salary) \vee$$
$$(\neg is\text{-}manager \wedge has\text{-}manager\text{-}salary).$$

Notice the case-analysis. If the equivalence was included, the programmer could write

$$is\text{-}manager \equiv \neg has\text{-}manager\text{-}salary,$$

and if the discrepancy was included, the programmer could write simply[5]

$$is\text{-}manager \not\equiv has\text{-}manager\text{-}salary.$$

---

[4]Instead a direct appeal to $A \equiv B$, an appeal is made to the equivalent, but longer, $(A \Rightarrow B) \wedge (B \Rightarrow A)$. This is what is behind the last two examples.

[5]Besides omitting the equivalence and the discrepancy, some of these "query" languages even omit the negation! Although sold under the heading of "user-friendliness", some users don't find them friendly at all!

Case-analyses are often forced upon programmers who do not consider 0 to be natural: We have all seen 0 treated as a special case. Sometimes even 1 is treated as a special case! Consider a program that selects, by some criterion, a list of names (from somewhere), and then sorts them. With a "sort" that (only) works for lists of length at least 1, we would be forced to code this as

    select a list of names
    ; <u>if</u> list is empty   → *skip*
      ▯ list is non-empty → sort the list
      <u>fi</u>

If the "sort" handled lists of length 0, we could write[6]

    select a list of names
    ; sort the list

For another example, and this leads to case explosion, consider proving the validity of a boolean expression in N variables by enumerating all possible combinations of values. Since each variable can take on two values (*true* or *false*), N variables can take on 2^N combinations. Using a case-analysis we would have to enumerate all 2^N cases. Such enumerations are known as "truth-tables" and are the usual way in which boolean expressions are introduced (unfortunately)!

⋆   ⋆

Programmers often argue that (avoidable) case-analyses are desirable for reasons of efficiency. Their reasoning should be considered very carefully. For example, a programmer once encountered the problem of searching a list that was often empty. He proposed maintaining an extra variable that held its length. His reason was that a search of the list using

    <u>if</u> list-length $= 0$ → "search unsuccessful"
    ▯ list-length $\neq 0$ → search the list
    <u>fi</u>

would be more efficient than

    search the list .

---

[6] Notice that the expression "list is empty" no longer has to be provided.

An investigation revealed that evaluating the expression "list-length=0" required as much time as a search of an empty list. (After all, the list was empty!) In other words, his program was no improvement in the case of the empty list. In the case of the non-empty list it was worse, since it had to evaluate "list-length=0" every time. In other words, his proposal actually *decreased* efficiency. (Things got even worse, since "list-length" had to be updated whenever the list's length was changed).

The moral, of course, is that avoidable case-analyses should be ... avoided!

9.4   An example — Integer-division improved (and postponing design decisions)

We assume familiarity with the previous solution to "integer-division". In that development we arrived at

$$\{x \geq 0 \ \wedge \ y > 0\}$$
$$q, r := 0, x$$
$$\{inv \ P: \ 0 \leq r \ \wedge \ q * y + r = x\}$$
$$;\underline{\text{do}} \ r \geq y \ \rightarrow \ r, q := r - k, E \ \underline{\text{od}}$$
$$\{R\}$$

where our bound function was

$$bound \ t: \quad r$$

and where k and E had to satisfy

$$0 < k \ \wedge \ k \leq r \ \wedge \ E = q + k/y. \tag{0}$$

On account of the bound function, progress is made by the decrease of r by k. In our earlier development we chose $k = y$. Here we will go after a larger value for k, hence a larger decrease of r, and therefore a program requiring a smaller number of repetitions.

We continue by solving (0), keeping in mind that we would prefer as large a k as possible. Recall, also, that division is not an admissible operation.

★   ★

To eliminate the division from (0), we must choose for k some multiple of y. Since we are after a large multiple, and since a suitably large candidate is not obvious, we postpone this choice. We do so by introducing fresh variable d satisfying $k = d * y$. Continuing:

$$0 < k \ \wedge \ k \leq r \ \wedge \ E = q + k/y$$
$$\equiv \qquad \langle \text{ Using } k = d * y \ \rangle$$
$$0 < d * y \ \wedge \ d * y \leq r \ \wedge \ E = q + (d * y)/y$$
$$\equiv \qquad \langle \ 0 < y, \text{ hence } 0 < d, \text{ therefore } 1 \leq d \ ; \text{ by arithmetic} \rangle$$
$$1 \leq d \ \wedge \ d * y \leq r \ \wedge \ E = q + d$$
$$\equiv \qquad \langle \text{ Assume } d \text{ satisfies } 1 \leq d \ \wedge \ d * y \leq r; \text{ by arithmetic} \rangle$$
$$E = q + d$$

And so for S we have arrived at[7]

$$\{P \wedge r \geq y\}$$
$$\|[\underline{\text{var}} \ d : int$$
$$; S0 : \text{ Choose } d \text{ to satisfy } 1 \leq d \ \wedge \ d * y \leq r$$
$$; r, q := r - d * y, q + d$$
$$]\|$$
$$\{P\}$$

To eliminate the multiplication $d * y$ from the decrease of r we introduce additional fresh variable dd and revise this to

$$\{P \wedge r \geq y\}$$
$$\|[\underline{\text{var}} \ d, dd : int$$
$$; S0 : \text{ Choose } d, dd \text{ to satisfy } 1 \leq d \ \wedge \ d * y \leq r \ \wedge \ dd = d * y$$
$$; r, q := r - dd, q + d$$
$$]\|$$
$$\{P\}$$

Note, in particular, that r is decreased by dd, which is equal to $d * y$. In our earlier solution we effectively chose 1 for d, resulting in a decrease of r by y. What remains is the development of $S0$, in which we will look for a larger value for d, and hence a larger decrease of r.

★ ★

Program $S0$ must assign to d and dd to establish the conjunction of[8]

---

[7]The bracket pair "$\|[\ \ldots \ ]\|$" is used to introduce fresh variables, just like Pascal's "BEGIN ... END".

[8]We introduce separate names for ease of future reference.

$R0: \ 1 \leq d$
$R1: \ d*y \leq r$
$R2: \ dd = d*y$

We would also prefer a large value for d. Since the largest d satisfying $R1$ (and $R0$) is the smallest d satisfying $r < (d+1)*y$, we might apply the Linear Search. We might, were it not for the fact that this would boil down to finding a large d using repeated increases by 1.

The way out is to constrain d in such a way that it can be increased very quickly, i.e. using a small number of operations. Recalling that powers of 2 fall into this category, we further constrain d to satisfy

$R3: \ (d$ is a power of 2$)$.

Finally, we constrain d to be the largest possible power of 2. On account of $R1$, we see that this boils down to requiring d to additionally satisfy

$R4: \ r < 2*d*y$.

What remains is the development of $S0$, which must now establish

$RR: \ R0 \ \wedge \ R1 \ \wedge \ R2 \ \wedge \ R3 \ \wedge \ R4$.

$$\star \qquad\qquad\qquad \star$$

We will establish RR using a repetition. The first step then is to choose an invariant. Which conjunct do we delete from RR? Conjuncts $R0$ and $R3$ tell us too much about d, and $R2$ is the only one that mentions dd. Of the remaining two, we somewhat arbitrarily delete $R4$. In other words, for our invariant we propose

$PP: \ R0 \ \wedge \ R1 \ \wedge \ R2 \ \wedge \ R3$.

We observe that the assignment $d, dd := 1, y$ establishes PP. It clearly establishes $R0$, $R2$, and $R3$, and on account of $S0$'s precondition (i.e. $r \geq y$), establishes $R1$ as well.

Choosing, as usual, the negation of the deleted conjunct for the guard, for $S0$ we have arrived at

$$d, dd := 1, y$$
$$\{inv: \ PP\}$$
$$;\underline{do} \ r \geq 2 * d * y \ \rightarrow \ SS \ \underline{od}$$

Remark   Because of the invariance of $dd = d * y$, the guard can be rewritten as $r \geq dd + dd$.   □

What remains is the development of SS.

★   ★

To guarantee termination, SS must eventually falsify $r \geq 2 * d * y$. On account of the fact that r and y are constants in $S0$, our only choice is to increase d.

This increase must also maintain PP. Towards avoiding a calculation, we observe that any increase maintains $R0$, and that $R3$ requires that d remain a power of 2. Therefore, the simplest way to maintain $R0$ and $R3$ is to double d. Because $R2$ must be maintained, we see that a doubling of d must be accompanied by a doubling of dd. On account of the guard (i.e. $r \geq 2 * d * y$), we see that this doubling also maintains $R1$. And so, for SS we propose

$$SS: \ d, dd := 2 * d, 2 * dd$$

Remark   These multiplications can be replaced by additions.   □

This completes the development.

★   ★

The final solution is:

$$q, r := 0, x$$
$$;\underline{do} \ r \geq y \ \rightarrow$$
$$\quad \|[\underline{var} \ d, dd : int$$
$$\quad ; d, dd := 1, y$$
$$\quad ;\underline{do} \ r \geq dd + dd \ \rightarrow \ d, dd := d + d, dd + dd \ \underline{od}$$
$$\quad ; r, q := r - dd, q + d$$
$$\quad]|$$
$$\underline{od}$$

We compare our two solutions by comparing their respective numbers of arithmetic operations. Since our first solution was at its worst when x was significantly greater than y, we constrain ourselves to a few such cases. A little calculation reveals the following:

x	y	Improvement
1000	3	9-fold
4096	2	114-fold
2^{20}	3	17,000-fold

The improvement is indeed a substantial one! Notice that it was obtained in a straightforward way. The critical step was postponing which multiple of y to choose for k. This was accomplished by introducing fresh variable d satisfying $k = d * y$. It gave us great freedom, and leads us to propose the following heuristic:

| Heuristic | Do not make a design decision until absolutely necessary.[9] |

As far as the rest of the development was concerned, the only rabbit-out-of-the-hat was the further constraint that d be a power of 2, and this wasn't much of a rabbit at all. It was all but forced upon us: We wanted to generate a large d using a small number of arithmetic operations, and powers of 2 are the obvious choice. In particular, this additional restriction allowed a large d to be found using a logarithmic number of arithmetic operations, when otherwise a linear number would be required.

⋆   ⋆

Ex 9.7   Develop a different solution to $S0$. In particular, arrive at a different invariant by deleting the conjunct $R1$ from RR. Division of a power of 2 by 2 is allowed, but exponentiation is not.   □

---

[9]Many efforts in industry are started with the purchase of computer X and software package Y. The result is that programmers must constrain their solutions to fit these choices. This often entails great pain, great expense, and many times leads to overly complicated solutions. The cost of such premature design decisions should not be underestimated.

10

Loops B — On replacing constants by fresh variables

10.0 Introduction

The first step in loop development is to choose invariant P and guard B from postcondition R to satisfy

$$P \land \neg B \Rightarrow R$$

If R happens to be a conjunction, then this is easy. Choose for P one of the conjuncts, and choose for B the negation of the other conjunct, as we have seen.

What if R is not a conjunction? Perhaps we can make it into one. Consider being given function f, and postcondition

$$x = f.N \tag{0}$$

With the aid of a fresh variable we can rewrite (0) as

$$x = f.n \ \land \ n = N$$

where n is the fresh variable. Since this is a conjunction, we can proceed as before and delete a conjunct to arrive at, for example

    invariant: $x = f.n,$ and
    guard: $n \neq N$

⋆   ⋆

One more thing: Suppose that function f is not "total", i.e. is defined only at certain points. For example, suppose that f is given as $f(i : 0 \leq i \leq M)$, for some M. Observe, in this case, that $f.n$, from the invariant, is defined only when $0 \leq n \leq M$. As a result, we should strengthen our invariant in order to keep $f.n$ defined. In this case we would strengthen it to

$$x = f.n \;\; \wedge \;\; 0 \leq n \leq M \tag{1}$$

In other words, appropriate constraints should be placed on freshly introduced variables.

⋆   ⋆

Remark   We will usually write (1) as

> $P0$: $x = f.n$
> $P1$: $0 \leq n \leq M$

which we deem to be shorthand for $P0 \wedge P1$. Splitting the invariant in this way will ease calculations. For example, instead of the hint "Using P, in particular $x = f.n$", we can write the much shorter "Using $P0$".   □

⋆   ⋆

In summary, an invariant can be obtained from postcondition R by replacing constants in R by fresh variables, and putting appropriate constraints on the fresh variables.

Remark   We usually omit the step of making the postcondition into a conjunction, and directly obtain our invariant by replacing constants in the postcondition by fresh variables. For our first two examples, however, we will explicitly show this step.   □

10.1   An example — Evaluating a polynomial

We are asked to solve

> <u>var</u> $b : array\ of\ int$ $\{0 \leq \#b\}$
> ; <u>var</u> $x : int$
> ; <u>var</u> $y : int$
> ; $y : R$

where for R we are given

> R : $y = f.0$

and where function f is given by

$$f.k = \underline{\text{if}}\ k = \#b \qquad \rightarrow\ 0$$
$$\square\ 0 \leq k < \#b \ \rightarrow\ f.(k+1) * x + b.k$$
$$\underline{\text{fi}}$$

The program text cannot contain function f.

Remark   If it could, then $y := f.0$ would solve the problem. $\square$

★   ★

Since the postcondition is not a conjunction, we will make it into one. In particular we introduce fresh variable n, and rewrite R as

$$y = f.n \ \wedge\ n = 0.$$

Next we find an invariant by deleting a conjunct. We delete the second conjunct to arrive at

$$y = f.n.$$

Because the definition of f tells us that $f.n$ is defined only when n satisfies $0 \leq n \leq \#b$, this constraint must also be added. In other words, for our invariants we choose

$P0:\ y = f.n$
$P1:\ 0 \leq n \leq \#b$ (so $f.n$ is defined in $P0$).

Choosing, as always, the negation of the deleted conjunct as the guard, we arrive at:

$|[\underline{\text{var}}\ n : int$
$;S0\ \{inv:\ P0 \wedge P1\}$
$;\underline{\text{do}}\ n \neq 0 \ \rightarrow\ S\ \underline{\text{od}}$
$\{P0 \wedge P1 \wedge n = 0,\ hence\ R\}$
$]|$

The remaining tasks, namely the developments of $S0$ and SS, are as before. In other words, the rest of the development should be straightforward.

★   ★

Program $S0$ must establish the invariants initially. Since the definition of f tells us that $f.\#b = 0$, we can establish $P0$ using the assignment $n, y := \#b, 0$. On account of the fact that $0 \leq \#b$, we see that this establishes $P1$ as well. Thus for $S0$ we propose

$$S0: \quad n, y := \#b, 0$$

What remains is the development of S.

⋆   ⋆

To guarantee termination, S must eventually falsify $n \neq 0$. Since n is initially $\#b$, which is at least 0, this can be accomplished by decreasing n. The definition of f suggests a decrease by 1.

S must also maintain the invariants, which name variables n and y. Thus for S we envision

$$S: \quad n, y := n - 1, E,$$

where E must be chosen to maintain the invariants.

Towards simplifying the calculation for E, observe that n is the only variable named in $P1$. On account of the guard, we see that $0 < n \ \wedge \ n \leq \#b$ is a precondition of S, and therefore that the decrease of n by 1 maintains $P1$. With the required maintenance of $P1$ taken care of, we need only solve for an E that maintains $P0$. We calculate as usual:

$$\quad wp.(n, y := n - 1, E).P0$$
$$\equiv \quad \langle \text{ Definitions of } P0 \text{ and assignment } \rangle$$
$$\quad E = f.(n - 1)$$

This is perfectly good solution, except for the fact that f is disallowed in the program. Observing that $f.(n - 1)$ can be eliminated if it can be rewritten in terms of $f.n$ which, by $P0$, equals y, we find that

$$\quad f.(n - 1)$$
$$= \quad \langle \text{ The only way to rewrite this is to appeal to the definition}$$
$$\qquad \text{of } f. \text{ Since } f \text{ has two cases, we must determine which}$$
$$\qquad \text{case this falls into. By } P1 \text{ and the guard, namely } n \neq 0,$$
$$\qquad \text{we see that } 0 < n \leq \#b, \text{ in which case } 0 \leq n - 1 < \#b.$$
$$\qquad \text{Using the definition of } f. \ \rangle$$
$$\quad f.n * x + b.(n - 1)$$
$$= \quad \langle P0 \rangle$$
$$\quad y * x + b.(n - 1)$$

This completes the development. The final solution is

$$
\begin{aligned}
&\|[\underline{\text{var}}\ n : int \\
&;n, y := \#b, 0 \\
&;\underline{\text{do}}\ n \neq 0\ \rightarrow\ n, y := n - 1, y * x + b.(n - 1)\ \underline{\text{od}} \\
&]|
\end{aligned}
$$

★   ★

The entire development was a standard one, with the exception of the technique used to choose the invariant.

In summary, when given a postcondition that is not a conjunction, make it into one. In general, this boils down to rewriting the postcondition as a conjunction (with the aid of fresh variables), and then deleting a conjunct. Because the invariant obtained must be defined, it is necessary to add appropriate constraints to the fresh variables. Once obtained, we can proceed as before, i.e. by establishing it initially, and so on.

★   ★

Although it may not have been obvious from the specification, the problem was one of evaluating a polynomial. Consider the case $\#b = 3$:

$$
\begin{aligned}
&f.0 \\
=\ &\quad \langle\,\text{Definition of }f\,\rangle \\
&f.1 * x + b.0 \\
=\ &\quad \langle\,\text{Definition of }f\,\rangle \\
&(f.2 * x + b.1) * x + b.0 \\
=\ &\quad \langle\,\text{Definition of }f\,\rangle \\
&((f.3 * x + b.2) * x + b.1) * x + b.0 \\
=\ &\quad \langle\,\text{Definition of }f,\ f.3 = 0\,;\text{ arithmetic}\,\rangle \\
&((0 * x + b.2) * x + b.1) * x + b.0 \\
=\ &\quad \langle\,\text{Arithmetic}\,\rangle \\
&b.2 * x^2 + b.1 * x^1 + b.0 * x^0
\end{aligned}
$$

This method of evaluating a polynomial is called *Horner's rule*, after W.G. Horner who used it in 1819. It has also been attributed to Isaac Newton.[0]

Notice that the solution correctly solves the problem for the case of 0 coefficients (i.e. $\#b = 0$). We need to look no further than the precondition to see this.

---

[0]The discovery of useful rules like Horner's is a major part of programming. Because this is a study all by itself, we save it until later.

Also notice that no insights into the specification's "meaning" were needed. Given the specification, we simply developed the program. The fact that it was a specification of a program to evaluate polynomials was irrelevant.

10.2   An example — The minimum value

We are asked to solve:

> $\underline{var}\ b : array\ of\ int\quad\{\#b \geq 0\}$
> $;\underline{var}\ x : int$
> $;x :\ R$

where R is given by

> $R:\ x\ =\ (\underline{MIN}\,i : 0 \leq i\ \wedge\ i < \#b : b.i)\,.$

*   *

The obvious solution, namely

> $x := (\underline{MIN}\,i : 0 \leq i\ \wedge\ i < \#b : b.i)$

we disallow under the reasonable assumption that quantifications are not allowed in programs.[1] As a result, we will establish R using a repetition. Our first step, of course, is to choose an invariant.

*   *

Because R is not a conjunction, we will make it into one. For reasons of simplicity, we will allow only a single fresh variable, in which case the following possibilities present themselves:

> $x\ =\ (\underline{MIN}\,i : n \leq i\ \wedge\ i < \#b : b.i)\ \wedge\ n = 0$ $\hspace{2cm}$ (0)
> $x\ =\ (\underline{MIN}\,i : 0 \leq i\ \wedge\ i < n : b.i)\ \wedge\ n = \#b$ $\hspace{2cm}$ (1)

We arbitrarily[2] choose (1). By deleting a conjunct, we propose the following for our invariant:

---

[1]From now on we implicitly disallow quantifications from programs.

[2]The choice is completely arbitrary. The other choice would lead to a different solution.

$$x = (\underline{\text{MIN}}\, i : 0 \le i \,\wedge\, i < n : b.i).$$

Because the quantification is defined only when $0 \le n \,\wedge\, n \le \#b$,[3]   we add the following constraints

$$0 \le n \,\wedge\, n \le \#b.$$

In other words, for our invariants we propose

$$P0: \quad x = (\underline{\text{MIN}}\, i : 0 \le i \,\wedge\, i < n : b.i)$$
$$P1: \quad 0 \le n \,\wedge\, n \le \#b$$

Remark   From now on, we will omit the step of making the postcondition into a conjunction. We will simply replace constants in the post-condition by fresh variables, and then suitably constrain these fresh variables.   □

Using these invariants, we arrive at the program

$$\begin{array}{l}
|[\underline{\text{var}}\ n : int \\
;S0\ \{inv : P0\ \wedge\ P1\} \\
;\underline{\text{do}}\ n \ne \#b\ \rightarrow\ S\ \underline{\text{od}} \\
\quad \{P0\ \wedge\ P1\ \wedge\ n = \#b,\ hence\ R\} \\
]|
\end{array}$$

What remains are the developments of $S0$ and S.

★   ★

Recalling that a minimization with an empty range equals $+inf$, for $S0$ we propose

$$S0: \quad n, x := 0, +inf$$

---

[3]The first conjunct guarantees that the range is at least empty. When not empty, we must guarantee that $b.i$ is defined for all i in the range. This boils down to guaranteeing that i be less than $\#b$. Since $i < n$, we see that n can be at most $\#b$.

Remark   If $\#b > 0$ was the precondition, then $n, y := 1, b.0$ would also
       do the job.   □

$$\star \qquad\qquad \star$$

Our next task is to choose a bound function. Since $n = \#b$ must eventually
be truthified, the obvious choice is

$$\text{bound } t : \ \#b - n \,.$$

Because $\#b$ is a constant, the only way to decrease t is to increase n.
What remains is the development of loop body S.

$$\star \qquad\qquad \star$$

For S, we envision

$$S : \ n, x := n + 1, E$$

where E must be chosen to maintain $P0$ and $P1$.

Towards simplifying the calculation for E, observe that n is the only variable named in $P1$. On account of the guard, we see that $0 \leq n \ \wedge \ n < \#b$
is a precondition of S, and therefore that the increase of n by 1 maintains
$P1$.

With the required maintenance of $P1$ taken care of, we need only solve for
an E that maintains $P0$. We calculate:

$$wp.S.P0$$
$$\equiv \qquad \langle \text{ Definitions of } S, \ P0, \text{ and assignment} \rangle$$
$$E \ = \ (\underline{\text{MIN}}\, i : 0 \leq i \ \wedge \ i < n + 1 : b.i)$$

Thus we have solved for E. The only problem is that E is a quantification, and we do not allow quantifications in our programs. Towards its
elimination, we find that:

$$(\underline{\text{MIN}}\, i : 0 \leq i \ \wedge \ i < n + 1 : b.i)$$
$$= \qquad \langle \text{ Rewrite range} \rangle$$
$$(\underline{\text{MIN}}\, i : 0 \leq i \ \wedge \ (i < n \ \vee \ i = n) : b.i)$$
$$= \qquad \langle \ \wedge \ \text{ distributes over } \ \vee \ \rangle$$
$$(\underline{\text{MIN}}\, i : (0 \leq i \ \wedge \ i < n) \ \vee \ (0 \leq i \ \wedge \ i = n) : b.i)$$
$$= \qquad \langle \text{ Split range} \rangle$$
$$(\underline{\text{MIN}}\, i : 0 \leq i \ \wedge \ i < n : b.i) \ \ min \ \ (\underline{\text{MIN}}\, i : 0 \leq i \ \wedge \ i = n : b.i)$$
$$= \qquad \langle \text{ On account of } P0 \rangle$$
$$x \ \ min \ \ (\underline{\text{MIN}}\, i : 0 \leq i \ \wedge \ i = n : b.i)$$

$$= \qquad \langle\, \text{Rewrite range} \,\rangle$$
$$x \ \ min \ \ (\underline{\text{MIN}}\, i \ : \ 0 \le n \ \wedge \ i = n \ : \ b.i\,)$$
$$= \qquad \langle\, \text{From } P1, \text{ namely } 0 \le n \,\rangle$$
$$x \ \ min \ \ (\underline{\text{MIN}}\, i \ : \ i = n \ : \ b.i\,)$$
$$= \qquad \langle\, \text{1-point rule} \,\rangle$$
$$x \ \ min \ \ b.n$$

The initial steps boiled down to factoring out the quantification that appears in $P0$. Once factored out, it could be replaced by x. Since our aim was to eliminate a quantification, this was the obvious way to proceed. Four steps were required to accomplish this. In the future, we will combine these steps.

With the quantification eliminated, the development is complete. The final solution is:

$$|[\underline{\text{var}} \ n : int$$
$$;n, y := 0, +inf$$
$$;\underline{\text{do}} \ n \ne \#b \ \rightarrow \ n, x := n+1, x \ min \ b.n \ \underline{\text{od}}$$
$$]|$$

$$\star \qquad\qquad \star$$
$$\star$$

Ex 10.0   Solve:

$$\underline{\text{var}} \ b : array \ of \ int$$
$$;\underline{\text{var}} \ x : int$$
$$;x : \ x = (\underline{\text{MIN}}\, i \ : \ 0 \le i \ \wedge \ i < \#b \ : \ b.i\,)$$

Choose a different invariant than the one we chose in our previous solution to this problem. □

Ex 10.1   Solve:

$$\underline{\text{var}} \ f : array \ of \ int$$
$$;\underline{\text{var}} \ s : int$$
$$;s : \ s = (\Sigma\, i \ : \ 0 \le i \ \wedge \ i < \#f \ : \ f.i\,)$$

□

Ex 10.2   Find a different solution to the previous exercise. □

Ex 10.3   Solve:

> <u>var</u> f : *array of int*
> ; <u>var</u> s, t : *int*
> ; s, t : $s = (\underline{\text{MIN}}\, i : 0 \le i \ \wedge\ i < \#f : f.i)\ \wedge$
> $t = (\underline{\text{MAX}}\, i : 0 \le i \ \wedge\ i < \#f : f.i)$

□

Ex 10.4   Solve:

> <u>var</u> N : *int* $\{N \ge 0\}$
> ; <u>var</u> z : *int*
> ; z : $z = f.N$

where we are given that

> $f.k = \underline{\text{if}}\ k = 0\ \rightarrow\ 1$
> $\quad\ \Box\ k > 0\ \rightarrow\ k * f.(k-1)$
> $\quad\ \underline{\text{fi}}$

The solution cannot contain f.   □

Ex 10.5   Solve:

> <u>var</u> N : *int* $\{N \ge 0\}$
> ; <u>var</u> x : *int*
> ; x : $x = (\Pi i : 1 \le i \ \wedge\ i < N+1 : i)$

□

Ex 10.6   Solve:

> <u>var</u> f : *array of bool*
> ; <u>var</u> z : *bool*
> ; z : $z \equiv (\forall i : 0 \le i \ \wedge\ i < \#f : f.i)$

□

Ex 10.7   Solve:

> <u>var</u> X, Y : *int* $\{X \ge 0 \ \wedge\ Y \ge 0\}$
> ; <u>var</u> z : *int*
> ; z : $z = X * Y$

The solution cannot contain multiplication.   □

10.3   An example — Determining the multiple

We are asked to prove the following:

> For any integer X and natural N,
> $X^N - 1$ is a multiple of $X - 1$.

A PROOF BY WRITING A PROGRAM

As programmers we have an interesting way to prove this. We can construct a program that given integer X and natural N, determines the multiple of $X - 1$ that equals $X^N - 1$. Because the program will determine this multiple (i.e. establishes its postcondition) for *any* integer X and natural N proves the theorem. In other words, the existence of such a program is a proof of the theorem!

⋆   ⋆

We begin by casting the problem into a specification:

> <u>var</u> $N, X, z : int$ $\{N \geq 0\}$
> $; z :\ z * (X - 1) = X^N - 1$

This is a specification of a program to set z to the multiple of $X - 1$ that equals $X^N - 1$. Our proof has reduced to finding a solution to this specification.

A FIRST ATTEMPT

Our first proposal is the program

> $z := (X^N - 1)/(X - 1)$

Unfortunately, the division is only legal if $X^N - 1$ is a multiple of $X - 1$, which begs the problem in the first place. As a result, we will disallow division from our solution.

A SECOND ATTEMPT

We will establish our postcondition using a loop. Our first step is to choose an invariant. By the technique of replacing constants by fresh variables, we propose replacing N by fresh variable n to arrive at invariants

$$P0: \ z * (X - 1) = X^n - 1$$
$$P1: \ 0 \le n \le N$$

and the program

```
|[var n : int
;n, z := 0, 0  {P0 ∧ P1}
;do n ≠ N → S od
]|
```

What remains is the development of S.

★   ★

S must increase n and must also maintain the invariants. As the only variables named in the invariants are n and z, an increase to n must be accompanied by some assignment to z. Thus we envision

$$S: \ n, z := n + 1, E \quad \text{for some } E.$$

On account of $P1$ and the guard, we see that the increase of n maintains $P1$. Therefore we need only solve for an E that maintains $P0$:

$$wp.(n, z := n + 1, E).P0$$
$\equiv \quad \langle\,\text{Definitions of } P0 \text{ and assignment}\,\rangle$
$$E * (X - 1) = X^{n+1} - 1$$
$\equiv \quad \langle\,\text{Arithmetic, towards factoring out } X^n - 1\,\rangle$
$$E * (X - 1) = X * (X^n - 1) + X - 1$$
$\equiv \quad \langle\,\text{Using } P0\,\rangle$
$$E * (X - 1) = X * z * (X - 1) + X - 1$$
$\equiv \quad \langle\,\text{Arithmetic}\,\rangle$
$$E * (X - 1) = (X * z + 1) * (X - 1)$$
$\Leftarrow \quad \langle\,\text{Leibniz}\,\rangle$
$$E = X * z + 1$$

This completes the development, and so proves the theorem.

$\star$ $\star$

Notice that we did not write the last step of our calculation as

$$E * (X - 1) = (X * z + 1) * (X - 1)$$
$$\equiv \quad \langle \text{Arithmetic} \rangle$$
$$E = X * z + 1$$

The reason is that for $X = 1$ we would have had a divide by 0. In other words, the equivalence is too strong. For many problems we have a choice, but when the equivalence is too strong, we must apply Leibniz's rule.

Remark   This theorem can also be proved using mathematical induction. Our proof by writing a program has an advantage though: not only do we know that there is always a multiple, we also know how to determine it in every instance! Such a proof is called *constructive*: instead of asserting that "given so-and-so, there exists something", it shows us how to determine the "something" given the "so-and-so". □

$\star$ $\star$

Ex 10.8   Prove, for any integer x, that $x^2 + x$ is even (i.e. is a multiple of 2) by solving:

> var $x : int$
> ; var $z : int$
> ; $z : \ 2 * z = x^2 + x$

Although it can be nicely solved without a repetition, a repetition is desired. □

10.4   An example — A table of cubes

The table of cubes of the natural numbers is the sequence

$0, \ 1, \ 8, \ 27, \ 64, \ \ldots.$

Given integer $N \geq 0$, we are asked to establish

R: the first N entries in the table of cubes are printed.

Further, we are not allowed to use exponentiation or multiplication in the solution.

★   ★

From R we find an invariant by replacing the constant N by fresh variable n to arrive at invariants

> $P0$: the first n entries in the table of cubes are printed
> $P1$: $n \geq 0$ (so $P0$ is defined)

and the program:

$$
\begin{aligned}
&|[\underline{\text{var}}\ n : int \\
&;n := 0\ \ \{P0 \wedge P1\} \\
&;\underline{\text{do}}\ n \neq N\ \rightarrow \\
&\qquad print.(n^3) \\
&\qquad ;n := n + 1 \\
&\underline{\text{od}} \\
&\{P0\ \wedge\ n = N,\ hence\ R\} \\
&]|
\end{aligned}
$$

The only problem is that the program contains an exponentiation, which is disallowed. Towards its elimination, we introduce fresh variable x, and rewrite our program as:

$$
\begin{aligned}
&|[\underline{\text{var}}\ n, x : int \\
&;n := 0\ \ \{P0 \wedge P1\} \\
&;\underline{\text{do}}\ n \neq N\ \rightarrow \\
&\qquad print.x \\
&\qquad ;n := n + 1 \\
&\underline{\text{od}} \\
&\{P0\ \wedge\ n = N,\ hence\ R\} \\
&]|
\end{aligned}
$$

— a program which does the job only if

> $P2$: $x = n^3$

is a precondition of *print.x* . One way to guarantee that $P2$ is a precondition of *print.x* is to maintain the invariance of $P2$. This we will do, to arrive at:

```
|[var n, x : int
;n, x := 0, 0  {P0 ∧ P1 ∧ P2}
;do n ≠ N →
      print.x
    ;n, x := n + 1, E
 od
]|
```

where E must be chosen to maintain $P2$. We solve for an E that maintains $P2$:

$$wp.(n, x := n + 1, E).P2$$
$$\equiv \qquad \langle \text{Definitions of } P2 \text{ and assignment} \rangle$$
$$E = (n + 1)^3$$

Unfortunately, this expression includes an exponentiation, which is disallowed. Towards its elimination we find:

$$(n + 1)^3$$
$$= \qquad \langle \text{Arithmetic} \rangle$$
$$n^3 + 3 * n^2 + 3 * n + 1$$
$$= \qquad \langle P2, \text{ to eliminate an exponentiation} \rangle$$
$$x + 3 * n^2 + 3 * n + 1$$
$$= \qquad \langle P3, \text{ see below, to eliminate the exponentiation}$$
$$\qquad\qquad \text{and the multiplications} \rangle$$
$$x + y$$

where the $P3$ mentioned in the hint is:

$$P3: \quad y = 3 * n^2 + 3 * n + 1.$$

In order to eliminate the exponentiation and multiplications from E, we invented and assumed that $P3$ holds. Thus we must guarantee that it does. A simple way to accomplish this is to maintain $P3$'s invariance. Adding $P3$ to the invariant we arrive at:

```
|[var n, x, y : int
;n, x, y := 0, 0, 1  {P0 ∧ P1 ∧ P2 ∧ P3}
;do n ≠ N →
      print.x
    ;n, x, y := n + 1, x + y, E
 od
]|
```

where E must be chosen to maintain the invariance of $P3$. We solve for an E that maintains $P3$:

$$
\begin{array}{ll}
& wp.(n, y := n + 1, E).P3 \\
\equiv & \langle\,\text{Definitions of } P3 \text{ and assignment}\,\rangle \\
& E = 3 * (n + 1)^2 + 3 * (n + 1) + 1
\end{array}
$$

Towards eliminating the exponentiation and multiplications, we find:

$$
\begin{array}{ll}
& 3 * (n + 1)^2 + 3 * (n + 1) + 1 \\
= & \langle\,\text{Arithmetic}\,\rangle \\
& 3 * n^2 + 9 * n + 7 \\
= & \langle\,P3\,\rangle \\
& y + 6 * n + 6
\end{array}
$$

Clearly, $6 * n$ can be rewritten without multiplication, but for fun we go round once more:

$$
\begin{array}{ll}
& y + 6 * n + 6 \\
= & \langle\,P4\,,\ \text{see below}\,\rangle \\
& y + z
\end{array}
$$

where the $P4$ mentioned in the hint is:

$$
P4: \quad z = 6 * n + 6.
$$

Adding $P4$ to the invariant we arrive at:

$$
\begin{array}{l}
|[\,\underline{\text{var}}\ n, x, y, z : int \\
;\, n, x, y, z := 0, 0, 1, 6\ \ \{P0\ \wedge\ P1\ \wedge\ P2\ \wedge\ P3\ \wedge\ P4\} \\
;\, \underline{\text{do}}\ n \neq N\ \rightarrow \\
\qquad print.x \\
\qquad ;\, n, x, y, z := n + 1, x + y, y + z, E \\
\quad\ \underline{\text{od}} \\
]|
\end{array}
$$

Solving for an E that maintains $P4$, we find:

$$
\begin{array}{ll}
& wp.(n, z := n + 1, E).P4 \\
\equiv & \langle\,\text{Definitions of } P4 \text{ and assignment}\,\rangle \\
& E = 6 * (n + 1) + 6
\end{array}
$$

Towards eliminating the multiplication, we find:

$$6 * (n + 1) + 6$$
$$= \quad \langle \text{ Arithmetic } \rangle$$
$$6 * n + 12$$
$$= \quad \langle P4 \rangle$$
$$z + 6$$

This completes the development. The final solution is

$$\begin{aligned}
&\|[\underline{\text{var}}\ n, x, y, z : int \\
&;n, x, y, z := 0, 0, 1, 6 \\
&;\underline{\text{do}}\ n \neq N\ \rightarrow \\
&\qquad print.x \\
&\qquad ;n, x, y, z := n + 1, x + y, y + z, z + 6 \\
&\quad \underline{\text{od}} \\
&]|
\end{aligned}$$

$\star$ $\qquad$ $\star$

Notice that the postcondition is established on account of $P0$ (and $n = N$) only. The need for additional invariants (i.e. $P2$, $P3$, and $P4$) was revealed by our calculations. In other words, we obtained them in a straightforward way.

In general, the technique of adding invariants is called *strengthening the invariant*. This technique we add to our repetioire.

$\star$ $\qquad$ $\star$

Ex 10.9 Solve:

$$\begin{aligned}
&\underline{\text{var}}\ N, X : int \quad \{N \geq 0\} \\
&;\underline{\text{var}}\ y : int \\
&;y:\ y = (\Sigma i\ :\ 0 \leq i < N\ :\ X^i)
\end{aligned}$$

The solution cannot include exponentiation. □

Ex 10.10 Solve:

$$\begin{aligned}
&\underline{\text{var}}\ b : array\ of\ int \quad \{0 \leq \#b\} \\
&;\underline{\text{var}}\ x : int \\
&;\underline{\text{var}}\ y : int \\
&;y:\ y = (\Sigma i\ :\ 0 \leq i < \#b\ :\ b.i * x^i)
\end{aligned}$$

The solution cannot include exponentiation. Interpreting this specification, we see that we are asked to evaluate a polynomial. □

10.5   An example — The maximum section sum

Given is integer array b. The sections of b are the $b(k : i \leq k < j)$, for each pair i,j that satisfies $0 \leq i \ \wedge \ i \leq j \ \wedge \ j \leq \#b$. A section's sum is the sum of the section's elements. Desired is the maximum section sum in b.[4] In other words, we are asked to solve:

> $\underline{\text{var}}\ b : \ array\ of\ int \quad \{0 \leq \#b\}$
> $;\underline{\text{var}}\ x : \ int$
> $;x : \ \ x = (\underline{\text{MAX}}\, i,j \ : \ 0 \leq i \ \wedge \ i \leq j \ \wedge \ j \leq \#b \ : \ f.i.j\,)$

where $f.i.j$ is the sum of section $b(k : i \leq k < j)$, i.e.

> $f.i.j = (\Sigma k \ : \ i \leq k \ \wedge \ k < j \ : \ b.k\,) \quad$ for $0 \leq i \leq j \leq \#b$.

Remark   The number of non-empty sections is proportional to $\#b^2$. Calculation of the sum of each section requires on average a number of additions proportional to $\#b$. Thus we might expect a solution to require a number of additions proportional to $\#b^3$. We will arrive at a solution significantly better than this.   □

⋆   ⋆

From the postcondition we replace the constant $\#b$ by a fresh variable to arrive at invariants

> $P0 : \ \ x = (\underline{\text{MAX}}\, i,j \ : \ 0 \leq i \ \wedge \ i \leq j \ \wedge \ j \leq n \ : \ f.i.j\,)$
> $P1 : \ \ 0 \leq n \ \wedge \ n \leq \#b$

and the program

> $|[\underline{\text{var}}\ n : int$
> $;n,x := 0,0 \ \ \{P0 \ \wedge \ P1\}$
> $;\underline{\text{do}}\ n \neq \#b \ \rightarrow \ S \ \underline{\text{od}}$
> $\ \ \{P0 \ \wedge \ n = \#b,\ hence\ R\}$
> $]|$

---

[4]We are after the maximum section sum only, and not the particular sections having this sum. The former is unique, while there may be many instances of the latter.

What remains is the development of loop body S.

⋆ ⋆

For S we envision:

$$S : x, n := E, n + 1 .$$

We solve for an E that maintains $P0$:

$$
\begin{aligned}
&wp.(x, n := E, n + 1).P0 \\
\equiv\quad &\langle \text{ Definitions of } P0 \text{ and assignment} \rangle \\
&E = (\underline{\text{MAX}}\, i, j : 0 \le i \,\wedge\, i \le j \,\wedge\, j \le n + 1 : f.i.j)
\end{aligned}
$$

To eliminate the quantification, we find that:

$$
\begin{aligned}
&(\underline{\text{MAX}}\, i, j : 0 \le i \,\wedge\, i \le j \,\wedge\, j \le n + 1 : f.i.j) \\
=\quad &\langle \text{ Split range} \rangle \\
&(\underline{\text{MAX}}\, i, j : 0 \le i \,\wedge\, i \le j \,\wedge\, j \le n : f.i.j)\ \ max \\
&(\underline{\text{MAX}}\, i, j : 0 \le i \,\wedge\, i \le j \,\wedge\, j = n + 1 : f.i.j) \\
=\quad &\langle\, P0, \text{ to eliminate a quantification} \rangle \\
&x\ \ max\ \ (\underline{\text{MAX}}\, i, j : 0 \le i \,\wedge\, i \le j \,\wedge\, j = n + 1 : f.i.j) \\
=\quad &\langle \text{ Dummy elimination rule} \rangle \\
&x\ \ max\ \ (\underline{\text{MAX}}\, i : 0 \le i \,\wedge\, i \le n + 1 : f.i.(n + 1)) \\
=\quad &\langle \text{ Assume } P2\,(n := n + 1),\ \text{see below} \rangle \\
&x\ \ max\ \ y
\end{aligned}
$$

where we define:

$$P2 : y = (\underline{\text{MAX}}\, i : 0 \le i \,\wedge\, i \le n : f.i.n) .$$

Remark The question might arise as to why the following was not chosen instead:

$$y = (\underline{\text{MAX}}\, i : 0 \le i \,\wedge\, i \le n + 1 : f.i.(n + 1)) . \tag{$*$}$$

The reason is that $(*)$ cannot be established initially. Since n is initially 0, the assignment $y := f.0.1\ max\ f.1.1$ would be needed to establish $(*)$. By the definition of f, this boils down to $y := b.0\ max\ 0$. Unfortunately, $b.0$ is undefined when $\#b = 0$.

The problem, of course, is the $f.i.(n + 1)$. Had we chosen $(*)$, this would have been discovered, and we would have been forced to continue our calculation with the aim of factoring out an expression having $f.i.n$ for the term. We would also have discovered that is advantageous to keep the quantifications in "sync", which is a useful heuristic.

And so, it was with some forsight that we chose $P2$ directly. This choice will allow us to streamline the presentation. $\square$

Maintaining $P2$'s invariance, we arrive at:

$$
\begin{aligned}
&|[\underline{\text{var}}\ n, y : int \\
&;n, x, y := 0, 0, 0\ \{P0 \wedge P1 \wedge P2\} \\
&;\underline{\text{do}}\ n \neq \#b \rightarrow \\
&\qquad \{P2\}\ S0\ \{P2\,(n := n + 1)\} \\
&\qquad ;x, n := x\ max\ y, n + 1 \\
&\ \underline{\text{od}} \\
&]|
\end{aligned}
$$

where $S0$ has been added to guarantee that $P2\,(n := n + 1)$ is a precondition of the assignment to x. ($P2$ is a precondition of $S0$ because $P2$ is an invariant).

What remains is the development of $S0$.

$$\star \qquad\qquad \star$$

For $S0$ we envision

$$S0 : \quad y := E .$$

We solve for E to establish $P2\,(n := n + 1)$:

$$
\begin{aligned}
&wp.(y := E).(P2.(n := n + 1)) \\
\equiv\quad &\langle\,\text{Definitions of } P2 \text{ and assignment}\,\rangle \\
&E = (\underline{\text{MAX}}\,i : 0 \leq i \wedge i \leq n + 1 : f.i.(n + 1))
\end{aligned}
$$

Towards eliminating the quantification, we find:

$$
\begin{aligned}
&(\underline{\text{MAX}}\,i : 0 \leq i \wedge i \leq n + 1 : f.i.(n + 1)) \\
=\quad &\langle\,\text{Towards factoring out the quantification in } P2,\ \text{split range}\,\rangle \\
&(\underline{\text{MAX}}\,i : 0 \leq i \wedge i \leq n : f.i.(n + 1))\ max \\
&(\underline{\text{MAX}}\,i : 0 \leq i \wedge i = n + 1 : f.i.(n + 1))
\end{aligned}
$$

$=$ ⟨ But first we eliminate the second quantification:
$\quad$ $P1$, in particular $n \geq 0$, hence $0 \leq n+1$ ⟩
$(\text{MAX}\, i : 0 \leq i \wedge i \leq n : f.i.(n+1))\ \ max$
$(\text{MAX}\, i : i = n+1 : f.i.(n+1))$

$=$ ⟨ 1-point rule ⟩
$(\text{MAX}\, i : 0 \leq i \wedge i \leq n : f.i.(n+1))\ \ max\ \ f.(n+1).(n+1)$

$=$ ⟨ Property of f: $f.z.z = 0$, for any z. (see below) ⟩
$(\text{MAX}\, i : 0 \leq i \wedge i \leq n : f.i.(n+1))\ \ max\ \ 0$

$=$ ⟨ Towards getting the term to $f.i.n$, property of f:
$\quad f.i.(n+1) = f.i.n + b.n$ ⟩
$(\text{MAX}\, i : 0 \leq i \wedge i \leq n : f.i.n + b.n)\ \ max\ \ 0$

$=$ ⟨ $+$ distributes over MAX with non-empty range. By $P1$,
$\quad$ the range is non-empty ⟩
$(b.n + (\text{MAX}\, i : 0 \leq i \wedge i \leq n : f.i.n))\ \ max\ \ 0$

$=$ ⟨ $P2$ ⟩
$(b.n + y)\ \ max\ \ 0$

Our remaining obligations are proofs of the properties of f appealed to in this calculation. These proofs are left as exercises (see below). Thus the development is complete.

★   ★

The final solution is

```
|[var n, y : int
;n, x, y := 0, 0, 0
;do n ≠ #b →
      y := (b.n + y) max 0
    ;x, n := x max y, n + 1
  od
]|
```

— a program requiring a number of additions proportional to $\#b$!

★   ★

Ex 10.11 With $f.i.j = (\Sigma k : i \leq k \wedge k < j : b.k)$, prove:

(a) $f.i.i = 0$.
(b) $f.i.(n+1) = f.i.n + b.n$ for $0 \leq i \leq n < \#b$.

These are the properties of f appealed to in the last calculation. □

Ex 10.12   Solve:

> <u>var</u> $f : array\ of\ int$ $\{0 \le \#f\}$
> ; <u>var</u> $s : bool$
> ; $s : s \equiv (\forall i, j : 0 \le i \ \wedge \ i \le j \ \wedge \ j < \#f : b.i \le b.j)$

□

Ex 10.13   Solve:

> <u>var</u> $b : array\ of\ bool$ $\{0 \le \#b\}$
> ; <u>var</u> $x : bool$
> ; $x : x \equiv (\forall i, j : 0 \le i \ \wedge \ i \le j \ \wedge \ j < \#b : b.i \Rightarrow b.j)$

This problem has the curious name "imptest".   □

Ex 10.14   Solve: (due to Jan L.A. van de Snepscheut)

> <u>var</u> $N : int$ $\{N \ge 1\}$
> ; <u>var</u> $X, Y : int$
> ; <u>var</u> $x : int$
> ; $x : x = (\Sigma i : 0 \le i \ \wedge \ i \le N : f.i * f.(N - i))$

where function f is defined by

> $f.0 = 0$
> $f.1 = 1$
> $f.(k + 2) \ = \ X * f.k \ + \ Y * f.(k + 1)$ for $k \ge 0$.

Function f cannot appear in the program text. (This problem is known as "Fibolucci".)   □

Ex 10.15   Solve:

> <u>var</u> $N : int$ $\{N \ge 0\}$
> ; <u>var</u> x
> ; $x : x = f.N$

where function f is defined by

> $f.n = (\underline{OP}\,i, j : 0 \le i \ \wedge \ i \le j \ \wedge \ j \le n \ \wedge \ g.i.j : h.i.j),$

for any $n \ge 0$. $\underline{OP}$ is an arbitrary quantifier having underlying operator op, and all we know about g and h are that

- Both are defined when $0 \le i \le j \le N$.

- Both have appropriate types, i.e. g is of type boolean, and h is of the same type as the quantification.

- $g.z.z$ holds, for any z.

Function f is not allowed in the program, but function d, defined by

$$d.n = (\underline{OP}\, i : 0 \le i \,\wedge\, i \le n \,\wedge\, g.i.n : h.i.n) \quad \text{for } n \ge 0,$$

is allowed. This is a "generic" section problem, of which the maximum section sum problem is but an instance. □

10.6 An example — The binary search (and its numerous applications)

Given boolean function $b(k : 0 \le k < \#b)$, we are asked to establish

$$R: \; b.x \,\wedge\, \neg b.(x+1) \,\wedge\, -1 \le x \,\wedge\, x < \#b.$$

★   ★

We head for an invariant by replacing a constant by a fresh variable. There are many choices here.[5] Because no choice seems better than another, we choose to replace the most complicated constant, namely $x+1$, by fresh variable y, to arrive at invariant

$$b.x \,\wedge\, \neg b.y \,\wedge\, -1 \le x \,\wedge\, x < \#b$$
$$\wedge \; x+1 \le y \,\wedge\, y \le \#b.$$

Remark The bounds on y were found as follows: Since y replaces $x+1$, the largest value for y is 1 more than that of x, and the smallest value for y is $x+1$. □

For ease of future manipulation we rearrange this invariant into

$$P0: \; b.x \,\wedge\, \neg b.y$$
$$P1: \; -1 \le x \,\wedge\, x < y \,\wedge\, y \le \#b$$

---

[5]The bounds on x should remain. In $b.x$, we have the x. In $b.(x+1)$ we have the x, the 1 and the $x+1$.

to arrive at the program

```
|[var y : int
;S0  {P0 ∧ P1}
;do y ≠ x + 1 → SS od
 {P0 ∧ P1 ∧ y = x + 1, hence R}
]|
```

Our remaining tasks are the developments of $S0$ and SS.

⋆   ⋆

We begin by developing $S0$, namely establishing our invariants initially. For S we envision

$$S0: \quad x, y := E, F \quad \text{for some } E \text{ and } F.$$

We solve for E and F to establish the invariants:

$$
\begin{aligned}
& wp.(x, y := E, F).(P0 \wedge P1) \\
\equiv & \quad \langle \text{Definitions of } P0, P1, \text{ and assignment} \rangle \\
& b.E \ \wedge \ \neg b.F \ \wedge \ -1 \le E \ \wedge \ E < F \ \wedge \ F \le \#b \\
\equiv & \quad \langle \text{Let } F = \#b \text{ to truthify } F \le \#b \rangle \\
& b.E \ \wedge \ \neg b.\#b \ \wedge \ -1 \le E \ \wedge \ E < \#b \\
\equiv & \quad \langle \text{Let } E = -1 \text{ to truthify } -1 \le E \rangle \\
& b.(-1) \ \wedge \ \neg b.\#b \ \wedge \ -1 < \#b \\
\equiv & \quad \langle \text{Arithmetic} \rangle \\
& b.(-1) \ \wedge \ \neg b.\#b \ \wedge \ 0 \le \#b
\end{aligned}
$$

Thus we see that our invariants can be established if

$$Q: \ b.(-1) \ \wedge \ \neg b.\#b \ \wedge \ 0 \le \#b$$

holds initially. To satisfy this requirement we will take Q as our precondition. Q, however, refers to elements outside of the range of b. We will assume the existence of these fictitious elements, and will postulate that they satisfy the first two conjuncts of Q. We promise not to refer to them in our program!

What remains is the development of SS.

⋆   ⋆

Loop body SS must eventually truthify $y = x + 1$. On account of $P1$ we see that $x < y$, and therefore that this can be accomplished by decreasing

bound t : $y - x$.

We can decrease t by setting either x or y to a value intermediate to the two. An intermediate value is guaranteed to exist because of the truth of

$$x < y \;\land\; x + 1 \neq y.$$

Postponing this choice, we introduce fresh variable m to hold the intermediate value, to arrive at the following for SS:

$$
\begin{aligned}
&\|[\underline{var}\ m : int \\
&;m := E \ \{x < m < y\} \\
&;\underline{if}\ B0\ \rightarrow\ x := m \\
&\quad \square\ B1\ \rightarrow\ y := m \\
&\quad \underline{fi} \\
&]|
\end{aligned}
$$

Our remaining tasks are the choices for E, $B0$ and $B1$.

$$\star \qquad\qquad \star$$

We begin with the guards, which must be chosen to maintain $P0$. ($P1$ is maintained by the assignment to m). We solve for $B0$ first:

$$
\begin{aligned}
&wp.(x := m).P0 \\
\equiv\quad &\langle\,\text{Definitions of } P0 \text{ and assignment}\,\rangle \\
&b.m \;\land\; \neg b.y \\
\equiv\quad &\langle\,\text{From } P0\colon\ \neg b.y\,\rangle \\
&b.m
\end{aligned}
$$

Thus we have determined

$$B0 \;\equiv\; b.m.$$

By a similar calculation we would determine

$$B1 \;\equiv\; \neg b.m.$$

Because of $P1$ and $x < m < y$, we see that $0 \leq m < \#b$, and therefore that $b.m$ is not a fictitious element. Because the disjunction of these guards universally holds, the IF is not an *abort* either.

What remains is the choice of E in the assignment to m.

★   ★

The value E must be chosen to satisfy $x < E < y$. One choice is $x + 1$. Another is $y - 1$. Why choose one over the other? For reasons of symmetry we choose their "average", namely

$$E \; = \; (x + y) \; div \; 2 \, .$$

Remark   If "overflow" might be a problem, then $x + (y - x) \; div \; 2$ could be used instead. Also convince yourself that $x < E < y$ is satisfied even if *div* rounds up.   □

This completes the development.

★   ★

To summarize: Given boolean function $b(k : 0 \leq k < \#b)$ that satisfies

$$Q : \; b.(-1) \; \wedge \; \neg b.\#b \; \wedge \; 0 \leq \#b$$

the Binary Search

```
|[var y : int
;x, y := −1, #b
;do y ≠ x + 1 →
    |[var m : int
    ;m := (x + y) div 2
    ;if   b.m  →  x := m
     ☐ ¬b.m  →  y := m
     fi
    ]|
 od
]|
```

will establish

$$R: \quad b.x \; \wedge \; \neg b.(x+1) \; \wedge \; -1 \leq x \; \wedge \; x < \#b.$$

Although we chose $y - x$ as bound function, observe that each repetition of the Binary Search halves $y - x$, and so a tighter bound function is $log.(y - x)$ (we mean the base 2 logarithm) which is decreased by 1 each repetition. Since initially $x, y = -1, \#b$, the Binary Search requires $log.(\#b + 1)$ repetitions. It is its bound function that makes the Binary Search so useful.

With a solution in hand, we look at some of its applications. Observe that applying the Binary Search boils down to choosing a suitable boolean function b and a suitable value for $\#b$. These choices must satisfy precondition Q, of course. Also notice that a small value for $\#b$ guarantees a small number of repetitions.

A FIRST APPLICATION OF THE BINARY SEARCH

The integer square-root of N is the largest integer at most the $\sqrt{N}$. Given $N \geq 0$, we are asked to develop a program that determines the integer square-root of N. Square-roots cannot appear in the program.

By the definition of integer square-root we see that we are asked to establish

$$x \leq \sqrt{N} \; \wedge \; \sqrt{N} < x + 1$$

which, to eliminate the square-root, is equivalent to

$$R0: \quad x^2 \leq N \; \wedge \; N < (x+1)^2.$$

First we transform the postcondition of the Binary Search into $R0$:

$$
\begin{array}{ll}
& b.x \; \wedge \; \neg b.(x+1) \; \wedge \; -1 \leq x \; \wedge \; x < \#b \\
\equiv & \quad \langle \text{ Choose } b.x \; \equiv \; x^2 \leq N \, \rangle \\
& x^2 \leq N \; \wedge \; N < (x+1)^2 \; \wedge \; -1 \leq x \; \wedge \; x < \#b \\
\Rightarrow & \quad \langle \, P \wedge Q \Rightarrow P \, \rangle \\
& R0
\end{array}
$$

Thus if the postcondition of this Binary Search holds, then so does $R0$, our desired postcondition.

As for the choice for $\#b$ we might choose $\#b = +inf$, since b is defined for all integers. Instead we will seek as small a value as possible: The Binary Search requires $log.(\#b + 1)$ repetitions, so a small value for $\#b$ guarantees a minimum number of repetitions.

We recall from the Binary Search's precondition that $\#b$ must satisfy $\neg b.\#b$ and $0 \leq \#b$. We investigate with the aim of minimizing $\#b$:

$$\neg b.\#b \ \wedge \ 0 \leq \#b$$
$$\equiv \quad \langle \text{In this case: } b.x \ \equiv \ x^2 \leq N \rangle$$
$$\#b^2 > N \ \wedge \ 0 \leq \#b$$
$$\equiv \quad \langle \text{Choose } \#b = N+1, \text{ the smallest value}$$
$$\text{satisfying } \#b^2 > N. \rangle$$
$$0 \leq N+1$$
$$\equiv \quad \langle \text{From the precondition: } 0 \leq N \rangle$$
$$\textit{true}$$

This completes the development. The final solution is the Binary Search with

$$
\begin{array}{lll}
b.m & \text{replaced by} & m^2 \leq N \quad \text{and} \\
\#b & \text{replaced by} & N+1
\end{array}
$$

— a program requiring $log.(N+2)$ repetitions.

Remark For $N=1,000,000$, this solution requires only 20 repetitions. Notice that a Linear Search would require $\sqrt{N}$, or 1000! □

Remark Convince yourself that for $N < 0$ this program will establish $x = -1$. This is nice, since the original postcondition has no solution in this case. The general observation, and we omit its proof, is that when $\neg b.0$ holds initially, the Binary Search will establish $x = -1$, and when $b.0$ holds initially, it will establish $0 \leq x$. In this case, $\neg b.0 \equiv N < 0$. □

THE MOST COMMON APPLICATION OF THE BINARY SEARCH

Given integer N and integer array $f(k : 0 \leq k < \#f)$, where $\#f \geq 0$, we are asked to determine whether N occurs in f. More precisely, we are asked to assign to boolean variable p to establish

$$RR: \quad p \ \equiv \ (\exists k : 0 \leq k < \#f : f.k = N).$$

If N occurs in f we see no way to establish RR without determining where N occurs, that is, by exhibiting an x that satisfies

$$f.x = N \ \wedge \ 0 \leq x \ \wedge \ x < \#f.$$

If N does not occur in f, however, then this relation is too strong. There is no x that would satisfy it. What needs weakening is the first conjunct, and we observe that if we can establish the slightly weaker

$$R0: \ \ f.x \leq N \ \wedge \ N < f.(x+1) \ \wedge \ 0 \leq x \ \wedge \ x < \#f,$$

then if N occurs in f, and if f happens to be ascending, then N will occur at $f.x$. Relation $R0$ defines x as where N *should occur*, provided that f is ascending. From here it is easy to determine whether N does occur: We need only check whether $f.x = N$. In other words, the program

$$\text{Establish } R0 \ ; \ p := f.x = N$$

will establish RR, provided that "f is ascending" is a precondition of the assignment to p.

There is one little problem with this solution: Our precondition is $\#f \geq 0$, and relation $R0$ cannot be established when $\#f = 0$. In particular, there would be no way to satisfy $R0$'s last two conjuncts. Observing that the last conjunct can be satisfied if $x = -1$ is allowed, we will weaken $R0$ to allow $x = -1$. What we will weaken it to is

$$R1: \ \ f.x \leq N \ \wedge \ N < f.(x+1) \ \wedge \ -1 \leq x \ \wedge \ x < \#f.$$

Remark   The question might arise as to whether the first two conjuncts can be satisfied for any x that satisfies the last two. We ask that this question be put aside for now.   □

With $R0$ changed to $R1$, we must change the assignment to p to

$$\begin{aligned}
&\underline{\text{if }} 0 \leq x \quad \rightarrow \ p := f.x = N \qquad\qquad \text{(Assignment to } p\text{)}\\
&\square \ \ x = -1 \ \rightarrow \ p := \textit{false}\\
&\underline{\text{fi}}
\end{aligned}$$

— a program we call the "Assignment to p". To summarize what we have accomplished, we see that the program

$$\text{Establish } R1 \ ; \ \text{Assignment to } p$$

will establish RR, provided that "f is ascending" is a precondition of "Assignment to p". Our remaining task is to develop "Establish $R1$".

★   ★

Observing that $R1$ is an instance of the Binary Search's postcondition, we begin by transforming the latter into the former:

$$b.x \;\land\; \neg b.(x+1) \;\land\; -1 \leq x \;\land\; x < \#b$$
$$\equiv \qquad \langle\, \text{Choose } b.x \;\equiv\; f.x \leq N \,\rangle$$
$$f.x \leq N \;\land\; N < f.(x+1) \;\land\; -1 \leq x \;\land\; x < \#b$$

In other words, with $b.x \;\equiv\; f.x \leq N$, the Binary Search will establish $R1$.

Our final task is to choose for $\#b$ a value that satisfies the Binary Search's precondition:

$$\neg b.\#b \;\land\; 0 \leq \#b$$
$$\equiv \qquad \langle\, \text{In this case: } b.x \;\equiv\; f.x \leq N \,\rangle$$
$$f.\#b > N \;\land\; 0 \leq \#b$$
$$\equiv \qquad \langle\, \text{Knowing nothing about } f, \text{ choose } \#b = \#f \,\rangle$$
$$f.\#f > N \;\land\; 0 \leq \#f$$
$$\equiv \qquad \langle\, f.\#f \text{ is fictitious, so by postulate} \,\rangle$$
$$0 \leq \#f$$
$$\equiv \qquad \langle\, \text{By the precondition} \,\rangle$$
$$true$$

Thus a Binary Search with

$b.m$	replaced by	$f.m \leq N$
$\#b$	replaced by	$\#f$

(Binary Search 0)

is a solution to "Establish $R1$". This completes the development.

★   ★

To summarize: Given ascending array f, $\#f \geq 0$, the program

Binary Search 0 ; Assignment to p (Binary Search for N)

sets boolean variable p to the truth of "N occurs in f". We will refer to this program as the "Binary Search for N". It is the most common application of the Binary Search. Because we will soon compare it to some other solutions, we give its code:

```
|[var y : int
;x, y := −1, #f
;do  y ≠ x + 1 →
     |[var m : int
     ;m := (x + y) div 2
     ;if  f.m ≤ N  →  x := m
      ▯ N < f.m  →  y := m
      fi
     ]|
  od
]|
;if  0 ≤ x   →  p := f.x = N
 ▯ x = −1  →  p := false
 fi
```

Remark The Binary Search's postcondition (i.e. R) seems at first glance to be a rabbit-out-of-the-hat. It isn't. Had we been asked to solve this "most common application", we would have discovered $R1$. The generalization from $R1$ to R is an obvious step. ☐

Remark By our little observation at the end of the square-root example (that if $b.0$ holds initially, then $x \geq 0$ will be established), we see that when given that $f.0 \leq N$, we can simplify the assignment to p to $p := f.x = N$, and can change $x := -1$ to $x := 0$. ☐

REMARKS ON THE "BINARY SEARCH FOR N"

• Given an ascending array, the "Binary Search for N" is a great improvement over the Linear Search. The Linear Search decreases the search space by 1 element per repetition, while the "Binary Search for N", because it is a Binary Search, halves the search space each repetition. In the case of an array of length 1,000,000, a linear search might require 1,000,000 repetitions, while the "Binary Search for N" requires $log.(1,000,001)$, or 20. This is remarkable!

• This presentation of the "Binary Search for N" had a few aims:

The first was to show that the "Binary Search for N" is but a single application of the Binary Search. Many presentations treat the "Binary Search for N" as if it were the *only* Binary Search. The Binary Search has other applications. We have already seen one. Others can be found in the exercises.

The second was that many presentations of the "Binary Search for N" draw on f's ascendingness all over the place. As we have seen, f's ascendingness is required in one place only, viz. as precondition of the "Assignment to p", and here only if N occurs in f.

• Many books give the repetition of the "Binary Search for N" as some variation of

$$
\begin{aligned}
&\underline{\text{do}}\ x + 1 \neq y\ \rightarrow \\
&\quad |[\underline{\text{var}}\ m : int \\
&\quad ;m := (x + y)\ div\ 2 \\
&\quad ;\underline{\text{if}}\ f.m < N\ \rightarrow\ x := m \\
&\quad \Box\ f.m = N\ \rightarrow\ x := m\ ;\ terminate \\
&\quad \Box\ f.m > N\ \rightarrow\ y := m \\
&\quad \underline{\text{fi}} \\
&\quad]| \\
&\underline{\text{od}}
\end{aligned}
$$

— a program that we will refer to as the "improvement", because at first glance it appears to be an improvement. It terminates early, in particular, as soon as N is encountered. As our solution does not terminate early, how does it compare? How many repetitions does the "improvement" save?

Towards answering this question, we observe that if N does not occur in f, then no repetitions are saved, and the "improvement" is no improvement at all. In fact, it is worse if execution of its loop body is more expensive than ours.

If N occurs in f, we observe that

> for $1/2$ of the elements, zero repetitions are saved,
> for $1/4$ of the elements, one repetition is saved,
> for $1/8$ of the elements, two repetitions are saved, and so on.

A simple calculation reveals that, on average, about one repetition is saved. Since this savings is at the expense of a more complicated loop body we are led to investigate the loop bodies.

We will ignore the assignment to m. As for the IFs, we let $C3$ be the cost of the IF in the "improvement", and let $C2$ be the cost of our original IF. If $C3 = C2$ we see that the "improvement" is more efficient: it saves one repetition at no additional expense.

Next we investigate $C3 > C2$, which is the case in many implementations. Because our solution requires $log.(\#f + 1)$ repetitions, we see that its cost is

$$C2 * log.(\#f + 1).$$

Because the "improvement" saves one repetition, we see that its cost is

$$C3 * (log.(\#f + 1) - 1).$$

When[6] $C3 = 3/2 * C2$, we find:

$$C3 * (log.(\#f + 1) - 1) > C2 * log.(\#f + 1)$$
$$\equiv \quad \langle \text{ Assume } C3 = 3/2 * C2 \text{; by arithmetic omitted here } \rangle$$
$$\#f > 7$$

This calculation reveals that the "improvement" may actually be *less* efficient for arrays of more than a few elements. Although billed as an "early termination" version, it may actually terminate *later*! The moral is "keep it simple". Clever tricks in the name of efficiency often lead to *less* efficient (and more complicated) programs.

★   ★

Ex 10.16   Most published solutions of the Binary Search do not distinguish it from the "Binary Search for N". Even so, what do the programs look like? Are they correct? Do they work for the empty array? How disentangled are their developments? Do they assume f's ascendingness throughout? Do they "terminate early"? Do they have scattered additions and subtractions of 1 and if so why? Answer these questions for as many published solutions as you can.   □

Ex 10.17   In our choice of invariant for the Binary Search we replaced in R the constant $x + 1$ by fresh variable y. Instead replace the 1 by y, and complete the development. An alternative solution to the Binary Search will be revealed.   □

Ex 10.18   In our choice of invariant for the Binary Search we replaced in R the constant $x + 1$ by fresh variable y. Instead replace the 1 by y, maintain additional invariant "y is a power of 2", and complete the development. Yet another solution to the Binary Search will be revealed.   □

---

[6]We are thinking of an implementation in which the 2-way IF evaluates exactly one guard, and the 3-way IF evaluates 3/2 guard. In other words, the 3-way IF sometimes evaluates 1 guard, and sometimes evaluates 2. The average of 1 and 2 is 3/2.

Ex 10.19   Given $N \geq 0$, develop a program that determines whether N is the cube of some integer. The program should require a logarithmic number of repetitions.   □ ‚

Ex 10.20   Given character array f which contains a possibly empty sequence of non-blank characters followed by a possibly empty sequence of blanks. Specify and then develop a program that determines the number of non-blank characters in f. The program should require a logarithmic number of repetitions. (This exercise is due to C. Bron. Its solution shows a nice way to determine the length of a string that is stored in a known-length character array.)   □

Ex 10.21   The distances from Earth in light-years of $\#d \geq 0$ stars are stored in ascending array $d(k : 0 \leq k < \#d)$. Given N, develop a program that determines the number of stars more than N light-years from Earth. The program should require a logarithmic number of repetitions.   □

Ex 10.22   Solve: (due to W.H.J. Feijen)

> $\underline{\text{var}} \ N : int \quad \{N \geq 1\}$
> $; \underline{\text{var}} \ f(i : 0 \leq i \leq N) : int \quad \{f.0 < f.N\}$
> $; \underline{\text{var}} \ x : int$
> $; x : \ f.x < f.(x+1) \ \wedge \ 0 \leq x \ \wedge \ x < N$

The program should require a logarithmic number of repetitions. In this case we recommend that the solution be developed anew, and not by direct application of the Binary Search. Be sure that your program does not abort!   □

10.7   An example — Rearranging an array

We are asked to solve

> $\underline{\text{var}} \ f(i : x \leq i < y) : int \quad \{x \leq y \ \wedge \ bag.f = F\}$
> $; \underline{\text{var}} \ v : int$
> $; \underline{\text{var}} \ p : int$
> $; p, f : \ R \ \wedge \ bag.f = F$

where for R we are given

$$R: \quad x \leq p \leq y \; \wedge$$
$$(\forall i : x \leq i < p : f.i \leq v) \; \wedge$$
$$(\forall i : p \leq i < y : v < f.i).$$

Remark The conjunct $bag.f = F$ in the both the pre- and postcondition means that upon termination f must have the same bunch of values as it had initially. Thus the problem is one of rearranging the values in array f. Because of R, this rearrangement is one where the values in the first part of f, namely $f(i : x \leq i < p)$, must be at most (given) value v, and the values in the second part of f, namely $f(i : p \leq i < y)$, must exceed value v. □

★   ★

The conjunct $bag.f = F$ must hold upon termination. This can be accomplished by maintaining its invariance. One operation that maintains the invariance of $bag.f = F$ is a swap of a pair of elements of f. In light of this we propose maintaining the invariance of $bag.f = F$ by constraining the allowable operations on array f to swaps of pairs of f-elements. Thus we have transformed our problem into one of establishing

$$p, f : \quad R$$

where the only operations allowed on array f are swaps of pairs of f-elements.

Remark This is a standard trick. By constraining the allowable operations, we no longer have to drag along the expression $bag.f = F$, and hence no longer have to worry about maintaining its invariance. This trick is quite common in the development of programs that rearrange arrays. (Because array rearrangements, like the problem at hand, are often the central idea in sorting algorithms, such tricks are prevelant in the development of sorting algorithms too.) □

★   ★

Next we must find an invariant from postcondition R. The obvious candidate constants for replacement by fresh variables are x, y, and the two occurrences of p. We somewhat arbitrarily select one of the occurrences of p. Introducing fresh variable z, we arrive at invariant P, the conjunction of

$P0$: $x \leq p \leq y \ \wedge \ x \leq z \leq p$ (or $x \leq z \leq p \leq y$)
$P1a$: $(\forall i : x \leq i < z : f.i \leq v)$
$P1b$: $(\forall i : p \leq i < y : v < f.i)$

— an invariant which is broken up for ease of future manipulation, and the program

$$|[\text{var } z : int$$
$$; z, p := x, y \ \{ P0 \ \wedge \ P1a \ \wedge \ P1b \}$$
$$; \underline{\text{do}} \ z \neq p \ \rightarrow \ S \ \underline{\text{od}}$$
$$]|$$

Ex 10.23   If our invariant was found by replacing both occurrences of p in R by the same fresh variable, where in the development would we run into difficulties? Find out by trying it.   □

What remains is the development of loop body S.

$$\star \qquad\qquad \star$$

Loop body S must satisfy

$$\{ P \ \wedge \ z \neq p \} \ S \ \{ P \}.$$

It must also decrease some yet to be chosen bound function. Decrease of the bound function must eventually falsify $z \neq p$. Given that $z \leq p$ (from $P0$), the obvious choice is

bound t : $p - z$.

Bound function t can be decreased by either increasing z or by decreasing p. In light of the required invariance of $z \leq p$, we envision two possible operations:[7]

(a) $z := z + 1$ and
(b) $p := p - 1$.

---

[7]In other words, we avoid operations like $z := z + 2$ and $p := p - 2$, since they could easily falsify $z \leq p$.

Constraining ourselves to (a) for a moment, we note that since z is not named in $P1b$, (a) cannot falsify it. In light of $P0$, in particular $z \leq p$, and $z \neq p$, (a) trivially maintains $P0$ too. Thus, as far as (a) is concerned, we need only concern ourselves with $P1a$. We calculate:

$$wp.(z := z + 1).P1a$$
$\equiv$ ⟨ Definitions of $P1a$ and assignment ⟩
$$(\forall i : x \leq i < z + 1 : f.i \leq v)$$
$\equiv$ ⟨ Split range ⟩
$$(\forall i : x \leq i < z : f.i \leq v) \wedge (\forall i : i = z : f.i \leq v)$$
$\equiv$ ⟨ $P0 \wedge z \neq p$, hence $x \leq z < y$ (i.e. $f.z$ is defined);
    by the 1-point rule ⟩
$$(\forall i : x \leq i < z : f.i \leq v) \wedge f.z \leq v$$
$\equiv$ ⟨ Assuming $P1a$ ⟩
$$f.z \leq v$$

Thus, along with the fact that $z := z + 1$ maintains $P0 \wedge P1b$, we have derived:

$$\{P \wedge z \neq p \wedge f.z \leq v\}\ z := z + 1\ \{P\}.$$

Now we turn to (b), the assignment $p := p - 1$. By similar steps we would derive:

$$\{P \wedge z \neq p \wedge v < f.(p - 1)\}\ p := p - 1\ \{P\}.$$

Thus for S we consider building the following IF:

$$\textbf{if } f.z \leq v \quad\quad \to\ z := z + 1$$
$$\textbf{[]}\ v < f.(p - 1) \to\ p := p - 1$$
$$\textbf{fi}$$

Both alternatives maintain the invariant, and both decrease the bound function. The only problem is that this IF could abort if neither guard holds. Thus we consider expanding it to

$$\textbf{if } f.z \leq v \quad\quad\quad\quad\quad\quad \to\ z := z + 1$$
$$\textbf{[]}\ v < f.(p - 1) \quad\quad\quad\quad\quad \to\ p := p - 1$$
$$\textbf{[]}\ f.z > v \wedge v \geq f.(p - 1) \to\ SS$$
$$\textbf{fi}$$

where the new guard covers those cases that the first two omit, i.e. it is the negation of the disjunction of the first two guards. What remains is the development of SS.

★   ★

Program SS must maintain the invariance of P while decreasing t. From our previous calculations we know that $z := z+1$ maintains P if $f.z \leq v$, and $p := p-1$ maintains P if $f.(p-1) > v$. Note that the guard on SS guarantees exactly the reverse situation! So if $f.z$ and $f.(p-1)$ are swapped, we can either increase z or decrease p. Either will maintain the invariant. Either will decrease the bound function.

Actually, after such a swap, we can do both, since $f.z$ and $f.(p-1)$ cannot be the same element (since they differ in value: one exceeds v and the other is at most v). Thus for SS we propose:

$$SS: \quad f : swap(z, p-1) \; ; \; z, p := z+1, p-1$$

This completes the development. The entire solution is

```
|[var z : int
;z, p := x, y
;do z ≠ p →
      if f.z ≤ v                    → z := z + 1
      [] v < f.(p − 1)              → p := p − 1
      [] f.z > v  ∧  v ≥ f.(p − 1)  → f : swap(z, p − 1)
                                      ;z, p := z + 1, p − 1
      fi
   od
]|
```

Remark We aren't quite satisfied with the development of SS. It is a bit too informal for our taste. □

★   ★

Ex 10.24   Solve: (due to W.H.J. Feijen)

$$\underline{var} \; f(i : 0 \leq i < 2*N) : bool \quad \{0 \leq N \; \wedge \; bag.f = F\}$$
$$;f : \; bag.f = F \; \wedge \; (R0 \; \vee \; R1)$$

where we are given

$$R0: \ (\forall i : 0 \leq i < N : f.(2 * i))$$
$$R1: \ (\forall i : 0 \leq i < N : \neg f.(2 * i + 1))$$

This, of course, is another problem in array rearrangement. □

10.8 An example — The bounded linear search

Given $N \geq 0$ and boolean function $f(i : 0 \leq i < N)$ we are asked to determine the smallest natural solution of function $g(i : 0 \leq i \leq N)$, defined by

$$g.x \ \equiv \ x = N \ \vee \ f.x .$$

Thus we are asked to set x to N if f has no solution, and otherwise to the smallest solution of f. Since the first disjunct of g (i.e. $x = N$) guarantees that g has a solution, we are led to apply the Linear Search, to arrive at

$$x := 0 \ ; \ \underline{\text{do}} \ x \neq N \ \wedge \ \neg f.x \ \rightarrow \ x := x + 1 \ \underline{\text{od}}$$

This program has a little problem: its execution may evaluate an undefined expression. In particular it may evaluate $f.N$.

Remark   The general problem comes up when the precondition of an expression does not guarantee that all the expression's subexpressions are defined. In this case the precondition of the guard does not guarantee that all the guard's subexpressions are defined. In particular, $0 \leq x \leq N$ does not guarantee that $f.x$ is defined. At $x = N$ it is not. □

SOME SOLUTIONS TO THIS LITTLE PROBLEM

A common solution is to extend f with a so-called "sentinel", that is, to extend f with $f.N$ and to set $f.N \ \equiv \ true$. The sentinel guarantees that f has a smallest solution, thus allowing the Linear Search to be applied. Although this trick solves the problem, it easily leads to complications elsewhere. Such a trick is known as a "hack".[8]

---

[8]Consider a search of a linked list for some value. For *each* search a sentinel would have to be added. To add a sentinel, the entire list would have to be

Another common solution is to introduce a new logical operator *cand* (for "conditional and"), and define it by

$$X \ cand \ Y \ \equiv \ \underline{if} \ \neg X \ \rightarrow \ false$$
$$\Box \quad X \ \rightarrow \ Y$$
$$\underline{fi}$$

and recode the Bounded Linear Search as

$$x := M \ ; \ \underline{do} \ x \neq N \ cand \ \neg f.x \ \rightarrow \ x := x + 1 \ \underline{od}$$

The advantage of a *cand* is that its second "conjunct" is not evaluated if the first is *false*. Note that a conjunction can always be replaced by a *cand*.

The arguments against a *cand* (and its dual, the *cor*, which does not evaluate its second argument if the first is *true*), are that they change our logic to a three-valued one (with values *true*, *false*, and *undefined*), and that they lack all sorts of convenient properties. For example, neither is symmetric. The "conjunctions" in many well-known programming languages are in fact *cands*.[9]

⋆   ⋆

Yet another approach is to develop an entirely new solution for the Bounded Linear Search. We begin by specifying it as:

---

traversed. To avoid these traversals, a common trick is to add a variable that always "points" to the last element of the list. Besides the fact that there may be no last element, note that this extra variable's definition would have to be maintained by other operations on the list, for example by operations that add or delete elements, thus complicating these other operations. This leads us to the following definition of a "hack": a trick that solves one problem at the expense of generating many new ones!

[9]The "conjunction" in Modula-2 and "C" is actually a *cand*. Pascal's conjunction is not. In Modula-2 and C we must exercise extreme care so as not to appeal to invalid properties. For example, C's *cand* is written $A \ \&\& \ B$, which in general is not equal to $B \ \&\& \ A$. On a related topic, most implementations of C are inconsistent in the way they treat undefined expressions. They typically yield meaningless values for "array subscript out-of-range", but abort on "divide by 0". We also point out that C does not include booleans. Instead, integers are employed, with *false* denoted by 0, and *true* denoted by any non-zero value. A possible explanation as to why booleans are not included may be that C is 20 years old, and at the time we did not know how to calculate our programs. On the other hand, the designers of many of its predecessors, for example ALGOL 60, had already seen the need for booleans!

Given $N \geq 0$ and boolean function $f(i : 0 \leq i < N)$, we are asked to assign to x a value that will establish:

$$R: \quad 0 \leq x \leq N \ \land \ (x = N \ \lor \ f.x) \ \land \ (\forall i : 0 \leq i < x : \neg f.i).$$

Towards choosing an invariant we see that the third conjunct can be established by $x := 0$, the second by $x := N$, and the first by either $x := 0$ or $x := N$.

If we delete a conjunct it must be the second or third, since there is no way to establish both at once. If we delete the second we reintroduce the problem of the evaluation of $f.N$. If we delete the third we end up with a quantification in the guard. We might remove this quantification by introducing additional invariant

$$z \ \equiv \ (\forall i : 0 \leq i < x : \neg f.i)$$

but how would we establish this *and* establish the other two conjuncts? Thus deleting the third returns us to our original problem.

Because we find no invariant by deleting a conjunct, we are led to consider replacing constants by fresh variables. We can easily truthify the first and third conjuncts by $x := 0$. Because $x := 0$ does not truthify the second conjunct, we consider "relaxing" the second conjunct by replacing its occurrences of constant x by a fresh variable. We must replace both occurrences of x: the first because we cannot guarantee the validity of $0 = N$, and the second because we cannot guarantee the validity of $f.0$. This leads us to consider invariant

$$0 \leq x \leq N \ \land \ (m = N \ \lor \ f.m) \ \land \ (\forall i : 0 \leq i < x : \neg f.i)$$
$$\land \ x \leq m \leq N$$

where m is the fresh variable. For ease of future reference we rearrange this into

$$P0 : \ 0 \leq x \leq m \leq N$$
$$P1 : \ m = N \ \lor \ f.m$$
$$P2 : \ (\forall i : 0 \leq i < x : \neg f.i)$$

to arrive at the program

```
|[var m : int
;x, m := 0, N  {P0 ∧ P1 ∧ P2}
;do m ≠ x → S od
 {P0 ∧ P1 ∧ P2 ∧ m = x, hence R}
]|
```

What remains is the development of S.

⋆   ⋆

S must decrease $m - x$. This can be accomplished by either increasing x or decreasing m.

Looking at $P2$ we see that x can safely be increased by 1 if $\neg f.x$ holds. That $\neg f.x$ is defined follows from $P0$ and the guard of the repetition, which together guarantee $0 \leq x < N$. These observations lead us to consider for S the program

```
if ¬f.x → x := x + 1
 []   f.x → SS
fi
```

where the second guarded command has been introduced to handle the case that the first does not handle.

What remains is the development of SS which must maintain the invariants and must also decrease $m - x$. Because of the initial truth of $f.x$, and our prior observation that $\neg f.x$ is necessary for an increase of x, we see that SS must decrease $m - x$ via a decrease of m.

An assignment to m must also maintain $P1$. A quick glance at $P1$ shows that, because of the guard $f.x$, SS can maintain $P1$ via the assignment $m := x$. This assignment maintains $P1$ by truthifying $P1$'s second disjunct. It must also maintain $P0$ and $P2$. It clearly maintains $P0$, and because m does not occur in $P2$, $P2$ is maintained as well.

Our final obligation is to show that $m := x$ decreases $m - x$. That this is so follows from $P0$ and the guard of the repetition, which together guarantee that $x < m$.

This completes the development.

⋆   ⋆

In summary, given $N \geq 0$ and given boolean function $f(i : 0 \leq i < N)$, the Bounded Linear Search:

```
|[var m : int
;x, m := 0, N
;do m ≠ x →
    if ¬f.x → x := x + 1
    ▯   f.x → m := x
    fi
od
]|
```

sets x to the smallest natural solution of $i : i = N \lor f.i$.

In other words, it establishes $x = N$ when $f(k : 0 \leq k < N)$ has no solution, otherwise it sets x to the smallest solution of f.

APPLYING THE BOUNDED LINEAR SEARCH, AN EXAMPLE

Given natural BR and BC, and boolean matrix

$$B(i, j : 0 \leq i < BR \land 0 \leq j < BC),$$

we are asked to print the number of the first all-true row of B if there is one, and otherwise are asked to print "No all-true row". In $B.i.j$, i is the row number.

★   ★

Since there may not be an all-true row, we are led to apply the Bounded Linear Search. Defining function $g.i$ by

$$g.i \equiv \text{"row } i \text{ is all-true"} \qquad \text{for } 0 \leq i < BR,$$

we immediately propose the program

```
|[var x : int
;S : Set x to the smallest natural solution of i : i = BR ∨ g.i
;if x = BR → print."No all-true row"
 ▯ x ≠ BR → print.x
 fi
]|
```

Since the Bounded Linear Search

sets x to the smallest natural solution $i : i = N \lor f.i$

we see that S is simply a Bounded Linear Search with

$$
\begin{array}{lll}
N & \text{replaced by} & BR \\
f & \text{replaced by} & g\,.
\end{array}
$$

In other words, for S we have arrived at

```
|[var m : int
;x, m := 0, BR
;do m ≠ x →
      if ¬g.x → x := x + 1
      ▯  g.x → m := x
      fi
  od
]|
```

What remains is the elaboration of function g, for which we propose:

$$
\begin{array}{ll}
 & g.i \\
\equiv & \langle\, \text{Definition of } g \,\rangle \\
 & \text{row } i \text{ is all-true} \\
\equiv & \langle\, \text{Definition of an all-true row} \,\rangle \\
 & (\forall k : 0 \le k < BC : B.i.k)
\end{array}
$$

Substituting this expression for the occurrences of g in our program, however, puts quantifications into the guards. These can be eliminated in a number of steps. First we replace the body of S by

```
|[var c : bool
;Establish c ≡ g.x
;if ¬c → x := x + 1
 ▯  c → m := x
 fi
]|
```

— in other words, with the aid of fresh variable c we remove the occurrences of g from the guards. What remains is a solution to "Establish $c \equiv g.x$", which can be nicely solved as

||[**var** $z : int$
;$S1$: Set z = smallest natural solution of i : $i = BC \lor \neg B.x.i$
;$c := z = BC$
]|

Program $S1$, in turn, is simply a Bounded Linear Search with

x	replaced by	z
N	replaced by	BC
$f.x$	replaced by	$\neg B.x.z$.

This completes the development. The entire solution is simply a nested application of the Bounded Linear Search.

Remark This problem was the subject of an article in the Communications of the ACM (in 1987) in which its author claimed that additional programming language features were required in order to arrive at a "clean" solution. As we have seen, it can be nicely solved, without additional features, by a nested application of the Bounded Linear Search.[10] □

⋆ ⋆

Ex 10.25 Given integer G and integer array $g(k : 0 \le k < \#g)$, $\#g \ge 0$, develop a program that sets boolean z to the truth of "G occurs in g". Apply the Bounded Linear Search. □

Ex 10.26 The number of rabbits on an island at month x, for $0 \le x < 100$ is given by $R.x$. The number of foxes on an island at month x, for $0 \le x < 100$ is given by $F.x$. The rabbits are *stable* at month x, for $0 \le x < 99$, when $R.x = R.(x+1)$, and the foxes are stable at month x, for $0 \le x < 99$, when $F.x = F.(x+1)$.

Desired is a program that prints the number of the earliest month when both rabbits and foxes are stable, or if no such month exists, prints "rabbits (and foxes) are never stable". Apply the Bounded Linear Search. □

---

[10]That article presented a number of "solutions", at least one of which was incorrect, and generated a lot of comments, mostly about the features of this or that programming language. Since the problem boiled down to a nested application of the Bounded Linear Search, a discussion about programming probably would have been more fruitful than a discussion about various programming language features!

Ex 10.27 Given that functions R and F are defined by

$$R.x = \underline{\text{if }} x = 0 \;\rightarrow\; R0$$
$$ \square \;\; x > 0 \;\rightarrow\; R.(x-1) * (a - b * F.(x-1))$$
$$ \underline{\text{fi}}$$

$$F.x = \underline{\text{if }} x = 0 \;\rightarrow\; F0$$
$$ \square \;\; x > 0 \;\rightarrow\; F.(x-1) * (c - d * R.(x-1))$$
$$ \underline{\text{fi}}$$

where $R0$, a, b, $F0$, c, and d are given integer constants, eliminate the occurrences of R and F from your solution to the previous exercise. (This exercise has nothing to do with the Bounded Linear Search). □

11

Mainly on recursion

11.0   Introduction

Many functions are defined recursively. Consider exponentiation: for integer x and natural y, we have

$$x^y = \text{if } y = 0 \rightarrow 1$$
$$\quad \text{[] } y \neq 0 \rightarrow x * x^{y-1}$$
$$\underline{\text{fi}}$$

In other words, exponentiation is defined recursively.

There are many classes of recursively defined functions, and we are often asked to develop programs to evaluate them. Here we will restrict ourselves to functions having the following shape:

$$H.x = \text{if } \neg b.x \rightarrow c.x$$
$$\quad \text{[] } b.x \rightarrow H.(d.x)$$
$$\underline{\text{fi}}$$

A lot of problems boil down to evaluating functions of this shape. Although not apparent at this point, exponentiation has this shape. Other examples include reversing sequences (lists), tree traversals, polynomial evaluation, searching, sorting, and many more. Once we have a program that evaluates H, we will be able to apply it in all[0] of these instances.

In this chapter we present a program for evaluating H. Afterwards we apply it to a number of examples. In most examples, the functions we will be asked to evaluate will not have H's shape. In these instances, we will first have to transform the problem into one of evaluating a (more general) function that does have H's shape.

---

[0]Well, almost all!

11.1   The general solution

We are given value X and are asked to evaluate $H.X$. When H is allowed in expressions (i.e. in programs), we have nothing to do. When it is not, we simply use the following program:[1]

```
|[var x : appropriate type
 ;x := X  {inv P :  H.x = H.X }
 ;do b.x  →  x := d.x  od
 {P ∧ ¬b.x,  hence c.x = H.X}
]|
```

The postcondition was obtained as follows:

$$
\begin{array}{ll}
& P \\
\equiv & \quad \langle\,\text{Definition of } P\,\rangle \\
& H.x = H.X \\
\equiv & \quad \langle\,\text{Using } \neg b.x\,,\ \text{apply } H\,\rangle \\
& c.x = H.X
\end{array}
$$

In other words, upon termination the value of $H.X$ is $c.x$. To set v, say, to the value of $H.X$, we need only follow the program by the assignment

$$v := c.x\,.$$

Since we don't want H in our program, we also require that

Restriction 0: H does not occur in function c.

Our last task is to guarantee termination, which boils down to finding an integer function that is decreased by each application of H's definition, and that is bounded from below by 0. In other words, for any x in H's domain, there must be some integer function $t.x$ that satisfies:

Restriction 1: $b.x \Rightarrow t.(d.x) < t.x$ (Progress)
Restriction 2: $b.x \Rightarrow t.x > 0$ (Boundedness)

The functions that have H's shape and that satisfy these three restrictions are called *tail-recursive*. Observe that we can evaluate *any* tail-recursive function by simply substituting into this program.

---

[1]We simply present this program. Its development is left as an exercise.

Remark   Although we have not mentioned it, we assume that H makes sense. In other words, for any x such that $H.x$ is defined, we assume that

> $b.x$ is defined,
> $\neg b.x$ implies that $c.x$ is defined and has appropriate type, and
> $b.x$ implies that $H.(d.x)$ is defined and has appropriate type.

From now on we leave these assumptions implicit.   □

We turn to some examples.

11.2   An example — The sum of digits

For natural x, function f is defined by

$$f.x = \underline{\text{if }} x = 0 \rightarrow 0$$
$$ \square \; x \neq 0 \rightarrow x \bmod 10 + f.(x \bmod 10)$$
$$ \underline{\text{fi}}$$

Given natural X, we are asked to determine the value of $f.X$.

Remark   Interpreting f, $f.X$ is the sum of the digits of the decimal representation of X.   □

⋆   ⋆

We begin by observing that f does not have H's shape. In other words, it is not tail-recursive. In particular, $f.x$ does not have the same shape as $x \bmod 10 + f.(x \bmod 10)$. Observe, however, that both are instances of an expression of shape $y + f.z$. The second clearly has this shape. As for the first, defining

$$H.y.z = y + f.z \qquad \text{for natural } y \text{ and } z,$$

notice that

$$H.0.x = f.x. \tag{0}$$

Therefore, evaluating $f.x$ boils down to evaluating $H.0.x$. We can evaluate $H.0.x$ using our program for evaluating tail-recursive functions, provided that we can construct a tail-recursive definition for H. Towards this end, we observe that

$$
\begin{aligned}
& H.y.z \\
= \quad & \langle\, \text{Definition of } H \,\rangle \\
& y + f.z
\end{aligned}
$$

Based on the definition of f, we continue in two cases, namely the case when $z = 0$, and the case when $z \neq 0$. When $z = 0$, we find:

$$
\begin{aligned}
& y + f.z \\
= \quad & \langle\, \text{Using } z = 0,\ \text{apply } f \,\rangle \\
& y + 0 \\
= \quad & \langle\, \text{Arithmetic} \,\rangle \\
& y
\end{aligned}
$$

When $z \neq 0$, we find:

$$
\begin{aligned}
& y + f.z \\
= \quad & \langle\, \text{Using } z \neq 0,\ \text{apply } f \,\rangle \\
& y + (z \ mod \ 10 + f.(z \ div \ 10)) \\
= \quad & \langle\, + \text{ is associative} \,\rangle \\
& (y + z \ mod \ 10) + f.(z \ div \ 10)) \\
= \quad & \langle\, \text{Definition of } H \,\rangle \\
& H.(y + z \ mod \ 10).(z \ div \ 10)
\end{aligned}
$$

With natural y and z what we have derived is

$$
\begin{aligned}
H.y.z. = \ \underline{\text{if}}\ & z = 0\ \rightarrow\ y \\
\ \square\ & z \neq 0\ \rightarrow\ H.(y + z \ mod \ 10).(z \ div \ 10) \\
\underline{\text{fi}}\ &
\end{aligned}
$$

Notice that H is tail-recursive. In particular, the definition is exhaustive, i.e. the guards cover all cases, and the three restrictions on H are met, in this instance:

Restriction 0: H does not occur in y,

and for any natural z:

Restriction 1: $z \neq 0 \ \Rightarrow\ z \ div \ 10 < z$ (Progress)
Restriction 2: $z \neq 0 \ \Rightarrow\ z > 0$ (Boundedness)

As a result, we can evaluate H by substituting it into our program for evaluating tail-recursive functions. Our interest, of course, is in evaluating $f.X$ which, by (0), boils down to evaluating $H.0.X$. By direct substitution into our program for evaluating tail-recursive functions, we arrive at the following program:

$$
\begin{aligned}
&\|[\underline{\text{var}}\ y, z : natural \\
&;y, z := 0, X \quad \{P:\ H.y.z = H.0.X\} \\
&;\underline{\text{do}}\ z \neq 0\ \rightarrow\ y, z := y + z\ mod\ 10, z\ div\ 10\ \underline{\text{od}} \\
&\quad\{P\ \wedge\ z = 0,\ hence\ y = f.X\} \\
&]|
\end{aligned}
$$

In other words, the program establishes $y = f.X$. We have solved our problem of evaluating $f.X$. This completes the development.

★   ★

When given a tail-recursive function, we simply apply our program for evaluating such functions. When asked to evaluate a function that is not tail-recursive, we must first transform the problem into one of evaluating a more general function that is tail-recursive. Towards choosing a more general function, we are inspired by the shape of the function we are given.

11.3   An example — Exponentiation

For integer x and natural y, x^y is defined by

$$
\begin{aligned}
x^y = &\underline{\text{if}}\ y = 0\ \rightarrow\ 1 \\
&\underline{\text{[}}\ y \neq 0\ \rightarrow\ x * x^{y-1} \\
&\underline{\text{fi}}
\end{aligned}
$$

Given integer X and natural Y, we are asked to evaluate X^Y.

We observe that x^y is not tail-recursive. In particular, x^y does not have the same shape as $x * x^{y-1}$. Observe, however, that both expressions have shape $a * b^c$. This is clearly true of the second. As for the first, defining

$$H.a.b.c = a * b^c \qquad \text{for integers } a,\ b \text{ and natural } c,$$

notice that

$$H.1.x.y = x^y .$$ (0)

Therefore, evaluating x^y boils down to evaluating $H.1.x.y$. We can evaluate $H.1.x.y$ using our program for evaluating tail-recursive functions, provided that we can construct a tail-recursive definition for H. Towards this end, we observe that

$$\begin{array}{ll} & H.a.b.c \\ = & \quad \langle \text{ Definition of } H \rangle \\ & a * b^c \end{array}$$

Based on the definition of b^c, we continue in two cases, namely the case when $c = 0$, and the case when $c \neq 0$. When $c = 0$, we find:

$$\begin{array}{ll} & a * b^c \\ = & \quad \langle \text{ Using } c = 0, \text{ apply } b^c \rangle \\ & a * 1 \\ = & \quad \langle \text{ Arithmetic} \rangle \\ & a \end{array}$$

When $c \neq 0$, we find:

$$\begin{array}{ll} & a * b^c \\ = & \quad \langle \text{ Using } c \neq 0, \text{ apply } b^c \rangle \\ & a * (b * b^{c-1}) \\ = & \quad \langle * \text{ is associative} \rangle \\ & (a * b) * b^{c-1} \\ = & \quad \langle \text{ Definition of } H \rangle \\ & H.(a * b).b.(c - 1) \end{array}$$

With integers a and b, and natural c, what we have derived is

$$\begin{array}{ll} H.a.b.c = & \underline{\text{if }} c = 0 \; \rightarrow \; a \\ & \;\; \underline{\mathbb{0}} \; c \neq 0 \; \rightarrow \; H.(a * b).b.(c - 1) \\ & \;\; \underline{\text{fi}} \end{array}$$

Notice that H is tail-recursive. In particular it is exhaustive, c is decreased by each application, and c is bounded from below by 0.

Our interest is in evaluating X^Y which, by (0), boils down to evaluating $H.1.X.Y$. By direct substitution into our program for evaluating tail-recursive functions, we arrive at the following program:

```
|[var a, b : int ; var c : natural
;a, b, c := 1, X, Y  {P :  H.a.b.c = H.1.X.Y }
;do c ≠ 0 → a, b, c := a * b, b, c − 1 od
 {a = X^Y}
]|
```

This completes the development.

AN IMPROVEMENT IN EXPONENTIATION

In our solution to exponentiation, progress is made by decreasing c by 1. A larger decrease of c would yield a more efficient program. Our aim is to find a larger decrease.

One way to decrease c by more than 1 is to decrease it by 2 or 3 or more. Recall, however, that c must remain natural, and these decreases may violate this. Since our interest is constrained to decreasing c when it is positive, we observe that c can be safely decreased, when it is positive, by dividing it by any integer greater than 1. The simplest case is division by 2, which we will adopt. Our problem has reduced to solving

$$H.a.b.c = H.E.F.(c \ div \ 2) \qquad \text{for some } E \text{ and } F.$$

In other words, we need a way to rewrite $H.a.b.c$ *and* divide c by 2. Because $H.a.b.c = a * b^c$, we massage the righthand side heading for an expression of shape $a * b^c$:

$$H.E.F.(c \ div \ 2)$$
$=$ 〈 Definition of H 〉
$$E * F^{c \ div \ 2}$$
$=$ 〈 Choose $F = b^2$, towards getting b^c 〉
$$E * (b^2)^{c \ div \ 2}$$
$=$ 〈 Arithmetic 〉
$$E * b^{2*(c \ div \ 2)}$$
$=$ 〈 Further assume that c is even, hence $2 * (c \ div \ 2) = c$ 〉
$$E * b^c$$
$=$ 〈 Choose $E = a$ 〉
$$a * b^c$$
$=$ 〈 Definition of H 〉
$$H.a.b.c$$

What we have discovered is that

$H.a.b.c = H.a.(b^2).(c \; div \; 2)$ providing c is even.

Incorporating this into H we get

$$H.a.b.c = \text{if } c = 0 \;\rightarrow\; a$$
$$\quad\quad\quad [\!] \; c \neq 0 \;\rightarrow$$
$$\quad\quad\quad\quad\quad \text{if } even.c \;\rightarrow\; H.a.(b^2).(c \; div \; 2)$$
$$\quad\quad\quad\quad\quad [\!] \; true \quad\rightarrow\; H.(a*b).b.(c-1)$$
$$\quad\quad\quad\quad\quad \text{fi}$$
$$\quad\quad\quad \text{fi}$$

By direct substitution into our program for evaluating tail-recursive functions, we arrive at:

$$|[\underline{\text{var}} \; a, b : int \;\; ; \underline{\text{var}} \; c : natural$$
$$; a, b, c := 1, X, Y \;\; \{P : \; H.a.b.c = H.1.X.Y \}$$
$$; \underline{\text{do}} \; c \neq 0 \;\rightarrow$$
$$\quad\quad \text{if } even.c \;\rightarrow\; a, b, c := a, b^2, c \; div \; 2$$
$$\quad\quad [\!] \; true \quad\rightarrow\; a, b, c := a * b, b, c - 1$$
$$\quad\quad \text{fi}$$
$$\underline{\text{od}}$$
$$\{ a = X^Y \}$$
$$]|$$

where the assignments can be simplified a little, and the guard equal to *true* can be safely strengthened to $\neg even.c$ (or $odd.c$). In fact, it *should* be strengthened, otherwise the program is no improvement over our first (and simpler) solution!

Also notice, by the equivalence between a single and a multiple guarded command repetition, that this program can be nicely captured as

$$|[\underline{\text{var}} \; a, b : int \;\; ; \underline{\text{var}} \; c : natural$$
$$; a, b, c := 1, X, Y$$
$$; \underline{\text{do}} \; c \neq 0 \;\wedge\; even.c \;\rightarrow\; a, b, c := a, b^2, c \; div \; 2$$
$$\quad\quad [\!] \;\; c \neq 0 \;\wedge\; odd.c \;\;\rightarrow\; a, b, c := a * b, b, c - 1$$
$$\quad\quad \underline{\text{od}}$$
$$\{ a = X^Y \}$$
$$]|$$

Remark   From now on we will combine these two steps. In other words, we will immediately write the multiple guarded command repetition, when there is one to be written.   □

A FURTHER IMPROVEMENT IN EXPONENTIATION

Observing that we can safely halve an even number, we might consider halving c, when odd, by the assignment $c := (c-1)$ *div* 2. When c is odd, $c-1$ is even and can be safely halved. The calculation in this case, and we will not show it, would yield

$$H.a.b.c = H.(a*b).(b^2).((c-1) \ div \ 2) \qquad \text{providing } c \text{ is odd} \\ \text{and positive.}$$

Direct substitution into our program for evaluating tail-recursive functions yields the program:

```
|[ var a, b : int  ; var c : natural
 ; a, b, c := 1, X, Y
 ; do  c ≠ 0 ∧ even.c  →  a, b, c := a, b², c div 2
    []  c ≠ 0 ∧ odd.c   →  a, b, c := a * b, b², (c − 1) div 2
    od
    { a = Xʸ }
]|
```

On account of the fact that c is halved each repetition, a tighter bound function is *log.c*, which is decreased by 1 each repetition. Since initially $c = Y$, this program requires *log.Y* repetitions. This is a remarkable improvement over our first solution, which requires Y. Indeed, for $Y = 1000$ our first solution requires 1000 repetitions, while this program requires only 10!

Remark   Our second solution was logarithmic too, although this is not as easy to see.   □

11.4   Introducing four new types

SEQUENCES

We admit variables of type *sequence*, which we denote by *seq* in declarations, as in

var X : *seq*   or   var X : *seq of int* .

We denote the number of elements in sequence X by $\#X$, and give this operator higher binding power than function application. A sequence of length 0 is called the *empty sequence* and is denoted by ϵ. Catenation of sequences is denoted by $\sim$, as in $X \sim Y$. Catenation is associative and has unit ϵ. It is not symmetric. We denote the sequence containing 1 element by that element enclosed in square-brackets. For example, we denote the sequence containing (only) element x by $[x]$.

BINARY TREES

We also admit variables of type *binary tree*, which we denote by *bintree* in declarations, as in

> <u>var</u> $X : bintree$ or   <u>var</u> $X : bintree\ of\ int$.

The empty binary tree is denoted by $\triangle$. Non-empty binary tree t is the triple

> $(t.l\,,\ t.v\,,\ t.r)$

where $t.l$ and $t.r$ are binary trees, called the left- and right- subtrees of t, respectively, and $t.v$ is some value associated with t. The type of $t.v$ comes from the declaration. For example, in

> <u>var</u> $t : bintree\ of\ bool$

$t.v$ is a boolean. When irrelevant we omit $t.v$'s type.

SETS

We admit variables of type *set*, which we denote by *set* in declarations, as in

> <u>var</u> $X : set$ or   <u>var</u> $X : set\ of\ int$.

We denote the number of elements in set X by $\#X$. The empty set is denoted by $\emptyset$. Set union, denoted by $\cup$, has unit $\emptyset$, and is symmetric, associative and idempotent. We denote the set containing 1 element by that element enclosed in braces. For example, we denote the set containing (only) element x by $\{x\}$.

BAGS

Although we will not use them, we admit variables of type *bag*, which we denote by *bag* in declarations, as in

<u>var</u> $X : bag$ or   <u>var</u> $X : bag\ of\ int$.

The number of elements in a bag X is $\#X$. The empty bag is denoted by $\emptyset$. Bag union, denoted by $\cup$, has unit $\emptyset$, and is symmetric and associative. It is not idempotent. We denote the bag containing 1 element by that element enclosed in braces. For example, we denote the bag containing (only) element x by $\{x\}$.[2]

11.5   An example — Reversing a sequence (and the importance of good notation)

Function *rev* on sequences is given by

$$rev.X = \underline{if}\ X = \epsilon\ \rightarrow\ \epsilon$$
$$\quad\quad\quad \Box\ X \neq \epsilon\ \rightarrow\ \text{Letting}\ X = [z] \sim Z :$$
$$\quad\quad\quad\quad\quad\quad\quad\quad rev.Z \sim [z]$$
$$\quad\ \underline{fi}$$

Given sequence X we are asked to evaluate $rev.X$.

"Letting $X = [z] \sim Z$" is simply a way to indicate that z is the first element and Z is the rest, of (non-empty) sequence X.

Remark   One advantage of this notation is that it is very general. We can write "Letting $X = Z \sim [z]$" to indicate that z is X's last element, and so on.

An alternative approach would be to use functions, for example, *first.X*, *rest.X*, and *last.X*, but notice that a new function must be introduced for every purpose.

---

[2]Informally, a bag is a set in which duplicates are allowed (which is why bag union is not idempotent). For this reason, bags are sometimes called multi-sets, although it has been suggested that sets be called uni-bags.

Another approach would be to use subscripts. For example, $X.0$ would be the first element, and $X.(\#X - 1)$ would be the last element, of (non-empty) sequence X. For another example, the post-condition of a program that given sequence X, arbitrarily assigns to sequences Y and Z to establish $X = Y \sim Z$, would have to be written as something like

$$(\exists k : 0 \leq k \leq \#X : Y = X(i : 0 \leq i < k) \,\wedge \\ Z = X(i : k \leq i < \#X)).$$

Compared to $X = Y \sim Z$, this is quite baroque. A further disadvantage, perhaps more important, is that it would be quite cumbersome to drag through calculations![3]

In many instances, it is the choice of notation that is the difference between a solution and no solution at all. It is for this reason that the design of good notations is a major part of programming.[4] □

$$\star \qquad\qquad \star$$

Returning to our problem of reversing a sequence, notice that *rev* is not tail-recursive. Observe, however, that both $rev.X$ and $rev.Z \sim [z]$ are instances of an expression of shape $rev.A \sim B$. In particular, defining

$$H.A.B = rev.A \sim B \qquad \text{for sequences } A \text{ and } B,$$

notice that

$$H.X.\epsilon = rev.X. \tag{0}$$

Therefore, evaluating $rev.X$ boils down to evaluating $H.X.\epsilon$. Towards finding a tail-recursive definition for H, we observe that

$$\begin{aligned}
& H.A.B \\
= \quad & \langle \text{ Definition of } H \,\rangle \\
& rev.A \sim B
\end{aligned}$$

---

[3]The malady characterized by the inappropriate use of subscripting is known as *indexitis* — a name due to D. Gries and W.H.J. Feijen.

[4]A special case of notation design is programming language design. Many programming language designers do not seem to realize the importance of good (i.e. simple and expressive) notation. As a result, many programming languages are complicated, unexpressive, and awkward to use. This is a shame, and also a burden to the programmers who must use these languages.

We continue in two cases based on the definition of rev. When $A = \epsilon$, we find:

$$rev.A \sim B$$
$$= \quad \langle \text{Using } A = \epsilon, \text{ apply } rev \text{ ; Property of catenation} \rangle$$
$$B$$

When $A \neq \epsilon$, we find:

$$rev.A \sim B$$
$$= \quad \langle \text{Using } A \neq \epsilon, \text{ letting } A = [z] \sim Z, \text{ apply } rev \rangle$$
$$(rev.Z \sim [z]) \sim B$$
$$= \quad \langle \text{Catenation is associative} \rangle$$
$$rev.Z \sim ([z] \sim B)$$
$$= \quad \langle \text{Definition of } H \rangle$$
$$H.Z.([z] \sim B)$$

What we have derived is:

$$H.A.B = \text{if } A = \epsilon \rightarrow B$$
$$\qquad \llbracket \ A \neq \epsilon \rightarrow \text{Letting } A = [z] \sim Z: \quad H.Z.([z] \sim B)$$
$$\qquad \underline{\text{fi}}$$

Notice that H is tail recursive. Indeed, it makes progress by decreasing $\#A$. Our interest is in evaluating $rev.X$ which, by (0), boils down to evaluating $H.X.\epsilon$. By direct substitution into our program for evaluating tail-recursive functions, we arrive at the following program:

$$\lVert [\underline{\text{var}} \ A, B : seq$$
$$; A, B := X, \epsilon \ \{P: \ H.A.B = H.X.\epsilon\}$$
$$; \underline{\text{do}} \ A \neq \epsilon \rightarrow \text{Letting } A = [z] \sim Z: \quad A, B := Z, [z] \sim B \ \underline{\text{od}}$$
$$\{B = rev.X\}$$
$$]\rvert$$

This completes the development.

ON THE IMPORTANCE OF GOOD NOTATION

Many programmers find the problem of reversing a linked list tricky. When asked, they aren't quite sure whether their program will work for the empty list or for lists of length 1. Their difficulties usually come from the fact that they confuse the notion of a list (or sequence) with a (possible) *implementation* using pointers, coupled with the fact that they have been taught to reason about pointers using *pictures*.

One reason for their difficulties is that pictures are usually overspecific, and thus misleading. For example, how do we draw a picture of an angle? Recall that an angle can be acute, right, or obtuse. A picture would reflect only one of these. Were we to reason from such a picture, we would probably be misled.

For another example, a picture of a list will probably reflect the non-empty list only, which is misleading. The program obtained from reasoning about such a picture is unlikely to handle the other case. One way out is to draw two pictures, one of the empty list and the other of the non-empty list. The resulting program, however, is likely to contain an avoidable case-analysis.

Yet another disadvantage of pictures — and for us this is a major one — is that pictures are awkward to calculate with. Combining these observations, we see that pictures invite many difficulties. A notation with so many shortcomings is best avoided.

Using sequence notation, the development was entirely straightforward, even trivial. If at this point we find that our sequences are to be implemented using pointers, our remaining task would simply be a translation of our sequence operations into the equivalent pointer operations. This would be a separate step, and would have nothing to do with the algorithm.

Translating the sequence operations into their equivalent pointer operations in some programming language is left as an exercise. (Because most famous programming languages (unfortunately) do not include multiple assignments, it might be wise to replace the multiple assignments by simple assignments first).

$$\star \qquad\qquad \star$$

Remark   Alternative definitions of *rev* include

$$rev.X = \underline{if}\ X = \epsilon \rightarrow \epsilon$$
$$[]\ X \neq \epsilon \rightarrow \text{Letting}\ X = Z \sim [z]:\ [z] \sim rev.Z$$
$$\underline{fi}$$

and

$$rev.X = \underline{if}\ \#X < 2 \rightarrow X$$
$$[]\ \#X \geq 2 \rightarrow \text{Letting}\ X = [a] \sim B \sim [c]:$$
$$[c] \sim rev.B \sim [a]$$
$$\underline{fi}$$

The developments of the two programs that result from these two definitions are left as exercises (at chapter end). The first can be translated to a program for reversing linked lists that are linked in reverse, and the second can be translated into a program that reverses an array. Our original definition, along with these two alternatives, is actually derived from the "official" definition, namely:

$$rev.X = \underline{if}\ X = \epsilon \qquad \rightarrow \epsilon$$
$$\hphantom{rev.X = \underline{if}\ } \square\ X = [x] \qquad \rightarrow [x]$$
$$\hphantom{rev.X = \underline{if}\ } \square\ X = Y \sim Z \rightarrow rev.Z \sim rev.Y$$
$$\hphantom{rev.X = \ } \underline{fi}$$

We leave as an exercise the derivation of the other definitions from this "official" one. □

11.6 An example — The post-order of a binary tree

There are a number of sequences defined on binary trees. Three famous ones include the *pre-order*, which is defined on binary tree t by

$$pr.t = \underline{if}\ t = \triangle \rightarrow \epsilon$$
$$\hphantom{pr.t = \underline{if}\ } \square\ t \neq \triangle \rightarrow [t.v] \sim pr.(t.l) \sim pr.(t.r)$$
$$\hphantom{pr.t = \ } \underline{fi}$$

the *in-order*, which is defined by

$$in.t = \underline{if}\ t = \triangle \rightarrow \epsilon$$
$$\hphantom{in.t = \underline{if}\ } \square\ t \neq \triangle \rightarrow in.(t.l) \sim [t.v] \sim in.(t.r)$$
$$\hphantom{in.t = \ } \underline{fi}$$

and the *post-order*, which is defined by

$$po.t = \underline{if}\ t = \triangle \rightarrow \epsilon$$
$$\hphantom{po.t = \underline{if}\ } \square\ t \neq \triangle \rightarrow po.(t.l) \sim po.(t.r) \sim [t.v]$$
$$\hphantom{po.t = \ } \underline{fi}$$

We will not develop the first two, but will develop a program to evaluate the last. In particular, given binary tree t, we are asked to evaluate $po.t$.

★   ★

We begin by observing that po, on account of the two occurrences of po in its righthand side, is not tail-recursive. Inspired by the definition of po, we consider defining

$$H.a.b.X = po.a \sim po.b \sim X \qquad \text{for binary trees } a, b,$$
$$\text{and sequence } X.$$

Notice that

$$H.\triangle.t.\epsilon = po.t.$$

Towards finding a tail-recursive definition of H, we observe that

$$H.a.b.X$$
$$= \qquad \langle \text{Definition of } H \rangle$$
$$po.a \sim po.b \sim X$$

We continue in a number of cases. When $a = \triangle$ and $b = \triangle$, we find:

$$po.a \sim po.b \sim X$$
$$= \qquad \langle \text{Using } a = \triangle \text{ and } b = \triangle \rangle$$
$$po.\triangle \sim po.\triangle \sim X$$
$$= \qquad \langle \text{Definition of } po, \text{ twice} \rangle$$
$$\epsilon \sim \epsilon \sim X$$
$$= \qquad \langle \text{Properties of catenation} \rangle$$
$$X$$

When $b \neq \triangle$, we find:

$$po.a \sim po.b \sim X$$
$$= \qquad \langle \text{Using } b \neq \triangle, \text{ apply } po \rangle$$
$$po.a \sim (po.(b.l) \sim po.(b.r) \sim [b.v]) \sim X$$
$$= \qquad \langle \text{Catenation is associative} \rangle$$
$$po.a \sim po.(b.l) \sim po.(b.r) \sim ([b.v] \sim X)$$

And we are stuck! In particular, on account of the extra po, we see no way to get back to H's definition. In other words, our H is inadequate, and we must choose another. Since the problem arose when the rightmost po was applied to a non-empty binary tree, we might get more insight into an appropriate choice by expanding this expression when its rightmost po is, in turn, applied to a non-empty binary tree. What we find is that:

$$po.a \sim po.(b.l) \sim po.(b.r) \sim ([b.v] \sim X)$$
$$= \quad \langle \text{ Assume } b.r \neq \triangle, \text{ apply } po \rangle$$
$$po.a \sim po.(b.l) \sim (po.(b.r.l) \sim po.(b.r.r) \sim [b.r.v]) \sim ([b.v] \sim X)$$
$$= \quad \langle \text{ Catenation is associative} \rangle$$
$$po.a \sim po.(b.l) \sim po.(b.r.l) \sim po.(b.r.r) \sim ([b.r.v] \sim [b.v] \sim X)$$

In other words, whenever the rightmost *po* is applied to a non-empty binary tree, another *po* appears on its left. This leads us to generalize H to

$$H.A.b.X = f.A \sim po.b \sim X \qquad \text{for } A : seq \ of \ bintree, \ b : bintree$$
$$\text{and } X : seq,$$

where f, in turn, is defined on sequences of binary trees by

$$f.A = \underline{\text{if }} A = \epsilon \qquad \rightarrow \epsilon$$
$$\quad \underline{\square} \ A = Y \sim y \ \rightarrow \ f.Y \sim po.y$$
$$\quad \underline{\text{fi}}$$

In other words, $f.A$ captures the freshly introduced *po*'s.

With this new H, notice that

$$H.\epsilon.t.\epsilon$$
$$= \quad \langle \text{ Definition of } H \rangle$$
$$f.\epsilon \sim po.t \sim \epsilon$$
$$= \quad \langle \text{ Apply } f \rangle$$
$$\epsilon \sim po.t \sim \epsilon$$
$$= \quad \langle \text{ Property of catenation} \rangle$$
$$po.t$$

In other words:

$$H.\epsilon.t.\epsilon = po.t. \tag{0}$$

Since evaluating $po.t$ boils down to evaluating $H.\epsilon.t.\epsilon$, our problem boils down to finding a tail-recursive definition for H. Towards this end, we observe that

$$H.A.b.X$$
$$= \quad \langle \text{ Definition of } H \rangle$$
$$f.A \sim po.b \sim X$$

We continue in a number of cases. When $A = \epsilon$ and $b = \triangle$, we find:

$$f.A \sim po.b \sim X$$
$$= \quad \langle \text{ Using } A = \epsilon \text{ and } b = \triangle \,\rangle$$
$$f.\epsilon \sim po.\triangle \sim X$$
$$= \quad \langle \text{ Apply } f \text{ and } po \,\rangle$$
$$X$$

— which covers the case that both A and b are empty. When $b \neq \triangle$, we find:

$$f.A \sim po.b \sim X$$
$$= \quad \langle \text{ Using } b \neq \triangle, \text{ apply } po \,\rangle$$
$$f.A \sim po.(b.l) \sim po.(b.r) \sim b.v \sim X$$
$$= \quad \langle \text{ Apply } f \,\rangle$$
$$f.(A \sim b.l) \sim po.(b.r) \sim b.v \sim X$$
$$= \quad \langle \text{ Definition of } H \,\rangle$$
$$H.(A \sim b.l).(b.r).(b.v \sim X)$$

For the other case, namely when $A \neq \epsilon$, we find:

$$f.A \sim po.b \sim X$$
$$= \quad \langle \text{ Using } A \neq \epsilon \text{ , let } A = Y \sim y \,\rangle$$
$$f.(Y \sim y) \sim po.b \sim X$$
$$= \quad \langle \text{ Apply } f \,\rangle$$
$$f.Y \sim po.y \sim po.b \sim X$$
$$= \quad \langle \text{ Further assume } b = \triangle, \text{ to eliminate a } po, \text{ apply } po \,\rangle$$
$$f.Y \sim po.y \sim X$$
$$= \quad \langle \text{ Definition of } H \,\rangle$$
$$H.Y.y.X$$

In other words, we have discovered the following definition of H:

$$
\begin{aligned}
H.A.b.X = \underline{\text{if}}\ &A = \epsilon \wedge b = \triangle \rightarrow X \\
[]\ &A \neq \epsilon \vee b \neq \triangle \rightarrow \\
&\underline{\text{if}}\ A \neq \epsilon \wedge b = \triangle \rightarrow \text{ Letting } A = Y \sim y:\ H.Y.y.X \\
&[]\ b \neq \triangle \qquad\qquad \rightarrow H.(A \sim b.l).(b.r).(b.v \sim X) \\
&\underline{\text{fi}} \\
\underline{\text{fi}}\ &
\end{aligned}
$$

Notice, by the complement rule, that the second case is exhaustive. Notice, also, that each application of H makes progress, and that this progress is bounded.[5] In other words, H is tail-recursive.

---

[5] We leave the discovery of a bound function as an exercise.

Our interest is in evaluating *po.t*, which by (0), boils down to evaluating $H.\epsilon.t.\epsilon$. By direct substitution into our program for evaluating tail-recursive functions, we arrive at:

$$\begin{aligned}
&|[\underline{\text{var }} A : seq\ of\ bintree\ ;\ \underline{\text{var }} b : bintree\ ;\ \underline{\text{var }} X : seq \\
&;\ A, b, X := \epsilon, t, \epsilon\ \ \{P:\ H.A.b.X = H.\epsilon.t.\epsilon\} \\
&;\underline{\text{do }}\ A \neq \epsilon \wedge b = \triangle\ \rightarrow\ \text{Letting } A = Y \sim y:\ \ A, b, X := Y, y, X \\
&\quad \Box\ \ b \neq \triangle\ \ \ \ \ \ \ \ \ \ \ \ \ \ \rightarrow\ A, b, X := A \sim b.l, b.r, b.v \sim X \\
&\underline{\text{od}} \\
&\{X = po.t\} \\
&]|
\end{aligned}$$

This completes the development.

★   ★

In this instance, our original choice for *H* was inadequate and had to be generalized. Expanding its definition revealed the appropriate generalization. One way to make a good choice from the outset is to expand the original function definition. This should reveal a satisfactory generalization, and will avoid unnecessary calculations.

11.7   An example — The depth of a binary tree

We are asked to evaluate function *d*, defined on binary trees by

$$\begin{aligned}
d.t = &\underline{\text{if }} t = \triangle\ \rightarrow\ 0 \\
&\Box\ t \neq \triangle\ \rightarrow\ 1 + d.(t.l)\ max\ d.(t.r) \\
&\underline{\text{fi}}
\end{aligned}$$

★   ★

We observe that *d* is not tail-recursive. Towards discovering a more general function that is, we expand *d.t* :

$$\begin{aligned}
&1 + d.(t.l)\ max\ d.(t.r) \\
=\ &\quad \langle\ \text{Expand this, i.e. assume } t.r \neq \triangle,\ \text{apply } d\ \rangle \\
&1 + d.(t.l)\ max\ (1 + d.(t.r.l)\ max\ d.(t.r.r)) \\
=\ &\quad \langle\ +\ \text{distributes over } max,\ \text{twice (about our only choice)}\ \rangle \\
&(1 + d.(t.l))\ max\ (2 + d.(t.r.l))\ max\ (2 + d.(t.r.r))
\end{aligned}$$

This gives us insight for non-empty binary trees. For insight when some binary tree is empty, assume, in turn, that $t.r.r = \triangle$:

$$(1 + d.(t.l)) \ max \ (2 + d.(t.r.l)) \ max \ (2 + d.(t.r.r))$$
$$= \qquad \langle \text{Assume that } t.r.r = \triangle \rangle$$
$$(1 + d.(t.l)) \ max \ (2 + d.(t.r.l)) \ max \ (2 + d.\triangle)$$
$$= \qquad \langle \text{Apply } d \rangle$$
$$(1 + d.(t.l)) \ max \ (2 + d.(t.r.l)) \ max \ (2 + 0)$$
$$= \qquad \langle \text{Arithmetic} \rangle$$
$$(1 + d.(t.l)) \ max \ (2 + d.(t.r.l)) \ max \ 2$$

Denoting the pair $(u : natural, \ v : bintree)$ by the name *pair*, these investigations lead us to define

$$H.A.y \ = \ (\underline{\text{MAX}}\, x : x \in A : f.x) \ max \ y \qquad \text{for } A : set \ of \ pair$$
$$\text{and } y : natural\,.$$

where function f is defined by

$$f.x = x.u + d.(x.v) \qquad \text{for } x : pair\,.$$

Observe that

$$H.\{(0, t)\}.0 = d.t \tag{0}$$

Towards discovering a tail-recursive definition for H, we find

$$H.A.y$$
$$= \qquad \langle \text{Definition of } H \rangle$$
$$(\underline{\text{MAX}}\, x : x \in A : f.x) \ max \ y$$

To continue, we distinguish a few cases. When $A = \emptyset$, we find:

$$(\underline{\text{MAX}}\, x : x \in A : f.x) \ max \ y$$
$$= \qquad \langle \text{Using } A = \emptyset \rangle$$
$$(\underline{\text{MAX}}\, x : x \in \emptyset : f.x) \ max \ y$$
$$= \qquad \langle \text{Property of sets} \rangle$$
$$(\underline{\text{MAX}}\, x : false : f.x) \ max \ y$$
$$= \qquad \langle \text{Empty range rule for the maximum of naturals} \rangle$$
$$0 \ max \ y$$
$$= \qquad \langle y \text{ is natural} \rangle$$
$$y$$

When $A \neq \emptyset$, we find:

$$
\begin{array}{ll}
& (\underline{\text{MAX}}\, x \,:\, x \in A \,:\, f.x) \ \textit{max}\ y \\
= & \quad \langle\, \text{Using } A \neq \emptyset,\ \text{let } A = Z \cup \{z\}\,\rangle \\
& (\underline{\text{MAX}}\, x \,:\, x \in Z \cup \{z\} \,:\, f.x) \ \textit{max}\ y \\
= & \quad \langle\, \text{Split range}\ ;\ \text{1-point rule}\,\rangle \\
& (\underline{\text{MAX}}\, x \,:\, x \in Z \,:\, f.x) \ \textit{max}\ f.z \ \textit{max}\ y \\
= & \quad \langle\, \text{Definition of } f\,\rangle \\
& (\underline{\text{MAX}}\, x \,:\, x \in Z \,:\, f.x) \ \textit{max}\ (z.u + d.(z.v)) \ \textit{max}\ y
\end{array}
$$

Inspired by the definition of d, we continue in two cases, namely the case when $z.v = \triangle$, and the case when $z.v \neq \triangle$. For the first case we find:

$$
\begin{array}{ll}
& (\underline{\text{MAX}}\, x \,:\, x \in Z \,:\, f.x) \ \textit{max}\ (z.u + d.(z.v)) \ \textit{max}\ y \\
= & \quad \langle\, \text{Using } z.v = \triangle,\ \text{apply } d\ ;\ \text{arithmetic}\,\rangle \\
& (\underline{\text{MAX}}\, x \,:\, x \in Z \,:\, f.x) \ \textit{max}\ z.u \ \textit{max}\ y \\
= & \quad \langle\, \text{Definition of } H\,\rangle \\
& H.Z.(\,z.u\ \textit{max}\ y\,)
\end{array}
$$

For the second case we find:

$$
\begin{array}{ll}
& (\underline{\text{MAX}}\, x \,:\, x \in Z \,:\, f.x) \ \textit{max}\ (z.u + d.(z.v)) \ \textit{max}\ y \\
= & \quad \langle\, \text{Using } z.v \neq \triangle,\ \text{apply } d\,\rangle \\
& (\underline{\text{MAX}}\, x \,:\, x \in Z \,:\, f.x) \ \textit{max} \\
& (\,z.u + (1 + d.(z.v.l)\ \textit{max}\ d.(z.v.r))\,) \ \textit{max}\ y \\
= & \quad \langle\, +\ \text{distributes over } \textit{max},\ \text{twice}\,\rangle \\
& (\underline{\text{MAX}}\, x \,:\, x \in Z \,:\, f.x) \ \textit{max} \\
& (z.u + 1 + d.(z.v.l)) \ \textit{max}\ (z.u + 1 + d.(z.v.r)) \ \textit{max}\ y \\
= & \quad \langle\, \text{Definition of } f,\ \text{twice}\,\rangle \\
& (\underline{\text{MAX}}\, x \,:\, x \in Z \,:\, f.x) \ \textit{max} \\
& f.(z.u + 1,\ z.v.l) \ \textit{max}\ f.(z.u + 1,\ z.v.r) \ \textit{max}\ y \\
= & \quad \langle\, \text{1-point and range rules, twice}\,\rangle \\
& (\underline{\text{MAX}}\, x \,:\, x \in Z \cup \{(z.u + 1,\ z.v.l)\} \cup \{(z.u + 1,\ z.v.r)\} \,:\, f.x) \\
& \textit{max}\ y \\
= & \quad \langle\, \text{Definition of } H\,\rangle \\
& H.(\,Z \cup \{(z.u + 1,\ z.v.l)\} \cup \{(z.u + 1,\ z.v.r)\}\,).y
\end{array}
$$

In other words, we have discovered the following definition of H:

$$
\begin{aligned}
& H.A.y = \\
& \underline{\text{if}}\ A = \epsilon \ \to\ y \\
& \square \ A \neq \epsilon \ \to\ \text{Letting } A = Z \cup \{z\} : \\
& \qquad \underline{\text{if}}\ z.v = \triangle \ \to\ H.Z.(\,z.u\ \textit{max}\ y\,) \\
& \qquad \square \ z.v \neq \triangle \ \to\ H.(\,Z \cup \{(z.u + 1,\ z.v.l)\} \cup \{(z.u + 1,\ z.v.r)\}\,).y \\
& \qquad \underline{\text{fi}} \\
& \underline{\text{fi}}
\end{aligned}
$$

We observe that H is tail-recursive.[6] Our interest is in evaluating $d.t$ which, by (0), boils down to evaluating $H.\{(0,t)\}.0$. By direct substitution we arrive at:

$|[$ var $A : seq\ of\ pair$; var $y : int$
$; A, y := \{(0,t)\}, 0$ $\{P:\ H.A.y = H.\{(0,t)\}.0\}$
$;$ do $A \neq \epsilon \rightarrow$ Letting $A = Z \cup \{z\}:$
$\qquad$ if $z.v = \triangle \rightarrow A, y := Z, z.u\ max\ y$
$\qquad \square\ z.v \neq \triangle \rightarrow A, y := Z \cup \{(z.u+1, z.v.l)\} \cup \{(z.u+1, z.v.r)\}), y$
$\qquad$ fi
$\quad$ od
$\quad \{y = d.t\}$
$]|$

This completes the development.

⋆   ⋆

In this instance, thoughtful expansion in the beginning revealed a satisfactory H. The expansions saved us a lot of avoidable calculations. Indeed, had we chosen the "obvious" generalization, our calculations would have forced us to generalize at least once, possibly even twice. Each generalization would require a number of calculations.

The labor involved in finding an appropriate tail-recursive function depends on the experience of the programmer. At first, a reasonable amount of labor is required. With experience the labor decreases drastically. For an experienced programmer the choice of function is often immediate. As with all such things, practice is required.

Remark   There are functions that cannot be evaluated using the technique described in this chapter. Very roughly, success is to be expected when the underlying operators are associative and have (appropriate) unit-elements. Although we omit a proof, it will work for

$$D.x = \text{if } \neg b.x \rightarrow e.x$$
$$\quad\ \square\quad b.x \rightarrow f.x \circ D.(g.x)$$
$$\quad \text{fi}$$

so long as operator $\circ$

$\qquad$ has a left-unit element,[7] and
$\qquad$ is associative.

---

[6]We leave the discovery of a bound function as an exercise.

We leave the discovery of the reasons why this is so as an exercise. (In particular, see the last two exercises below.)   □

11.8   Exercises

Ex 11.0   The greatest common divisor of two positive integers can be defined by

$$gcd.x.y = \underline{if}\ x = y\ \rightarrow\ x$$
$$\square\ x \neq y\ \rightarrow$$
$$\underline{if}\ x > y\ \rightarrow\ gcd.(x - y).y$$
$$\square\ y > x\ \rightarrow\ gcd.x.(y - x)$$
$$\underline{fi}$$
$$\underline{fi}$$

Given positive X and Y, develop a program to evaluate $gcd.X.Y$. (Since the definition is already tail-recursive, this problem is very easy.)   □

Ex 11.1   Multiplication of natural x and y can be defined by

$$x * y = \underline{if}\ y = 0\ \rightarrow\ 0$$
$$\square\ y \neq 0\ \rightarrow\ x + x * (y - 1)$$
$$\underline{fi}$$

Given natural X and Y, develop a program that evaluates $X * Y$.   □

Ex 11.2   Develop a program that evaluates $X * Y$ in a logarithmic number of repetitions, given natural X and Y.   □

Ex 11.3   The base 2 logarithm of a positive integer that is a power of 2 is given by

$$lg.x = \underline{if}\ x = 1\ \rightarrow\ 0$$
$$\square\ x \neq 1\ \rightarrow\ 1 + lg.(x\ div\ 2)$$
$$\underline{fi}$$

Develop a program that given positive integer X, a power of 2, evaluates $lg.X$.   □

---

[7]Element ul is a left-unit of o if $ul\ o\ X = X$, for all X.

Ex 11.4   Function $x!$ is defined on natural x by

$$x! = \underline{\text{if}}\ x = 0\ \rightarrow\ 1$$
$$\quad\quad \Box\ x \neq 0\ \rightarrow\ x * (x - 1)!$$
$$\underline{\text{fi}}$$

Given natural X, develop a program that evaluates $X!$. $\Box$

Ex 11.5   For natural i and j, the binomial coefficient $\binom{i+j}{i}$ is given by

$$bc.i.j = \underline{\text{if}}\ i = 0\ \lor\ j = 0\ \rightarrow\ 1$$
$$\quad\quad \Box\ i \neq 0\ \land\ j \neq 0\ \rightarrow\ bc.(i-1).j + bc.i.(j-1)$$
$$\underline{\text{fi}}$$

Given natural X and Y, develop a program that evaluates $bc.X.Y$.
$\Box$

Ex 11.6   Function s is defined on binary tree t by

$$s.t = \underline{\text{if}}\ t = \triangle\ \rightarrow\ 0$$
$$\quad\quad \Box\ t \neq \triangle\ \rightarrow\ s.(t.l) + 1 + s.(t.r)$$
$$\underline{\text{fi}}$$

Given binary tree T, develop a program that evaluates $s.T$. (Interpreting s, we are asked to determine the number of nodes (i.e. trees) in binary tree T.) $\Box$

Ex 11.7   Letting capitals denote sequences of (decimal) digits, and smalls denote (decimal) digits, and for $0 \leq c \leq 1$, function f is defined by:

$$f.A.B.c =$$
$$\quad \underline{\text{if}}\ A = \epsilon\ \land\ B = \epsilon\ \land\ c = 0\ \rightarrow\ \epsilon$$
$$\quad \Box\ A \neq \epsilon\ \lor\ B \neq \epsilon\ \lor\ c \neq 0\ \rightarrow$$
$$\quad\quad \text{Letting } X, x\ =\ \epsilon, 0 \text{ if } A = \epsilon, \text{ otherwise } A = X \sim x \text{ and}$$
$$\quad\quad\quad\quad\quad\quad Y, y\ =\ \epsilon, 0 \text{ if } B = \epsilon, \text{ otherwise } B = Y \sim y:$$
$$\quad\quad f.X.Y.((x + y + c)\ div\ 10) \sim ((x + y + c)\ mod\ 10)$$
$$\quad \underline{\text{fi}}$$

Develop a program that evaluates $f.M.N.0$. (Interpreting f, we are asked to determine the sum of decimal digit sequences (i.e. variable-length addition). On account of the fact that f is already tail-recursive, this problem is very easy.) $\Box$

Ex 11.8   Methodically eliminate *div* and *mod* from your solution to the previous exercise. $\Box$

Ex 11.9 Function *rev* can also be defined by

$$rev.X = \underline{if}\ X = \epsilon \rightarrow \epsilon$$
$$\Box\ X \neq \epsilon \rightarrow \text{Letting } X = Z \sim [z]:\ [z] \sim rev.Z$$
$$\underline{fi}$$

Given sequence X, develop a program that evaluates $rev.X$. □

Ex 11.10 Yet another definition of *rev* is

$$rev.X = \underline{if}\ \#X < 2 \rightarrow x$$
$$\Box\ \#X \geq 2 \rightarrow \text{Letting } X = [a] \sim B \sim [c]:$$
$$[c] \sim rev.B \sim [a]$$
$$\underline{fi}$$

Given sequence X, develop a program that evaluates $rev.X$. □

Ex 11.11 A *leaf* is a binary tree that has empty binary trees for both its subtrees. The number of leaves in binary tree t is given by

$$nl.t = \underline{if}\ t = \triangle \rightarrow 0$$
$$\Box\ t \neq \triangle \rightarrow$$
$$\underline{if}\ t.l = \triangle \wedge t.r = \triangle \rightarrow 1$$
$$\Box\ t.l \neq \triangle \vee t.r \neq \triangle \rightarrow nl.(t.l) + nl.(t.r)$$
$$\underline{fi}$$
$$\underline{fi}$$

Given binary tree T, develop a program that evaluates $nl.T$. □

Ex 11.12 The pre-order of binary tree t is the sequence defined by

$$pr.t = \underline{if}\ t = \triangle \rightarrow \epsilon$$
$$\Box\ t \neq \triangle \rightarrow [t.v] \sim pr.(t.l) \sim pr.(t.r)$$
$$\underline{fi}$$

Given binary tree y, develop a program to evaluate $pr.y$. □

Ex 11.13 The in-order of binary tree t is the sequence defined by

$$in.t = \underline{if}\ t = \triangle \rightarrow \epsilon$$
$$\Box\ t \neq \triangle \rightarrow in.(t.l) \sim [t.v] \sim in.(t.r)$$
$$\underline{fi}$$

Given binary tree y, develop a program to evaluate $in.y$. □

Ex 11.14   Develop a different solution to the previous exercise by inventing and evaluating a different tail-recursive function.   □

Ex 11.15   Function D is defined by

$$D.x = \underline{\text{if}} \; \neg b.x \; \rightarrow \; e.x$$
$$\square \quad b.x \; \rightarrow \; f.x \circ D.(g.x)$$
$$\underline{\text{fi}}$$

Develop a program that given X, evaluates $D.X$. In doing so, certain properties of $\circ$ will have to be assumed. In addition to developing the program, list these properties.   □

Ex 11.16   Function D is defined by

$$D.x = \underline{\text{if}} \; \neg b.x \; \rightarrow \; e.x$$
$$\square \quad b.x \; \rightarrow \; f.x \circ D.(g.x) \diamond h.x$$
$$\underline{\text{fi}}$$

Develop a program that given X, evaluates $D.X$. In doing so, certain properties of $\circ$ and $\diamond$ will have to be assumed. In addition to developing the program, list these properties.   □

12

Back to scratch

12.0 Introduction

In previous chapters we were asked to solve specifications for their programs. The specifications were given. Practicing programmers, however, are rarely given specifications. Usually we get informal problem statements.

This fact did not concern us in the previous chapters, since we were after *techniques* for solving certain classes of specifications. Here we address this new concern.

What do we do when confronted with an informal problem statement?

Because a program is a solution to a specification, our first task is to compose a specification. In doing so we may find that the informal problem statement is unclear or unsolvable. If it is unsolvable, there is nothing we can do. If it is unclear, we must ask the questions necessary to clarify it. When clear, we can compose a specification.

In composing a specification we choose appropriate notation. If the problem is in an unfamiliar domain, we might have to invent new notation. When we invent new notation, we have to discover its properties. These properties we will need in our calculations.

Here we start anew and solve a few problems from scratch. All but the first problem will be given informally, and so we will have to compose specifications. Because our specifications will include new notation, we will have to discover useful properties.

12.1 An example — Evaluating a polynomial (and the discovery of nice specifications)

Given integer x and integer array b, where $\#b \geq 0$, we are asked to establish

$$R: \ y = (\Sigma i : 0 \leq i < \#b : b.i * x^i)$$

In other words, we are asked to set y to the value of a $(\#b - 1)$st degree polynomial with coefficients b.

⋆   ⋆

By replacing the 0 by fresh variable k, we define

$$g.k = (\Sigma i : k \leq i < \#b : b.i * x^i) \quad \text{for } 0 \leq k \leq \#b.$$

and consider maintaining

$$P0: \ y = g.k$$
$$P1: \ 0 \leq k \leq \#b.$$

Because R, our original postcondition, can be replaced by the equivalent but simpler

$$R0: \ y = g.0$$

we will forget about R and investigate g. What we find is that

$g.k$
$=\qquad \langle\,$ Definition of $g\,\rangle$
$\qquad (\Sigma i : k \leq i < \#b : b.i * x^i)$
$=\qquad \langle\,$ The obvious choices are to split the range or to distribute
$\qquad\qquad$ some power of x out of the quantification. With this
$\qquad\qquad$ last choice the obvious candidates are x and x^k.
$\qquad\qquad$ We head for the latter. $\rangle$
$\qquad (\Sigma i : k \leq i < \#b : b.i * x^k * x^{i-k})$
$=\qquad \langle\, *$ distributes over $\Sigma\,\rangle$
$\qquad x^k * (\Sigma i : k \leq i < \#b : b.i * x^{i-k})$
$=\qquad \langle\,$ Definition of f, see below $\rangle$
$\qquad x^k * f.k$

where f is given by

$$f.k = (\Sigma i : k \leq i < \#b : b.i * x^{i-k}) \quad \text{for } 0 \leq k \leq \#b.$$

Since our interest is $g.0$, we find

$$g.0$$
$$= \quad \langle \text{By the last calculation} \rangle$$
$$x^0 * f.0$$
$$= \quad \langle \text{Arithmetic} \rangle$$
$$f.0$$

Therefore we can replace $R0$ by the equivalent

$$R1: \quad y = f.0$$

which allows us to forget about g and concentrate on f. Looking at the definition of f we see that

$$f.\#b = 0 \,.$$

Investigating $f.k$ for $0 \leq k < \#b$ we find:

$$f.k$$
$$= \quad \langle \text{Definition of } f \rangle$$
$$(\Sigma i : k \leq i < \#b : b.i * x^{i-k})$$
$$= \quad \langle \text{Split range} \rangle$$
$$(\Sigma i : k = i : b.i * x^{i-k}) + (\Sigma i : k+1 \leq i < \#b : b.i * x^{i-k})$$
$$= \quad \langle \text{Since } 0 \leq k < \#b, \ b.k \text{ is defined, so 1-point rule} \rangle$$
$$b.k * x^{k-k} + (\Sigma i : k+1 \leq i < \#b : b.i * x^{i-k})$$
$$= \quad \langle \text{Arithmetic} \rangle$$
$$b.k + (\Sigma i : k+1 \leq i < \#b : b.i * x^{i-k})$$
$$= \quad \langle \text{Towards replacing the quantification by } f \rangle$$
$$b.k + (\Sigma i : k+1 \leq i < \#b : b.i * x * x^{i-(k+1)})$$
$$= \quad \langle * \text{ distributes over } \Sigma \rangle$$
$$b.k + x * (\Sigma i : k+1 \leq i < \#b : b.i * x^{i-(k+1)})$$
$$= \quad \langle \text{Definition of } f \rangle$$
$$b.k + x * f.(k+1)$$

These last two results allow us to write the following definition of f:

$$f.k = \underline{\text{if }} k = \#b \quad \rightarrow 0$$
$$\text{▯} \ 0 \leq k < \#b \ \rightarrow b.k + x * f.(k+1)$$
$$\underline{\text{fi}}$$

which along with our postcondition, $R1$, is enough to develop the program.

★   ★

We will not develop a program from this specification because we have already done so. Recall that this was the specification for our earlier example of evaluating a polynomial.[0]

At the time of that earlier example we did not know what problem we were solving. From a given specification, we simply developed a program. At the end we were *told* that the specification was for a program for evaluating a polynomial. No proof was given. All we saw was an example.

One of the tasks of the programmer is to provide a convincing justification as to why a particular specification matches the problem statement. Here we did so. We started with a straightforward specification and transformed it into an equivalent one. The equivalent one yields a very nice program, a program we have already seen.

Notice also that we have discovered Horner's rule!

12.2   An example — Greatest common divisors (and the discovery of useful properties)

The *greatest common divisor* of two integers is the largest integer that divides them both. Given two integers, we are asked to determine their greatest common divisor.

⋆   ⋆

We start, of course, by composing a specification. We propose:

> $\underline{\text{var}}\ X, Y : int$
> ; $\underline{\text{var}}\ x : int$
> ; $x :\ \ x = X\ gcd\ Y$

where

> $A\ gcd\ B\ =\ $ greatest common divisor of A and B.

Remark   Although we will not prove this, *gcd* is associative, i.e.

---

[0]Notice also that f is an instance of a tail-recursive function and, as such, the program can be obtained by direct substitution into our program for evaluating such functions.

$$(A \ gcd \ B) \ gcd \ C = A \ gcd \ (B \ gcd \ C),$$

and is also symmetric (i.e. $A \ gcd \ B = B \ gcd \ A$). It is because it is associative that we wrote it as an infix operator. Because it is associative and symmetric, the greatest common divisor of a bunch of integers can be determined by repeatedly determining the greatest common divisors of integer pairs. □

A FIRST ATTEMPT

The obvious solution, namely

$$x := X \ gcd \ Y$$

we disallow under the reasonable assumption that gcd is not a primitive allowed in program texts. Since direct use of gcd is disallowed, we are forced to find useful properties — properties that we can exploit.

DISCOVERING PROPERTIES OF gcd

What can we discover about gcd?

Our first discovery is that because 0 has no largest divisor (everything is a divisor of 0), $0 \ gcd \ 0$ is undefined. As a result there is no solution for $X = 0 \ \wedge \ Y = 0$. Because the problem is unsolvable as given, we can either stop here, or can change the problem. As the required change is a small one, we choose the latter, and strengthen the precondition to

$$X \neq 0 \ \vee \ Y \neq 0.$$

Our next discovery is that the greatest divisor of a negative integer is its positive counterpart. Therefore, the greatest common divisor of a pair of integers is the greatest common divisor of their absolute values. In other words, we have discovered that

$$A \ gcd \ B \ = \ |A| \ gcd \ |B|. \tag{0}$$

This last result is helpful since it allows us to focus our attention on the greatest common divisor of natural arguments, at least one of which is non-zero, hence positive. What can we discover about the greatest divisor shared by two integers, one natural and the other positive?

One thing we know is that every integer divides 0. We also know that the largest divisor of a positive integer is itself. As a result we see that the greatest common divisor of 0 and a positive integer is the positive integer. In other words, we have discovered that

$$A \; gcd \; 0 \; = \; A \qquad \text{for positive } A. \tag{1}$$

Property (1) leads us to propose, for natural A and B, at least one non-zero, the following definition of gcd:

$$
\begin{aligned}
A \; gcd \; B \; = \; &\underline{\text{if}} \; B = 0 \; \rightarrow \; A \quad \text{(by (1))} \\
&\underline{} \; B \neq 0 \; \rightarrow \; \{A \geq 0 \; \wedge \; B > 0\} \; \ldots \\
&\underline{\text{fi}}
\end{aligned}
$$

What this strongly suggests is that we try to choose for the missing part an expression which yields a tail-recursive definition. This boils down to finding a rewriting of $A \; gcd \; B$ that maintains the naturalness of A and B, and also decreases B (to guarantee progress).

In light of this last requirement, the obvious choices are a decrease by subtraction or a decrease by division. Since gcd is fairly unfamiliar, and since the former is simpler, we start with subtraction, and postpone an investigation of division until later.

⋆   ⋆

The obvious candidate for subtraction from B is A. What properties does $B - A$ have? The obvious one is that any integer that divides both A and B also divides $B - A$. This leads us to observe that a common divisor of two integers is also a divisor of their difference, and therefore that their greatest common divisor is also. In other words, we have discovered that

$$A \; gcd \; B \; = \; A \; gcd \; (B - A).$$

While valid, this rewriting is unsuitable for our purposes. In particular it does not decrease B when $A = 0$. Since B is positive, we might instead subtract B from A using

$$A \; gcd \; B \; = \; (A - B) \; gcd \; B \tag{2}$$

were it not for the fact that this results in a decrease of A instead of a decrease of B. Since it does decrease *something*, one way out is to appeal to the symmetry of *gcd*, and propose a decrease of B using

$$A \ gcd \ B \ = \ B \ gcd \ (A - B).$$

This, of course, only does the job if $A - B < B$. We might continue by looking for a rewriting that decreases B when $A - B \geq B$, but instead propose using our newfound knowledge to investigate potentially larger decreases using division. Division, of course, is repeated subtraction, which is why we feel ready to investigate it.

★   ★

We observe that

$$
\begin{aligned}
&A \ gcd \ B \\
= \quad &\langle \text{Property (2), } q \text{ times (because it decreases } \textit{something}) \rangle \\
&(A - q * B) \ gcd \ B \\
= \quad &\langle \text{Symmetry of } gcd \text{ (since we are after a decrease of } B) \rangle \\
&B \ gcd \ (A - q * B)
\end{aligned}
$$

While valid for any q, our purposes require that B be decreased and also remain natural. In other words, q must be chosen to satisfy

    (a) $A - q * B < B$ and
    (b) $0 \leq A - q * B$.

We would also like the largest q possible, since such a q yields the largest possible decrease of B. Focusing our attention on (b), we see that the largest q that satisfies (b) is the quotient from integer-division of A by B. And when q is the quotient, $A - q * B$ is the remainder, a value we denote by $A \ mod \ B$. All that remains is to guarantee that (a), namely $A \ mod \ B < B$, is satisfied. This, in turn, is a basic property of *mod*, and so we are finished.

★   ★

In summary, what we have discovered is the following tail-recursive definition of *gcd*, defined for natural A and B, where at least one is non-zero:

$$
\begin{aligned}
A \ gcd \ B \ = \quad &\underline{\text{if}} \ B = 0 \ \rightarrow \ A \\
&\square \ B \neq 0 \ \rightarrow \ B \ gcd \ (A \ mod \ B) \\
&\underline{\text{fi}}
\end{aligned}
$$

WRITING THE PROGRAM

We were given integers X and Y, and asked to establish

$$x = X \; gcd \; Y.$$

Because *gcd* is undefined when both arguments are zero, we further require that at least one of these is non-zero.

★   ★

Because our tail-recursive definition is valid for natural arguments only, we find our program by first appealing to property (0), namely

$$A \; gcd \; B \; = \; |A| \; gcd \; |B|, \tag{0}$$

and then substituting into our program for evaluating tail-recursive functions. The result is

$$\{X \neq 0 \lor Y \neq 0\}$$
$$\|[\underline{var} \; x, y : int$$
$$; x, y := |X|, |Y| \; \{x \; gcd \; y \; = \; |X| \; gcd \; |Y|\}$$
$$; \underline{do} \; y \neq 0 \; \rightarrow \; x, y := y, x \; mod \; y \; \underline{od}$$
$$]|$$

Upon termination we have

$$\begin{aligned}
& x \; gcd \; y \; = \; |X| \; gcd \; |Y| \\
= \quad & \langle \, \text{By (0)} \, \rangle \\
& x \; gcd \; y \; = \; X \; gcd \; Y \\
= \quad & \langle \, \text{Using } y = 0, \text{ applying the definition of } gcd \, \rangle \\
& x \; = \; X \; gcd \; Y
\end{aligned}$$

which completes the development. The resulting program is known as *Euclid's Algorithm*, since it was discovered by Euclid over 2000 years ago!

MAINLY ON DISCOVERING USEFUL PROPERTIES

When confronted with an informal problem statement we must compose a specification. Sometimes we must invent new notation. To calculate with new notation, properties must be discovered. Such a discovery may take many routes:

• For familiar domains, the relevant properties will be common knowledge. For example, almost everyone knows that $\leq$ is transitive (for integers), and that 0 is the unit of addition. We have often appealed to such properties.

• For some domains, the relevant properties can be found. We can ask someone with expertise, or can look in a book. Although we didn't take this route, properties of *gcd* can be found in many books.

• For some domains we will have to discover them ourselves. For example, we discovered a number of properties of *gcd*.

• Yet another option is to transform the problem into an equivalent one in a familiar domain. Many computer network problems, for example, can be transformed into problems on graphs, since properties of graphs are well-known.

The discovery of properties does not have to be haphazard either. After a preliminary investigation, we decided to seek a tail-recursive definition of *gcd*. From this point we knew exactly what we were after, namely a rewriting of *gcd* which decreased its second argument. Further, we could discard properties that were useless for this purpose.[1]

Remark   On a related topic, some specifications have no solutions (i.e. are of uncomputable problems), and some are intractable (i.e. admit no reasonably efficient solutions). These areas have been well studied and come under the headings of *computability theory* and *computational complexity theory*. Knowing whether a problem falls into one of these classes is eminently practical. It saves us from laboring endlessly on problems that are inherently unsolvable.   □

★   ★
★

Ex 12.0   The *least common multiple* of a bunch of positive integers is the smallest positive integer that is a multiple of these integers. Given a pair of positive integers, specify and then develop a program that determines their least common multiple. In order to solve this problem, properties of least common multiples will have to be discovered.   □

---

[1]Observation courtesy of Vit Novak.

12.3   An example — All shortest paths
(and the specification as logical firewall)

A large company has a bunch of offices, and offices like to send messages
to other offices. The postal service was too slow, so the company installed
a number of high-speed one-way communications lines between pairs of
offices. Because the cost of line installation was high, only certain pairs of
offices had lines installed. This was done in such a way as to guarantee
that if office A had to send messages to office B, there was a way to do so.
Perhaps office A would send a message to office C which, in turn, would
forward it to office B.

As inevitably happens, economic hard times have hit. The offices must still
send messages, but would like to cut the costs of doing so. Someone noticed
that the cost of transmitting a message over a line was constant, although
this constant varied from line to line. As a result, the cost of message
transmittal from one office to another could be minimized by finding the
least-cost route between every pair of offices.

The company, being a conservative one, decides to commission a study to
determine, not the least-cost route between every pair of offices, but instead
the *costs* of these least-cost routes.

⋆   ⋆

As the informal problem statement is full of superfluous details, we look
at it carefully, and determine that solving it boils down to solving a more
concisely stated problem, namely:

> Given a directed graph, determine, for every pair of nodes i and j,
> the shortest path length from i to j. The length of a path is the
> sum of the lengths of the (directed) edges that comprise it. We are
> given the lengths of the edges.

Remark   We have taken the liberty of casting the problem in terms of
"nodes" instead of "offices", "directed edges" instead of "one-way
communications lines", and "shortest path lengths" instead of "costs
of least-cost routes". We do this with good reason. Introducing neu-
tral terminology, we avoid questions like "what if a communications
line fails?", something of no relevance to the problem at hand. We
also avoid the danger of unconsciously appealing to invalid properties.
□

Composing a specification

We start, of course, by composing a specification. We propose

Given, for each pair of nodes i and j, integer variable b_{ij} satisfying

$$b_{ij} = \text{"length of edge from } i \text{ to } j \text{"} \quad (= +inf \text{ if no edge)},^2$$

we are asked to establish

$$R: \quad b_{ij} = f.i.j \quad \text{for all } i, j,$$

where

$$f.i.j = \text{"shortest path length from } i \text{ to } j \text{"}.$$

A first attempt

The obvious program, namely

$$b_{ij} := f.i.j \quad \text{for all } i, j$$

we disallow under the reasonable assumption that f is not allowed in program texts. Since direct use of f is disallowed, we are forced to discover properties of f that we can exploit.

Discovering properties of f

Observing that the shortest path length from i to j is either the edge length from i to j (i.e. b_{ij}), or the shortest path length from i to j through some intermediate node, we are led to define

$$f.i.j = b_{ij} \ min \ (\underline{MIN} \, x : x \in G : f.i.x + f.x.j)$$

---

[2]Notice how the use of $+inf$ for the length of a non-existent edge avoids a case-analysis (i.e. one case if there is an edge, and another if there isn't).

where G is the set of nodes in the graph. As is, $f.i.j$ is a constant, and therefore is not amenable to manipulation. This suggests that we generalize it to something that is. Towards this end we observe that the G in the righthand side is almost begging to be replaced by a fresh variable, a variable that then becomes a parameter. In other words, the obvious generalization is:

$$g.i.j.X \; = \; b_{ij} \; min \; (\underline{\text{MIN}}\, x \, : \, x \in X \, : \, g.i.x.X \, + \, g.x.j.X\,) \qquad (0)$$

where X is some subset of G.

Remark The generalization from f to g is considered the key idea in the development of this program. The fact that f was not open to manipulation led us to generalize it, and (0) is the obvious generalization.

Function $g.i.j.X$ can be interpreted as the "shortest path length from i to j allowing only nodes in X as intermediate nodes". □

Towards discovering properties of g, we observe that

$$g.i.j.\emptyset \; = \; b_{ij}\,. \qquad (1)$$

When X is not empty, we find, for any $a \notin X$, that

$$
\begin{aligned}
& g.i.j.(X \cup \{a\}) \\
= \quad & \langle\,(0)\,\rangle \\
& b_{ij} \; min \\
& (\underline{\text{MIN}}\, x \, : \, x \in X \cup \{a\} \, : \, g.i.x.(X \cup \{a\}) \, + \, g.x.j.(X \cup \{a\})) \\
= \quad & \langle\,(3),\ \text{see below}\,\rangle \\
& b_{ij} \; min \\
& (\underline{\text{MIN}}\, x \, : \, x \in X \cup \{a\} \, : \, g.i.x.X \, + \, g.x.j.X\,) \\
= \quad & \langle\, \text{Split range ; 1-point rule}\,\rangle \\
& b_{ij} \; min \; (\underline{\text{MIN}}\, x \, : \, x \in X \, : \, g.i.x.X \, + \, g.x.j.X\,) \; min \\
& (g.i.a.X \, + \, g.a.j.X) \\
= \quad & \langle\,(0)\,\rangle \\
& g.i.j.X \; min \; (g.i.a.X \, + \, g.a.j.X)
\end{aligned}
$$

In other words, we have discovered that

$$g.i.j.(X \cup \{a\}) \; = \; g.i.j.X \; min \; (g.i.a.X \, + \, g.a.j.X) \qquad (2)$$

provided that the following also holds:

$$(\underline{\text{MIN}}\, x\ :\ x \in X \cup \{a\}\ :\ g.i.x.(X \cup \{a\}) + g.x.j.(X \cup \{a\})) \qquad (3)$$
$$= (\underline{\text{MIN}}\, x\ :\ x \in X \cup \{a\}\ :\ g.i.x.X + g.x.j.X).$$

In other words:

$$
\begin{array}{ll}
& (2) \\
\Leftarrow & \quad \langle\, \text{By this last calculation}\,\rangle \\
& (3)
\end{array}
$$

We observe that (3), in turn, holds when the shortest path length allowing a more than once is no longer than the shortest path length allowing a at most once. This, in turn, is guaranteed if the shortest path length allowing a more than once, namely:

$$g.i.a.X + g.a.a.(X \cup \{a\}) + g.a.j.X. \qquad (4)$$

is no smaller than the shortest path length allowing a *exactly once*, namely:

$$g.i.a.X + g.a.j.X. \qquad (5)$$

This leads us to discover that:

$$
\begin{array}{ll}
& (3) \\
\Leftarrow & \quad \langle\, \text{By the reasoning above}\ (*)\,\rangle \\
& (4) \geq (5) \\
\equiv & \quad \langle\, \text{By arithmetic}\,\rangle \\
& g.a.a.(X \cup \{a\}) \geq 0 \\
\Leftarrow & \quad \langle\, \text{This holds if there is no path from}\ a\ \text{to itself having} \\
& \qquad \text{negative length. Such a path is called a negative-lengthed} \\
& \qquad \text{cycle containing}\ a.\ \text{This, in turn, follows if the graph} \\
& \qquad \text{contains no negative-lengthed cycles.}\,\rangle \\
& \text{The graph contains no negative-lengthed cycles}
\end{array}
$$

In other words, if the graph contains no negative-lengthed cycles, then (2) holds.

Remark   We apologize for the way in which step $(*)$ was dealt with. Short of postulating (3) (or (2)), we were unable to do better.   □

Armed with property (1), which applies when X is empty, and property (2), which applies when X is non-empty, provided that the graph is without negative-lengthed cycles, we feel fairly certain that we can develop the program.

A SECOND ATTEMPT

Noticing that our original postcondition, namely

$$R: \quad b_{ij} = f.i.j \quad \text{for all } i, j$$

is equivalent to

$$R: \quad b_{ij} = g.i.j.G \quad \text{for all } i, j$$

we propose replacing G by a fresh variable, to arrive at invariants

$$P0: \quad b_{ij} = g.i.j.X \quad \text{for all } i, j$$
$$P1: \quad X \text{ is a subset of } G,$$

and the program

```
|[ var X : set of node
;X := ∅  {P0 ∧ P1, on account of property (1)}
;do X ≠ G →
     Letting a be any node in G not in X :
     S
     ;X := X ∪ {a}
  od
]|
```

What remains is the development of S.

Remark   If the nodes are numbered, then an integer variable, say k, can take on the roles of set X and node a. For instance:

$$X = \text{nodes } 0..k - 1 \quad \text{and}$$
$$a = \text{node } k,$$

in which case the program could be translated into:

$$\begin{aligned}
&\lVert[\underline{var}\ k : int \\
&; k := 0\ ; \underline{do}\ k \neq \#G\ \rightarrow\ S\ ; k := k+1\ \underline{od} \\
&]\rVert
\end{aligned}$$

This assumption is a common one. □

★   ★

S must maintain the invariants. In particular, it must satisfy

$$\{P0\}\ S\ \{P0(X := X \cup \{a\})\}\,.$$

Investigating the postcondition, we find that

$$\begin{aligned}
&P0(X := X \cup \{a\}) \\
\equiv\quad &\langle\,\text{Definition of } P0\,\rangle \\
&b_{ij}\ =\ g.i.j.(X \cup \{a\}) \quad \text{for all } i, j
\end{aligned}$$

Towards eliminating g we find, for all i, j, that

$$\begin{aligned}
&g.i.j.(X \cup \{a\}) \\
=\quad &\langle\,\text{Using (2)}\,\rangle \\
&g.i.j.X\ min\ (g.i.a.X\ +\ g.a.j.X) \\
=\quad &\langle\,P0,\ \text{thrice}\,\rangle \\
&b_{ij}\ min\ (b_{ia}\ +\ b_{aj})
\end{aligned}$$

What we have discovered is that the simultaneous assignment

$$b_{ij} := b_{ij}\ min\ (b_{ia}\ +\ b_{aj}) \quad \text{for all } i, j$$

is a solution for S. This we denote by

$$S:\ (\underline{forall}\ i, j\ :\ i \in G\ \wedge\ j \in G\ :\ b_{ij} := b_{ij}\ min\ (b_{ia} + b_{aj}))\,.$$

Letting N be the number of nodes in the graph, we see that each execution of S requires N^2 assignments. Because S is executed N times, we see that the program requires a total of N^3 assignments.

Remark   Because we appealed to property (2), we are obligated to require that the graph contain no negative-lengthed cycles. We do so by adding this restriction to the precondition. □

⋆   ⋆

Next we attempt to eliminate the <u>forall</u>. In other words, we will try to find a (sequential) ordering of its N^2 assignments.

We begin by observing that each execution of the <u>forall</u> assigns to each b_{ij} a value that depends on the values of b_{ij}, b_{ia} and b_{aj}. Because b_{ij} is assigned to only once, we see that the assignments in the <u>forall</u> can be executed in any order if the assignments to the b_{xa} (for all $x \in G$) and the assignments to the b_{ax} (for all $x \in G$) can be executed in any order.

The assignments to the b_{xa} can be executed in any order if they are empty assignments, i.e. if they do not change the values of the b_{xa}. Since the value assigned to each b_{xa} is

$$b_{xa}\ min\ (b_{xa} + b_{aa}),$$

we see that each b_{xa} is unchanged if

$$b_{xa}\ min\ (b_{xa} + b_{aa})\ =\ b_{xa}.$$

We calculate:

$$
\begin{array}{ll}
& b_{xa}\ min\ (b_{xa} + b_{aa})\ =\ b_{xa} \\
\equiv & \quad \langle\,P\ min\ Q = P\ \equiv\ Q \geq P\,\rangle \\
& b_{xa} + b_{aa} \geq b_{xa} \\
\equiv & \quad \langle\,P + Q \geq P\ \equiv\ Q \geq 0\,\rangle \\
& b_{aa} \geq 0
\end{array}
$$

What we have discovered is that the assignments in the <u>forall</u> can be executed in any order if $b_{aa} \geq 0$ is maintained.

Since b_{aa} is a shortest path length from node a to itself, we see that $b_{aa} \geq 0$ is maintained if the graph contains no negative-lengthed cycles. Recalling that we have already imposed this restriction, we see that the assignments in the <u>forall</u> can be executed in any order.

This completes the development.

⋆   ⋆

Ex 12.1   Extend the algorithm so that it determines instances of shortest paths also. Start by composing a specification.   □

Ex 12.2 Going back to our company and its offices. Given (only) boolean variables c_{ij}, satisfying

$$c_{ij} \equiv \text{truth of "there exists a one-way communications line}$$
$$\text{from office } i \text{ to office } j\text{",}$$

specify and then solve the problem of determining, for every pair of offices, whether or not there is a message transmittal route from one to the other. □

THE SPECIFICATION AS LOGICAL FIREWALL

When given a story, like that about our company and its offices, the first step is to collect the relevant facts. Once collected, the story can be forgotten. This is good, since stories are usually full of superfluous details, details that do not concern us, and would only serve to confuse us. Recall the "word-problems" in high-school mathematics and physics.

The same applies when we compose a specification. From an informal problem statement we compose a specification. We do so because we like to calculate our programs. Another reason is that it reveals ambiguities in the informal problem statement. There is yet another reason: The specification provides a "logical firewall" (a term due to E.W. Dijkstra) between problem statement and program. It shows us how to separate our task into two smaller ones. In doing the second, we can forget about the first. Such a separation of concerns is the hallmark of clear thinking. And clear thinking is the hallmark of a good programmer!

12.4 A final example — Shiloach's algorithm

Given two non-empty integer circular arrays of the same length, we are asked to determine whether they are equal.

Remark A circular array is like a normal array, except that it has no "last" element: If non-empty, then its last element is followed by its first. For example, the following two circular arrays are equal:

[7,9,1,7]   and   [7,7,9,1]

□

$$\star \qquad\qquad \star$$

We start by composing a specification. Let N be the number of elements in the circular arrays, and let (non-circular) arrays A and B hold them. We arrive at the specification

> <u>var</u> $N : int$ $\{N \geq 1\}$
> ; <u>var</u> $A, B(i : 0 \leq i < N) : array\ of\ int$
> ; <u>var</u> $z : bool$
> ; $z :\ R$

where postcondition R has yet to be formulated. Towards formulating R, we are led to define the ith *rotation* of A by

$$SA.i = A(k : i \leq k < i + N) \quad \text{for } 0 \leq i$$

where indices are reduced modulo N. Defining the ith rotation of B similarly, we can formulate R as

$$R:\quad z \ \equiv\ (\exists i,j : 0 \leq i \wedge 0 \leq j : SA.i = SB.j).$$

DEVELOPING THE PROGRAM

We see no way to establish R when A and B happen to be equal, short of exhibiting a pair (i, j) that satisfies

$$R0:\quad SA.i = SB.j \ \wedge\ 0 \leq i \ \wedge\ 0 \leq j.$$

Towards choosing an invariant, we investigate $R0$. What we find is that

$$
\begin{aligned}
&R0 \\
\equiv\quad &\langle \text{Definition of } R0 \rangle \\
&SA.i = SB.j \ \wedge\ 0 \leq i \ \wedge\ 0 \leq j \\
\equiv\quad &\langle \text{Definitions of } SA \text{ and } SB \rangle \\
&(\forall k : 0 \leq k < h : SA.i.k = SB.j.k) \ \wedge\ 0 \leq i \ \wedge\ 0 \leq j \ \wedge\ h \geq N
\end{aligned}
$$

Remark   The $h \geq N$ was used instead of $h = N$ on account of the arrays being circular.   □

By deleting a conjunct, we propose establishing $R0$ using invariant

$$P : \ (\forall k \ : \ 0 \le k < h \ : \ SA.i.k = SB.j.k\ ) \ \wedge \ 0 \le i \ \wedge \ 0 \le j.$$

This leads directly to:

```
|[var h, i, j : int
;h, i, j := 0, 0, 0  {P}
;do h < N → S  od
 {P ∧ h ≥ N, hence R0}
]|
```

What remains is the development of S.

⋆   ⋆

On account of the guard, we see that S must increase h. It must also maintain P. When $SA.i.h = SB.j.h$ this can be accomplished by an increase of h by 1. When $SA.i.h \ne SB.j.h$ the appropriate increase is not as apparent, and so we will calculate it. In other words, for S we propose

```
if SA.i.h = SB.j.h → h := h + 1
▯  SA.i.h ≠ SB.j.h → h := h + E   (for some E > 0)
fi
```

All that remains is to solve for E. What we find is that

$$wp.(h := h + E).P$$
$$\equiv \quad \langle\, \text{Definitions of } P \text{ and assignment} \,\rangle$$
$$(\forall k \ : \ 0 \le k < h + E \ : \ SA.i.k = SB.j.k\ ) \ \wedge \ 0 \le i \ \wedge \ 0 \le j$$
$$\equiv \quad \langle\, \text{Using } P, \text{ in particular its second conjunct} \,\rangle$$
$$(\forall k \ : \ 0 \le k < h + E \ : \ SA.i.k = SB.j.k\ )$$
$$\equiv \quad \langle\, \text{Towards using the first conjunct of } P \text{ and also the guard,}$$
$$\text{split range twice ; 1-point rule} \,\rangle$$
$$(\forall k \ : \ 0 \le k < h \ : \ SA.i.k = SB.j.k\ ) \ \wedge \ SA.i.h = SB.j.h \ \wedge$$
$$(\forall k \ : \ h + 1 \le k < h + E \ : \ SA.i.k = SB.j.k\ )$$
$$\equiv \quad \langle\, \text{On account of the guard, namely } SA.i.h \ne SB.j.h \,\rangle$$
$$\textit{false}$$

Thus there is no choice for E and, as a result, no way to increase h under the invariance of P when $SA.i.h \ne SB.j.h$. In other words, we are stuck.

This should not be surprising. We cannot expect to establish $R0$ when A and B differ. In other words, we cannot maintain $P0$ *and* establish $h \ge N$ in this case. What we need, of course, is a relation that can be established when A and B are different circular arrays. Our next task, then, is to discover such a relation.

Discovering what to establish when the arrays differ

Towards finding a relation we can establish when A and B differ, we begin by investigating the guard that got us into trouble, namely:

$$SA.i.h \neq SB.j.h.$$

Noticing that these elements are integers, we observe that if they differ, then one must exceed the other. For example:

$$SA.i.h > SB.j.h. \tag{0}$$

Introducing the $>$ leads us to consider introducing the relation $>$ between rotations. After all, if (0) holds then it seems very reasonable to let

$$SA.(i + h) > SB.(j + h)$$

hold as well. This leads us to define the relation $>$ between rotations. We give it the obvious meaning, namely

$SA.a > SB.b \equiv$ "There exists an $x \geq 0$ such that the first x elements of $SA.a$ and $SB.b$ are pairwise equal, and $SA.a.x > SB.j.x$".

With $>$ defined between rotations, we investigate its properties. We begin by observing that we are dealing with two finite, non-empty sets, the set of rotations of A and the set of rotations of B. What properties does a finite set of elements, ordered by $>$, have? Consider a finite, non-empty set of integers. What properties does it have? There is only one distinguished feature of such a set, namely that it has a smallest and a largest element. Can we exploit this fact to our advantage? We can as soon as we realize that if the respective smallest elements differ, then the two sets differ also.

In other words, with

$AA =$ smallest rotation of A and
$BB =$ smallest rotation of B,

we see that

$$AA \neq BB \;\Rightarrow\; A \neq B.$$

As a result, we can establish that A and B differ by establishing

$$AA \neq BB. \tag{1}$$

One way to establish (1) is to compute AA, BB, and then compare them. We might take this route, were it not for the fact that we have no interest in AA and BB — we are only interested in whether they differ. We can establish that they differ, without determining AA and BB, by establishing that either

All rotations of A exceed BB or	(2)
All rotations of B exceed AA.	(3)

Defining

$$QA: \; (\forall k: 0 \leq k < i: SA.i > BB) \quad \text{and}$$
$$QB: \; (\forall k: 0 \leq k < j: SB.j > AA),$$

we see that (2), in turn, can be established by establishing

$$QA \;\wedge\; i \geq N,$$

and that (3), in turn, can be established by establishing

$$QB \;\wedge\; j \geq N.$$

In summary, we can establish that the two arrays differ by establishing

$$R1: \; QA \;\wedge\; QB \;\wedge\; (i \geq N \;\vee\; j \geq N).$$

DEVELOPING THE PROGRAM

Now that we have a way to establish that the two circular arrays are equal, namely by establishing

$$R0: \; P \;\wedge\; h \geq N,$$

and a way to establish that they differ, namely by establishing

$$R1: \quad QA \;\wedge\; QB \;\wedge\; (i \geq N \;\vee\; j \geq N).$$

we are ready to develop our program. Without much ado, we propose

```
|[var h, i, j : int
;h, i, j := 0, 0, 0  {P ∧ QA ∧ QB}
;do h < N ∧ i < N ∧ j < N → S od
 {P ∧ QA ∧ QB ∧ (h ≥ N ∨ i ≥ N ∨ j ≥ N)}
;if h ≥ N             → {R0} z := true
 ▯ i ≥ N ∨ j ≥ N  → {R1} z := false
 fi
]|
```

What remains is the development of S.

Remark   We leave it to the reader to prove that the if can be replaced
by the simpler $z := h \geq N$. (With this replacement notice that the
program works for $N = 0$.)   □

Developing S

Towards developing S we observe that $h + i + j$ must be increased, an
increase that is bounded from above by the guard. In light of the invariants,
for S we propose

```
if SA.i.h = SB.j.h  →  S0
▯ SA.i.h > SB.j.h  →  S1
▯ SB.j.h > SA.i.h  →  S2
fi
```

where we can replace

$$
\begin{array}{llll}
SA.i.h & \text{by} & A.((i + h) \bmod N) & \text{and} \\
SB.j.h & \text{by} & B.((i + h) \bmod N).
\end{array}
$$

What remains are the developments of $S0$, $S1$, and $S2$.

DEVELOPING $S0$

For $S0$ we observe that $h := h + 1$ maintains P and, because h doesn't occur in them, maintains QA and QB as well. This assignment also increases $h + i + j$. Thus for $S0$ we propose

$$S0: \quad h := h + 1.$$

What remains are the developments of $S1$ and $S2$.

DEVELOPING $S1$ AND $S2$

For $S1$ we observe that:

  o Because $SA.i.h > SB.j.h$ we see that $SA.i > SB.j$, and therefore that $SA.i > BB$. Thus QA can be maintained by $i := i + 1$. Because i is not named in it, this assignment maintains QB as well.

  o P can be maintained by making it vacuously true, i.e. by $h := 0$.

The only problem is that $h + i + j$ is not increased. In particular, $h := 0$ decreases it by h. Thus the assignment to i must increase i by at least $h + 1$. Such an increase must also maintain QA. This leads us to solve

$$\{QA \wedge P \wedge SA.i.h > SB.j.h\} \; i := i + E \; \{QA\}$$

for some $E \geq h + 1$. Solving this boils down to solving

$$QA \wedge P \wedge SA.i.h > SB.j.h \;\Rightarrow\; QA(i := i + E) \quad \text{for } E \geq h + 1.$$

Because the lefthand side is the more complicated expression, we try to convert it into the righthand side. What we find is that

$$QA \wedge P \wedge SA.i.h > SB.j.h$$
$\Rightarrow \qquad \langle \text{Using } P \rangle$
$$QA \wedge (\forall k : 0 \leq k < h : SA.i.h = SB.j.h) \wedge SA.i.h > SB.j.h$$
$\Rightarrow \qquad \langle \text{The last two conjuncts imply } SA.(i + x) > SB.(j + x),$
    for any x satisfying $0 \leq x < h + 1 \rangle$
$$QA \wedge (\forall x : 0 \leq x < h + 1 : SA.(i + x) > SB.(j + x))$$

$\Rightarrow$ $\langle$ Definition of BB $\rangle$
$$QA \;\wedge\; (\forall x : 0 \leq x < h+1 : SA.(i+x) > BB)$$
$\equiv$ $\langle$ Dummy transformation, using $k := i+x$ $\rangle$
$$QA \;\wedge\; (\forall k : 0 \leq k-i < h+1 : SA.k > BB)$$
$\equiv$ $\langle$ Arithmetic $\rangle$
$$QA \;\wedge\; (\forall k : i \leq k < i+h+1 : SA.k > BB)$$
$\equiv$ $\langle$ Definition of QA $\rangle$
$$(\forall k : 0 \leq k < i : SA.k > BB) \;\wedge\;$$
$$(\forall k : i \leq k < i+h+1 : SA.k > BB\cdot)$$
$\equiv$ $\langle$ Join ranges $\rangle$
$$(\forall k : 0 \leq k < i+h+1 : SA.k > BB)$$
$\equiv$ $\langle$ Definition of QA $\rangle$
$$QA(i := i+h+1)$$
$\equiv$ $\langle$ Let $h+1 = E$, which certainly satisfies $E \geq h+1$ $\rangle$
$$QA(i := i+E)$$

Thus for $S1$ we propose

$$S1 : \quad i, h := i+h+1, 0.$$

★   ★

$S2$ follows from $S1$, by symmetry. In other words for $S2$ we propose

$$S2 : \quad j, h := j+h+1, 0.$$

This completes the development. This program is originally due to Y. Shiloach (in 1979).

HOW DOES THIS PROGRAM MEASURE UP?

Because of the guard and the fact that $h+i+j$ is increased by 1 each repetition, the program requires at most $N + (N-1) + (N-1) = 3*N-2$ repetitions.

Next we compare it with the naive solution, one that compares A with each rotation of B. In the worst case, the naive solution requires nearly $N^2/2$ array element comparisons. Assuming 1 pair of array elements can be compared each second, that Shiloach's solution requires 2 of these per repetition, and that all other operations are free, we obtain:

N	Naive solution	Shiloach's solution
1,000	5 days	2 hours
10,000	578 days	17 hours
100,000	158 years	7 days

It should be clear that the inefficiency of the naive solution is due to the fact that it does not take into account the fact that the circular arrays contain integers.

Remark   Since a polygon can be represented by a circular array of its vertices, one application of this algorithm is in determining whether two polygons are equal. (For those familiar with computational geometry, the general problem is whether two polygons are "similar"). This program might also have applications in computational biochemistry. □

Remark   For students with a prior exposure to programming, this problem makes an excellent first exercise. (They can be asked to find a solution for arrays of size 10,000 that executes in less than a year under the assumptions made above). If unable to arrive at a solution, they might be asked to describe what *approach* they took. In doing so they might realize, perhaps for the first time, that they do not know any methods for attacking problems for which cleverness is insufficient. (Also, they will be eager to see a solution!)   □

12.5   Additional exercises

Ex 12.3   Celebrity problem: A *celebrity* is someone who is known by everyone, but who knows no one. Given that there exists a celebrity amongst $N \geq 0$ people, and given boolean function b satisfying

$$b.i.j \equiv \text{``person } i \text{ knows person } j\text{''}$$

specify and then develop a program that determines a celebrity.   □

Ex 12.4   Sum of powers: Given natural N and integer X, develop a program that determines the value of

$$(\Sigma i : 0 \leq i < N : X^i)$$

The program should require a number of repetitions proportional to the logarithm of N.   □

Ex 12.5   *The majority value:* In an array containing N elements, a *majority value* is any value that occurs more than N *div* 2 times. Given that there is one, determine the majority value in a given array. A linear solution is desired.   □

Ex 12.6   *Sum of square-pairs:* Print for given $N \geq 0$, all natural solutions of

$$x, y : \ x^2 + y^2 = N \ \wedge \ x \leq y$$

□

Ex 12.7   *Largest true square:* Given natural M and N, and boolean array $b(i, j : 0 \leq i < M \ \wedge \ 0 \leq j < N)$, specify and then solve the problem of determining the size, i.e. the length of a side, of the largest square subarray of b in which all elements are *true*.   □

Ex 12.8   *Regular polygon on a circle:* A circle has on its circumference $N \geq 3$ points numbered clockwise from 0. Given N and given function d satisfying

$d.i = $ length of arc between point i and its clockwise neighbor,

and given integer k, satisfying $3 \leq k \leq N$, specify and then develop a program that determines whether there exists amongst the given points the vertices of a regular polygon having k sides.   □

Ex 12.9   The soon to be famous function *fusc* is defined by:

$$
\begin{aligned}
fusc.k = \ &\underline{\text{if}} \ k = 0 && \rightarrow \ 0 \\
&\square \ k = 1 && \rightarrow \ 1 \\
&\square \ k \geq 2 \ \wedge \ even.k && \rightarrow \ fusc.(k/2) \\
&\square \ k \geq 2 \ \wedge \ odd.k && \rightarrow \ fusc.((k-1)/2) \ + \\
& && \quad \ fusc.((k+1)/2) \\
&\underline{\text{fi}}
\end{aligned}
$$

Specify and develop a program that given $N \geq 0$, evaluates *fusc.N*. A logarithmic solution is desired.   □

Ex 12.10   *Halving the perimeter of a polygon:* The N vertices of a polygon are numbered clockwise from 0. The distance from vertex i to its clockwise neighbor is $d.i$, where $d.i > 0$. Specify and then develop a program that determines a pair of vertices that halve the perimeter as closely as possible.   □

Ex 12.11 *A proof about integers:* For every k and r satisfying

$$Q: \ 1 \le k \ \wedge \ (r \text{ is odd}) \ \wedge \ 1 \le r < 2^k$$

there exists an x satisfying

$$R: \ (x \text{ is odd}) \ \wedge \ 1 \le x < 2^k \ \wedge \ (x^3 - r \text{ is a multiple of } 2^k).$$

Prove this by constructing a program having precondition Q and postcondition R. A logarithmic solution is desired. ◻

Ex 12.12 *Two distinct values:* Develop a program that determines the length of the longest array section containing at most two distinct values. ◻

Ex 12.13 *Period of the decimal representation:* Develop a program that given integer $N \ge 1$, determines the period of the decimal representation of N. ◻

13

Where to go from here

13.0   On what we have learned

We have seen a number of methods. We have applied these methods to a number of examples. While the examples were not the subject matter, I have tried to choose generally useful ones.

Some major observations:

- A specification must be composed before a solution can be developed:

  Since our approach is based on calculation, the specification must be in a notation we can calculate with. Otherwise, there is nothing we can do (except guess). And in order to keep our calculations manageable, we aim for notations that are elegant and expressive.[0]

  As we have seen, specifications can be developed methodically, although there are often many possibilities. The ability to arrive at useful specifications comes, of course, from practice.

- Calculation is quite effective:

  A lot of algorithms that seemed to embody near genius, or were at least considered quite difficult, have turned out to be "matter of fact" when we calculate.

  There are, of course, problems that we cannot solve by calculation. At least, not yet. Outright invention may be required, invention that should be explicitly noted in a development. But even with invention, we can employ calculation to help with the rest of the development.

  That a lot of programming is straight calculation is good news. What used to be hard is now easy. We calculate expressions in assignments, and guards in IFs. We guess the invariant for a repetition, and from

---

[0]Recall that we avoid picture notations because they are difficult to calculate with (and are usually overspecific, and therefore misleading), and recall that we avoid notations suffering from indexitis because they make our calculations cumbersome.

there the development of the repetition is straightforward. And if the development reaches a point where it cannot continue, then we go back and guess another invariant. A bad guess leads to no solution, *not* to an incorrect program.

Much attention has been focussed on guessing the invariant. Our "guess" for an invariant is often not much of a guess at all. Our invariants are inspired by the shapes of our specifications. From the shape of a specification, we are usually led to a satisfactory invariant. Relevant techniques include deleting a conjunct and replacing constants by fresh variables.

With so much reduced to calculation, we can turn our attention to finding better solutions and to solving new problems. The guess and test approach was dull and frustrating. A scientific approach is much more exciting. It challenges the mind, not with avoidable puzzles, but with genuinely interesting problems.

- To be productive, work slowly:

With a calculational approach to programming, we need only to take care at each step. If we make an error, we can check our calculations. If we go slowly, write neatly,[1] and are very careful, we avoid introducing errors in the first place.

- Put efficiency in its place:

Real efficiency comes from a larger decrease of the bound function, (i.e. from algorithmic means), not from minor adjustments to the program. Compare a binary search to a linear search — a logarithmic solution is vastly superior to a highly-tuned linear one.

Another way to improve efficiency is to strengthen the invariant. Recall the problem of the maximum section sum in which we added a conjunct to the invariant to eliminate a quantification from an expression. Although motivated by simplicity, and not by efficiency, a linear solution came for free.

C.A.R. Hoare once said that "the price to be paid for reliablity is simplicity". Simplicity comes from a striving for elegance. We strive for elegance in our specifications and in our developments. Every symbol should have its place. In addition to a good eye, a lot of practice is required to meet this goal.

---

[1] There seems to be a direct correlation between neatness of writing and correctness of solutions!

13.1 Where to go from here

If there are other courses on programming, by all means take them. If not, then there are at least three alternatives:

- Teach a course.

  The best way to learn is to teach. Presenting material to others has an uncanny ability to improve it.

- Self study.

  There are a number of additional sources of examples and exercises, depending on your interests.

  > For the use of the predicate calculus, see [0], [3], and [4].
  >
  > For program development, see the references at the end.
  >
  > For the semantics of programs, see [4].
  >
  > For the streamlining of mathematical arguments, see [0], [3] and [4].

  If possible, a group of people can embark on a joint study. Such an approach has its advantages.

  Some additional suggestions for a self-study of programming:

  > Keep in mind that the older the published example, the more informal it tends to be. Trying to improve an older development is an excellent exercise.
  >
  > Another avenue is to try for a nice development for some important algorithm. Find one in an algorithm book. It is unlikely that it will include a workable specification, so the first step will be to formulate one.

  Start with easy problems, and work from there. By all means, don't get frustrated! A problem nicely solved is quite gratifying, but also requires care.

- Take a related course.

  Take another course. Develop nice solutions for the examples in the course text and for the exercises. They probably won't come with workable specifications, so most likely that job will be yours. (This is often the most challenging part.) In developing a specification, new notation may be required. Begin by discovering its properties. It is also likely that solutions will be required in a notation other than guarded commands. Develop them in guarded commands, since they were designed with programming in mind. When finished, translate your solution into Pascal (or whatever). The final translation is a simple task.

⋆   ⋆

Be selective about the courses you choose. Many courses on "programming" instead turn out to be surveys of the features of programming language X, for whatever X, combined with lessons on "style".

Language X is usually presented as a long sequence of features, e.g. "these are the 5 kinds of loops", along with an operational notion as to how each "works" (i.e. might execute on a computer, as in "a loop goes round and round"). The "style lessons" usually include how to comment, how to indent, how to write a header, why we should use mnemonic names, why not to use gotos, when it's acceptable to exit a loop in the middle, and so on.

As for learning the particulars of some programming language, look in a book! Once familiar with programming, the mastery of this or that programming language is an easy task. (Indeed, an introductory programming course supplemented with lectures and exercises on Pascal (say) will generate Pascal experts, and is probably the best way to satisfy such a requirement.)

As for the style lessons, most are rather silly. For example, we are told to use mnemonic names. In the absence of a definition, a mnemonic name can be misleading (e.g. what does "sum" mean), and if there is a definition, then a mnemonic name is simply excessive verbiage (e.g. "sum-of-first-k-elements-in-array-b"), which only serves to make the definition hard to read, and to give us writer's cramp when we try to manipulate it!

Such courses are readily identified by their names, typically "Introduction to programming in X". One reason for their prevalence is that when the "guess and test" approach is taken, there are no methods to be taught (except to be careful). Besides "style lessons" and surveys of language features (along with examples of their use, as in "here is an example of the use of pointers"), there really isn't much to say.

Remark   One result of such courses is that students, especially beginners, are led to confuse "style rules" with "method", and "programming in language X" with "programming". The student who is first taught programming is in a position to question, for example, the wisdom of

5 kinds of loops, or why experimentation is necessary to determine how some "feature" of language X might work on the computer, or even whether language X is suitable for programming at all!

Someone without any exposure cannot even ask these questions. For them, "programming" *is* "programming in language X". As a result, we meet "X programmers" who use "X style", and who endlessly argue with "Y programmers" on the merits of "X" over "Y". □

13.2 Be a little discriminating

In both its development and in its use, the cost of software to industry is enormous, and most of it is unreliable. That this is so is often blamed on a lack of good tools (e.g. programming languages, "software engineering environments", etc.), but the fundamental problem is a lack of appreciation of the challenge of programming.

One symptom of the latter is the common practice of non-programmer managers to "specify" and "write" programs — a phenomenon that would be unthinkable in other engineering professions.

Another symptom is the plethora of tools that purport to either make programming easier, or even to eliminate the programmer altogether.

We have "user-friendly" tools that are basically poorly designed programming languages. Their inadequacy being hidden behind extensive "feature lists" that include such entries as "multi-colored exploding data entry windows".

We have products that draw pictures. One picture is labeled "User Interface" and it is connected by special arrows to another called "Invoice Database". While these pictures look nice and are fun to draw, and seeing them gives the warm feeling that all is well, they are inadequate for doing programming.

We even have products called "expert systems" that "embody expert knowledge". We are told that "even non-programmers can develop these". An "expert system" is of course a program written in a specially restricted programming language. The programs are sets of "rules". How are non-programmers to write these programs? By guessing a set of rules! Take away the bit about "experts". Call it a programming language. Now consider the claim that "using our programming language, even non-programmers can develop systems that embody expert knowledge". It sounds absurd.

The lesson, of course, is to beware of promises of salvation. They can be recognized by their reassuring names (e.g. "expert system" or "software engineering"[2]). Stripping away the names, we often find something devoid of useful technical content.

The reason for pointing these things out (besides for fun) is so we do not waste too much time. There are always promises of salvation. A bit of discrimination saves us a lot of effort.

13.3   Inspirations and acknowledgements

Very little of the material in this book is my own. Most of it is due to others. My only contribution is to combine and present it in (hopefully!) a clear manner.

What can we learn from a cake?
The problem of the cake is due to E.W. Dijkstra. It can be found in [0], where its solution is attributed to A. Blokhuis. The quotation from C.A.R. Hoare is from an essay entitled "Programming is an engineering profession", which appears in [1]. The quotation from E.W. Dijkstra is from [2].

Preliminary notions, notations, and terminology
Once the usefulness of the uninterpreted manipulation of formulae is realized, our attention is drawn to notation and heuristics that increase our effectiveness in "letting the symbols do the work". I have been particularly inspired by Wim H.J. Feijen (see, for example, his contribution to [0]). Other inspirations have been the thesis of A.J.M. van Gasteren [3], and the writings of Edsger W. Dijkstra. Much of their recent research has been on the streamlining of mathematical arguments, a topic that will be of great interest to mathematicians in general, and one that arose from research on programming. Their observations permeate this book.

Specifically, the proof format, in particular, the inclusion of hints as a syntactic category, is due to Wim H.J. Feijen, a fact I learned from [3]. For further discussion see [3] and [4]. The arithmetic operator $\uparrow$ is also due to Feijen. The problems with the three dots, and the benefits of including 0 amongst the natural numbers, have been pointed out by E.W. Dijkstra. A nice essay on the latter appears in [0]. The example of Newton's law is due to Dijkstra too, as is the notation for function application. And it is A.J.M. van Gasteren (in [3]) who points out that operators with high binding powers should be given small symbols, as this makes formula parsing easy on the eye, an observation due to Jan L.A. van de Snepscheut.

---

[2]If we cannot develop programs, perhaps we can "engineer software"!

Predicates A — Boolean operators

The algebraic approach to the predicate calculus is due to E.W. Dijkstra (see [0] and [4]). He, and others, have observed that while often familiar with predicates, mathematicians in general, and programmers in particular, rarely *use* them in day-to-day work. One explanation, also due to Dijkstra, is that the subject is usually presented as a formalization of verbal reasoning, and not as a system of calculation. Because the equivalence has no verbal analogue, familiarity with the equivalence is rare. Indeed, in [4] we hear the story of the electrical engineer who called the equivalence the "exclusive nor"!

Predicates B — Quantified expressions

The notation for quantification is due to E.W. Dijkstra. The top-down presentation was inspired by A.J.M. van Gasteren [3], and was written with the aid of R.C. Backhouse's treatment in [5]. The top-down approach has the advantage of generality: a rich set of laws, generally applicable, can be presented very quickly. A recent treatment of quantification can be found in [4]. The exercises at the end come from a variety of programming problems.

Specifications

The Hoare triple is due to C.A.R. Hoare. It is from his seminal paper "An axiomatic basis for computer programming" (*Communications of the ACM 12*, Oct 1969) which has been widely reproduced (see [6], [1]). The use of equations in formulating specifications was inspired by J.M. Morris' contribution to [0]. The definition of an ascending function is from [7].

On the shapes of programs

The beautiful programming language of guarded commands is due to E.W. Dijkstra. It first appeared in [8] and [9], as did the predicate transformer $wp.S$ and its use in defining the semantics of programs. An in-depth study can be found in [4]. The definition of the loop in terms of wp, and a proof of the Invariance Theorem can be found in [10] and in [4] (where it is called the *Main Repetition Theorem*).

Remark The knowledgable reader probably noticed that we cheated in our definition of the Hoare triple. The definition should be the truth of "$wp.S.R$ holds in *all states in S's state space* where Q holds", a definition that is expressed by

$$\{Q\} \, S \, \{R\} \equiv (\forall s : Q : wp.S.R)$$

and where s ranges over all states in S's state space. By trading we see that the righthand side is equivalent to

$$(\forall s :: Q \Rightarrow wp.S.R)$$

We omitted the universal quantification. Another option, perhaps better, would have been to use Dijkstra and Scholten's "everywhere operator", a unary operator written with square brackets that has all of the properties of universal quantification over a non-empty range. Using "everywhere" we could write the last formula as

$[Q \Rightarrow wp.S.R]$

For further information, see [4].   □

Developing loopless programs and *Developing loops — an introduction*
The original masterpiece is of course E.W. Dijkstra's *A Discipline of Programming* (1976) [9]. The first text to be based on this material is David Gries' *The Science of Programming* (1981) [11], a book I have used with great success for many years. It has had an enormous influence on me, and I have borrowed heavily from it — for example, the taxonomy of techniques for weakening postconditions to arrive at invariants (deleting a conjunct, replacing constants by fresh variables). Gries' book was followed by a number of other excellent texts (e.g. [12], [13], [14], [5]). Yet another rich source of examples is Martin Rem's column "Small programming exercises" in the journal *Science of Computer Programming* [15].

Loops A — On deleting a conjunct
The example of *integer-division* was an important one for me. In presenting it several years ago, I "handwaved" the development of the loop body, which rightly bothered some students. It was Wim Feijen who showed me how to do it right. It was also his recommendation that I improve the algorithm. The *Linear Search* is from [9] and [11], and the proof that it terminates was inspired by Feijen. Few programmers are familiar with the *Linear Search*, perhaps because boolean functions are rarely understood, and end up reinventing it for each instance in which it is needed. A very nice treatment of the *Linear Search* can be found in [16]. An entirely different treatment, also very nice, can be found in [17]. The example *3-tuple sort* is based on *4-tuple sort*, which first appeared in [9]. It is included as an example of avoiding avoidable case-analyses, and not as a suggestion for sorting. Additional examples of avoidable case-analyses can be found by students, an exercise that they find quite illuminating.

Loops B — On replacing constants by fresh variables
The example of *evaluating a polynomial* appears in [11], though with a different specification. This particular specification was chosen because it was a bit difficult to interpret, allowing us to concentrate on an uninterpreted development. The *minimum value* was included at the request of several students. They thought that an example of quantification elimination would be helpful. *Determining the multiple* is from [18], where it is proved using

mathematical induction, and where X is (unnecessarily) contrained to be natural. It is mainly included to show an instance in which Leibniz's rule must be applied. An added benefit is that it is a nice example of a constructive existence proof. The *table of cubes* was from a well-received lecture by Wim Feijen at Harvard University in May 1988, a lecture that a number of students found illuminating. The *maximum section sum* problem was learned from David Gries. Its development first appeared in [19], in which its interesting history is discussed. It also appears in [0] and [14]. For the *Binary Search*, a truly remarkable program, I drew heavily from [14]. The idea to distinguish it from its most common application is due to Feijen. *Rearranging an array* was inspired by [20]. The *Bounded Linear Search* was inspired by [21]. Other treatments can be found in [17] and [16]. The latter includes an illuminating discussion of the problem of unevaluatable expressions.

Mainly on recursion

This chapter was originally two chapters. The first showed a rather ad-hoc technique for evaluating recursively defined functions, while the other showed what to do when the technique failed. As a result, I did not know for which functions the combination of techniques worked, and had to write a lot, since I kept developing the same program over and over without realizing it! It was only afterwards that I learned, from R. Hoogerwoord [22], that the class of functions for which the combination of techniques works is called tail-recursive, that all of these functions could be evaluated using the same program, and that when given a function that is not tail-recursive, the development effort boils down to discovering a more general function that is. The examples come from many places. The *sum of digits* is from [14]. A development of *exponentiation* appears in [9]. *Reversing a sequence* is, of course, an old problem, and is a nice example of the importance of appropriate notation. Many programmers find it tricky, usually because it is cast in terms of pointers, which are usually reasoned about using pictures. In terms of sequences it is very simple. The various orderings on binary trees (pre, in, and post) are usually called tree traversals. They come up in many areas, for example in programming language interpreters. The *post-order of a binary tree* was inspired by David Gries' development of the *in-order* in [0]. The problem of the *depth of a binary tree* was found in [23]. I was unable to solve it, and did what any self respecting instructor would do — I assigned it as an exercise! It was Haakon Chevalier who arrived at a solution. (His solution differed slightly in that he used two equal-lengthed sequences, rather than a set of pairs).

Back to Scratch

The derivation of *Horner's rule* for evaluating a polynomial was motivated by an omission pointed out by Wim Feijen, namely that the earlier specification came with no justification, only an example, and that the discovery of useful specifications is a major part of programming. *Euclid's algorithm* for the greatest common divisor goes back, of course, to Euclid. *All-pairs shortest paths* goes back to Floyd (in 1962, [24]), and was inspired by Jan L.A. van de Snepscheut's presentation of Warshall's algorithm for the transitive closure in [0] (and in [25]). (In [0] it is used as a stepping stone to a linear solution distributed over a network of cells. In [25] it is a stepping stone to an algorithm for the transitive reduction (i.e. eliminating redundant edges, while maintaining connectivity) of an acyclic graph). Shiloach's algorithm, a remarkable program, is due to Y. Shiloach [26]. More recent presentations appear in [3] and [27]. Regarding the exercises at the end: The *celebrity problem* is from [18] and [17]. The *largest true square* has appeared in many places. The *sum of powers* is from [22]. The *majority value* is originally from [28] and a generalization appears in [29] and in [0]. The *sum of square-pairs* and *proof about integers* are due to E.W. Dijkstra, as is the soon to be famous *fusc*. *Regular polygon on a circle, halving the perimeter of a polygon, two distinct values*, and *period of the decimal representation* are from [14].

13.4   Selected references

[0] Edsger W. Dijkstra (ed.), *Formal Development of Programs and Proofs*, Addison-Wesley 1989.

[1] C.A.R. Hoare and C.B. Jones (ed.), *Essays in Computing Science*, Prentice-Hall 1989.

[2] E.W. Dijkstra, On the cruelty of really teaching computing science, EWD 1036, The University of Texas at Austin, 1988.

[3] A.J.M. van Gasteren, *On the shape of mathematical arguments*, Ph.D. thesis, Eindhoven University of Technology, Eindhoven, The Netherlands, 1988. Also: Springer-Verlag Lecture Notes in Computer Science, 1990.

[4] Edsger W. Dijkstra and Carel S. Scholten, *Predicate Calculus and Program Semantics*, Springer-Verlag 1990.

[5] Roland C. Backhouse, *Program Construction and Verification*, Prentice Hall 1986.

[6] David Gries (ed.), *Programming Methodology*, Springer-Verlag 1978.

[7] E.W. Dijkstra, Ascending functions and The Welfare Crook, EWD 1031, The University of Texas at Austin, 1988.

[8] E.W. Dijkstra, Guarded commands, nondeterminacy and the formal derivation of programs, *Communications of the ACM 18* (1975), 453-7. (Also reproduced in [6].)

[9] Edsger W. Dijkstra, *A Discipline of Programming*, Prentice-Hall 1976.

[10] E.W. Dijkstra and A.J.M. van Gasteren, A simple fixpoint argument without the restriction to continuity, *Acta Informatica 23* 1986, 1-7.

[11] David Gries, *The Science of Programming*, Springer-Verlag 1981.

[12] John C. Reynolds, *The Craft of Programming*, Prentice-Hall 1981.

[13] Eric C.R. Hehner, *The Logic of Programming*, Prentice-Hall 1984.

[14] Edsger W. Dijkstra and W.H.J. Feijen, *A Method of Programming*, Addison-Wesley 1988. (Translated from 1984 Dutch edition).

[15] M. Rem, Small programming exercises, *Science of Computer Programming*. This is an on-going column. Problems posed in one column are solved in the subsequent one. Great attention is paid to "solution strategies".

[16] E.W. Dijkstra and W.H.J. Feijen, The linear search revisited, *Structured Programming 10* (1989), 5-9.

[17] Anne Kaldewaij and Barry Schoenmakers, Searching by elimination, *Science of Computer Programming*, to appear.

[18] Udi Manber, *Introduction to Algorithms*, Addison-Wesley 1989.

[19] D. Gries, A note on the standard strategy for developing loop invariants and loops, *Science of Computer Programming 2* (1984), 207-214.

[20] W.H.J. Feijen, A bagatelle (for the files), WF101, The University of Texas at Austin, 1988.

[21] John H. Remmers, A technique for developing loop invariants, *Information Processing Letters 18* (1984), 137-139.

[22] Rob Hoogerwoord, *The design of functional programs: a calculational approach*, Ph.D. thesis, Eindhoven University of Technology, Eindhoven, The Netherlands, 1989.

[23] Richard Bird and Phillip Wadler, *An Introduction to Functional Programming*, Prentice-Hall 1988.

[24] R.W. Floyd, Algorithm 97: Shortest Paths, *Communications of the ACM 5* (1962), 345.

[25] D. Gries, A.J. Martin, J.L.A. van de Snepscheut, J.T. Udding, An algorithm for transitive reduction of an acyclic graph, *Science of Computer Programming 12* (1989), 151-155.

[26] Yossi Shiloach, A fast equivalence checking algorithm for circular lists, *Information Processing Letters 8* (1979), 236-238.

[27] A.J.M. van Gasteren and W.H.J. Feijen, Shiloach's algorithm, taken as an exercise in presenting programs, *Nieuw Archief voor Wiskunde XXX* (1982), 277-282.

[28] R.S. Boyer and J.S. Moore, MJRTY, A fast majority-vote algorithm.

[29] J. Misra and David Gries, Finding repeated elements, *Science of Computer Programming 2* (1982), 143-152.

[30] Edsger W. Dijkstra, *Selected Writings on Computing*, Springer-Verlag 1982.

[31] D. Gries, What programmers don't and should know, Technical Report, Computer Science Department, Cornell University 1987.

[32] K. Mani Chandy and Jayadev Misra, *Parallel Program Design, A Foundation*, Addison-Wesley 1988.

13.5   If you find a nice example...

If you have a comment, a question, a nice development for some problem, or an interesting exercise, let me know. My address is: c/o Software Logic, PO Box 565, Brookline MA 02146, USA.

Index

Texts and Monographs in Computer Science

continued

Nissim Francez
Fairness
1986. XIII, 295 pages, 147 illus.

R.T. Gregory and E.V. Krishnamurthy
Methods and Applications of Error-Free Computation
1984. XII, 194 pages, 1 illus.

David Gries, Ed.
Programming Methodology: A Collection of Articles by Members of IFIP WG2.3
1978. XIV, 437 pages, 68 illus.

David Gries
The Science of Programming
1981. XV, 366 pages

Micha Hofri
Probabilistic Analysis of Algorithms
1987. XV, 240 pages, 14 illus.

A.J. Kfoury, Robert N. Moll, and Michael A. Arbib
A Programming Approach to Computability
1982. VIII, 251 pages, 36 illus.

E.V. Krishnamurthy
Error-Free Polynomial Matrix Computations
1985. XV, 154 pages

Ernest G. Manes and Michael A. Arbib
Algebraic Approaches to Program Semantics
1986. XIII, 351 pages

Robert N. Moll, Michael A. Arbib, and A.J. Kfoury
An Introduction to Formal Language Theory
1988. X, 203 pages, 61 illus.

Franco P. Preparata and Michael Ian Shamos
Computational Geometry: An Introduction
1988. XII, 390 pages, 231 illus.

Brian Randell, Ed.
The Origins of Digital Computers: Selected Papers, 3rd Edition
1982. XVI, 580 pages, 126 illus.

Thomas W. Reps and Tim Teitelbaum
The Synthesizer Generator: A System for Constructing Language-Based Editors
1989. XIII, 317 pages, 75 illus.

Texts and Monographs in Computer Science